A LIGHT
IN THE
NORTHERN
SEA

ALSO BY TIM BRADY

Three Ordinary Girls

A LIGHT IN THE NORTHERN SEA

*Denmark's Incredible Rescue of Their
Jewish Citizens During WWII*

TIM BRADY

CITADEL PRESS
Kensington Publishing Corp.
kensingtonbooks.com

CITADEL PRESS BOOKS are published by

Kensington Publishing Corp.
900 Third Avenue
New York, NY 10022

All Kensington titles, imprints, and distributed lines are available at special quantity discounts for bulk purchases for sales promotions, premiums, fund-raising, educational, or institutional use. Special book excerpts or customized printings can also be created to fit specific needs. For details, write or phone the office of the Kensington sales manager: Kensington Publishing Corp., 900 Third Avenue, New York, NY 10022, attn Sales Department; phone 1-800-221-2647.

CITADEL PRESS and the Citadel logo are Reg. U.S. Pat. & TM Off.

10 9 8 7 6 5 4 3 2 1

First Citadel hardcover printing: August 2025

Printed in the United States of America

ISBN: 978-0-8065-4342-0

ISBN: 978-0-8065-4344-4 (e-book)

Library of Congress Control Number: 2025934269

The authorized representative in the EU for product safety and compliance
is eucomply OU, Parnu mnt 139b-14, Apt 123,
Tallinn, Berlin 11317; hello@eucompliancepartner.com

CONTENTS

Maps / *ix*

PART 1
──────
Occupation

CHAPTER 1

April 9, 1940 / 3

CHAPTER 2

Ordinary Danes / 7

CHAPTER 3

The Jews of Denmark / 16

CHAPTER 4

Christian X Goes for a Ride / 21

CHAPTER 5

Movement / 29

CHAPTER 6

1943 / 38

CHAPTER 7

Bohr / 44

CHAPTER 8

August 1943 / 48

CHAPTER 9

Holger Danske 1 / 50

CHAPTER 10

Jorgen and Elsebet / 55

CHAPTER 11

State of Emergency / 59

CHAPTER 12

Duckwitz / 66

CHAPTER 13

Time to Act / 71

CHAPTER 14

The Germans Move Against the Jews / 77

PART 2

Exodus

CHAPTER 15

Finding a Way Out / 87

CHAPTER 16

Bispebjerg / 97

CHAPTER 17

Gerda III / 103

CHAPTER 18

Bohr Makes It to Scotland / 107

CHAPTER 19

Gestapo Juhl, Gilleleje, and the
Elsinore Sewing Club / 109

CHAPTER 20

Sweden: A Light in the Northern Sea / 120

CHAPTER 21

Theresienstadt / 121

PART 3
Resistance

CHAPTER 22
Holger Danske 2 / 139

CHAPTER 23
First Assignment / 144

CHAPTER 24
Setbacks / 150

CHAPTER 25
The First Death / 152

CHAPTER 26
Vengeance: First Attempt / 154

CHAPTER 27
New Territory / 157

CHAPTER 28
Menace of the Peter Group / 166

CHAPTER 29
The Demise of Holger Danske 2 / 171

CHAPTER 30
Refugees in Sweden / 181

CHAPTER 31
Resistance Continues / 187

CHAPTER 32
Vestre Faengsel / 190

CHAPTER 33
Strike / 199

CHAPTER 34
Froslev / 202

CHAPTER 35

The Police Are Arrested / 204

CHAPTER 36

The Flame / 206

CHAPTER 37

Aarhus / 207

CHAPTER 38

Porta Westfalica / 209

CHAPTER 39

Henny and Mix / 219

CHAPTER 40

Negotiations / 221

CHAPTER 41

Shellhus in Copenhagen / 225

CHAPTER 42

The White Buses / 227

CHAPTER 43

Porta Westfalica for a Last Time / 230

CHAPTER 44

Theresienstadt Once Again / 233

Acknowledgments / 237

Notes / 241

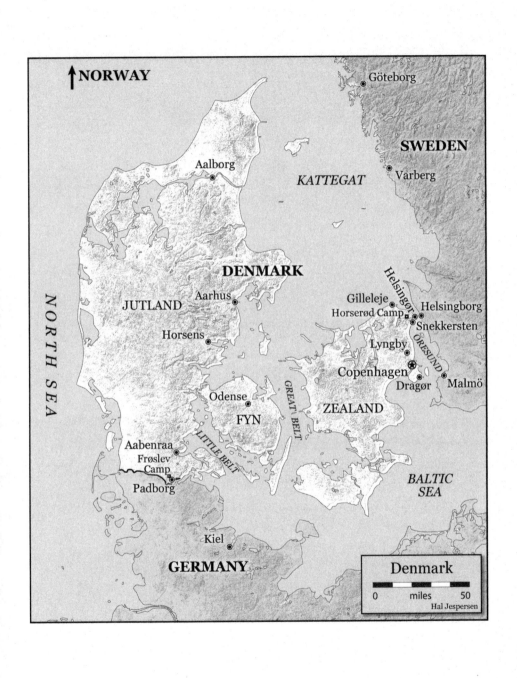

NORWAY

Göteborg

SWEDEN

Aalborg

KATTEGAT

Varberg

DENMARK

JUTLAND

Aarhus

Gilleleje
Horserød Camp

Helsingør

Helsingborg

Snekkersten

Horsens

Lyngby

ØRESUND

Odense

NORTH SEA

FYN

GREAT BELT

Copenhagen

Dragør

Malmö

ZEALAND

Aabenraa
Frøslev
Camp

LITTLE BELT

Padborg

BALTIC
SEA

Kiel

GERMANY

Denmark

0   miles   50

Hal Jespersen

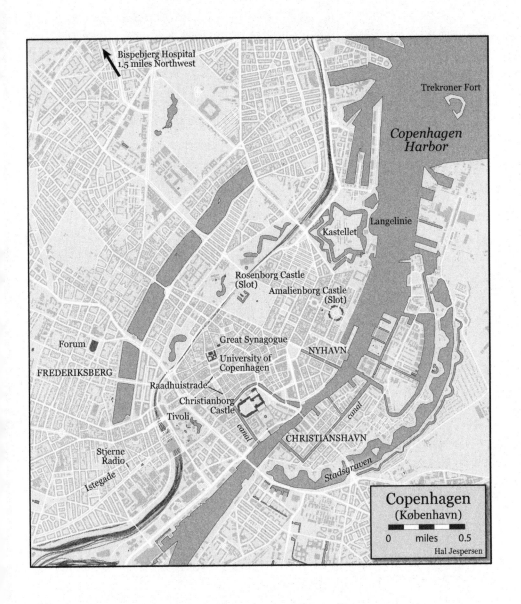

Bispebjerg Hospital
1.5 miles Northwest

Trekroner Fort

Copenhagen Harbor

Langelinie

Kastellet

Rosenborg Castle
(Slot)

Amalienborg Castle
(Slot)

Forum

Great Synagogue

NYHAVN

FREDERIKSBERG

University of
Copenhagen

Raadhuistrade

Christianborg
Castle

Tivoli

canal

canal

CHRISTIANSHAVN

Stjerne
Radio

Stadsgraven

Istegade

Copenhagen
(København)

0   miles   0.5

Hal Jespersen

A LIGHT
IN THE
NORTHERN
SEA

PART 1

Occupation

CHAPTER 1

April 9, 1940

SHORTLY AFTER FOUR O'CLOCK IN THE MORNING ON APRIL 9, 1940, HIT-ler's Germany sent a stream of motorized troops, including Panzer tank units, antitank weaponry, antiaircraft transport vehicles, and a thick convoy of troops on motorcycles, into southern Jutland, the Danish peninsula that extended north from Germany all the way to the North Sea. The soldiers wheeled through the heart of the city of Aabenraa, with hundreds of Danish citizens lining the streets and responding to the display in various poses from somber stances to enthusiastic waving to raising ramrod-straight salutes to Hitler in the Nazi style of the day. The Germans met only scattered resistance from the lightly armed Danish soldiers stationed along the way. In some instances, they were aided by Danish citizens, many of them German-speaking, ethnically aligned with Germany, and sympathetic to the German advance. Some even wore swastika armbands and helped guide the Germans through crossroads.

At the same time in Copenhagen, on the eastern edge of Denmark, a battalion of German soldiers, hidden within a troop ship that had just arrived at the Langelinie Pier in the Copenhagen harbor, spilled from the holds of the vessel and tromped through the center of the city. They were near all of Denmark's seats of power—political, monarchical, and militaristic. The troops quickly marched unencumbered toward the Citadel (Kastellet), near where the Royal Guard protected Christian X, the king of Denmark, night and day at the Amalienborg Palace.[1] A few shots were fired, but the Germans quickly overpowered the guards and took as prisoners about seventy Danish soldiers garrisoned there.

It was obvious that the Danish government had been woefully unprepared for any of what happened. Intelligence had suggested for weeks that German forces had been building on the border near Jutland in obvious preparation for an invasion, but Danish leaders in the foreign ministry had decided that any defense preparations would be viewed as provocative by Hitler, so they opted to do nothing, which left the Danish Army and Navy with their hands tied. There was no one in the field to tell the few troops there just what they were supposed to do to defend their nation.

All the missteps and dithering came home to roost that April morning. Inside the palace, the king was meeting with his cabinet in a chaotic, hastily gathered conference. Twenty minutes after the attack began, the German ambassador to Denmark visited the Danish foreign minister in Copenhagen and presented him with an ultimatum that read more like a fait accompli. The missive admitted that German troops were moving into Jutland, Fyn, and Zealand. They were doing so, it said, for Denmark's "own protection." As the logic of the Third Reich had it, Great Britain was the true threat to the nation, and Germany was doing the Danes a neighborly favor by usurping the Danish government and protecting them from Allied power.

The chief of Denmark's armed forces urged the king and cabinet to fight, but he was virtually alone in his sentiments. As the scattered gunfire at the Citadel was heard outside, the German ambassador assured the king and the Danish government that both he and it would be respected and allowed to continue as the political powers within Denmark and that Germany would only serve as protector against the Allies.

While the cabinet members and the king conferred, waves of German bombers could be heard passing over Copenhagen in the skies above, further emphasizing Denmark's helplessness in the face of the overwhelming power of the Reich, which was now occupying the country. Instead of bombs, the planes dropped thousands of leaflets that told the Danish people they were being occupied by the benevolent power to their south.

Given the choice of waging war against a country whose military was huge and primed for destruction when his own nation had done next to nothing to prepare for this invasion, the king and his council quickly decided to capitulate to German demands. Within two hours of the attack, King Christian ordered Danish forces to put down their arms in order to avoid any further bloodshed. Aside from the shooting outside the palace, the only resistance came from Danish troops in southern Jutland who skirmished with the Germans at a couple of outposts. Sixteen Danes were killed and twenty-three wounded in the fighting. In all, the Germans deployed about forty thousand troops to take Denmark and Norway. Eight hundred German soldiers poured from the ship at Langelinie Pier alone.[2] About four thousand Danish soldiers, most stationed in Jutland, stood against them.

It was decided that the king and the Danish prime minister should issue proclamations to the populace telling them what had happened, and a note was sent to the German government agreeing to their stipulations. The announcements were made in print and over the radio. The occupation of Denmark had begun.

Outside the palace, along the canals and piers and on the cobblestone streets of the city, the citizens of Copenhagen wandered stunned through their hometown, having a hard time understanding what had just happened. They'd gone to sleep a free people; now they faced a future of uncertainty, surrounded by jackbooted and heavily armed foreigners. They walked their bicycles among the German soldiers, gawking and trying to comprehend what had happened and what was to come.

For their part, the German soldiers had been given careful instructions on how to deal with the Danes they encountered. "The Dane is freedom-loving and self-aware," they were told in carefully printed instructions. "He rejects every Coercion and every Subordination. He lacks a sense of military discipline and authority. In other words: spare the commander, don't shout, this fills him with reluctance and is ineffective. Inform and convince in a matter-of-fact way. [Use] a humorous tone as far as possible. Unnecessary sharpness . . . must be avoided."[3]

Out in Jutland, especially along the border with Germany, many who came to observe already held pro-German, pro-Nazi feelings. Some continued to "Heil Hitler" with salutes to the German troops who were taking up positions along the roads and byways. Some offered helpful directions to the foreigners.

In Copenhagen, however, most Danes viewed the distinctive Stahlhelm helmets of the Wehrmacht troops and the black uniforms of the Gestapo with a sense of menace, as if aliens from some distant planet had just landed in their midst. It all seemed unreal.

CHAPTER 2

Ordinary Danes

A MONG THOSE JOINING THE CROWDS IN THE COPENHAGEN CENTRAL city were a brother and sister from the provincial town of Horsens in Jutland. Elsebet and Jorgen Kieler were both students at the nearby University of Copenhagen. Jorgen was twenty years old and was beginning to study medicine, his father's profession in Horsens. Elsebet, a year older than her brother, was a student of literature. They would soon be joined in Copenhagen by two more siblings—Flemming, another student of medicine, and sister Bente, who was studying to be a teacher.

That April morning, however, when it was just Jorgen and Elsebet in the streets of Copenhagen in the wake of the occupation, they came down from their shared flat after being awakened by the planes to find the sky filled with bombers flying low over the city. Like everyone else in the city, they felt that the presence of German troops standing guard in their Danish capitol city was unreal. Jorgen saw his first German soldier near the Royal Gardens, standing bold as you please with a bayonet fixed on his rifle and grenades dangling from his belt, right in the middle of the street. He was surrounded by staring cyclists.

Meanwhile, Elsebet had gone down to the port to see the German ship that had deposited its load of troops into the city. It was a chaotic scene but threatening only in the sense that German soldiers were guarding the streets as if they were their own. When the siblings met again in the central city, they got their hands on one of the circulars that was being passed around, announcing that Copenhagen had been occupied by the Germans to protect Denmark from the clutches of Great Britain.

Jorgen and Elsebet were hardly naïve witnesses to what was happening. The children of a comfortable professional-class upbringing and education in the provinces, both had traveled with the family to Germany as teenagers, and Jorgen had traveled by himself around Europe prior to beginning his studies at the university. In fact, he began his undergraduate work at the University of Munich in 1937, living with a German family and observing German politics and culture close-up and with a critical eye. He'd read *Mein Kampf* but "found it difficult to take seriously." Kieler had also gone to a famed exhibit of "decadent art" in the city—a collection of work by Jewish artists who were detested by Hitler. The art displayed was meant to highlight the emptiness and degeneration of Jewish culture, but to Kieler it was simply new and interesting.

Jorgen had also witnessed the historic meeting between Hitler and Mussolini in September 1937, during which both dictators gave speeches from the balcony overlooking the Konigsplatz square in Munich. Kieler was close enough to the fuhrer to see his "crudely chiseled, brutal and not particularly expressive" face, but he also sensed Hitler's power over the crowd when he spoke. Hitler used "mastered variations of vocal expression, mimicry and gesture" as he approached "his hysterical climax, the slogans, the unproved facts, the hate and self-glorification," all "showered down on the thousands of people on the Konigsplatz in whom they provoked a national orgasm."[1]

Jorgen traveled farther, to Paris and Cambridge in England, before returning to Horsens in Denmark, where he found the people of his hometown and home nation, like everyone else in Europe, in a state of anxiety over Hitler's ever-increasing bellicosity.

On the morning of the invasion, Jorgen and Elsebet returned to their flat with another circular in hand, this one a copy of the king's brief and hurriedly printed message to the people.

"To the Danish people!" it read. "German troops crossed the Danish border last night and landed in various places. The Danish Government has, under protest, decided to settle the country's situation in view of the occupation that has taken place, and in accordance with this the following is announced:

"The German troops who are now in this country are in contact with the Danish Armed Forces, and it is the duty of the population to refrain from any resistance to these troops. The Danish Government will try to secure the Danish people and our country against the accidents resulting from wartime conditions and therefore calls on the population to take a calm and controlled attitude towards these conditions which have now arisen.

"Peace and order must characterize the country, and loyal conduct must be shown towards all who have an authority to exercise."[2]

Now they knew with certainty what had happened to Denmark. That for the first time in its nearly thousand-year-old history, which included numerous wars with Sweden, Germany, and Norway, the Danish nation had been lost in its entirety to a foreign power. Jorgen would later remember feeling "boundless shame and sadness [as] he realized that Denmark had, in effect, capitulated without resistance, despite the assurances of politicians that they were going to defend us."[3]

ANOTHER FUTURE LEADER OF THE DANISH RESISTANCE HAD SIMILAR thoughts as he, too, was awakened by the sounds of German planes filling the skies above Copenhagen. Frode Jacobsen was a thirty-four-year-old scholar and budding politician. Prior to the war, he'd published a book on the German philosopher Nietzsche, but the esoterica of his studies were far from his mind that morning as he woke next to his wife, a woman of German descent from Hamburg. Outside, he could hear the excited chatter of Copenhagen citizens gathering in the streets. He quickly found one of the fliers in the street that the Kielers had spied, and all that was printed there confirmed what others were saying. He heard about the German ship docked on Langelinie and decided he needed to go down to the dock to see for himself what was happening.

Down at the harbor, he was disgusted to find a group of Danes gathered around the German soldiers, smiling, chatting them up, and sharing cigarettes. Some were even showing off by practicing the few phrases of the German language that they had at their command. Jacobsen spoke German fluently and, in fact, spoke the language around the house with his wife. To help vent his spleen, he spoke in German to one of the troopers standing there. "This is not the Danish people," he said contemptuously, warning them that there were harsher sentiments toward the occupation to be found in Denmark, "it's the Danish mob."

Jacobsen would ultimately have second thoughts about the sense of disappointment that he felt toward his fellow Danes in those first moments of occupation. "So unprepared were most people; so little did a large part of Denmark's population understand what had happened; so little had a majority grasped the nature of Nazism. And when the government had issued that statement [the announcement of capitulation.] It would not surprise me if some of those who gathered around the German soldiers that morning were a few years later in the ranks of the freedom movement."[4]

Later that day, Jacobsen reconnected with his wife, who had long since disassociated herself with what was happening in her native land. The two of them made a pact to no longer speak in German in their home. As it turned out, they kept this promise for the length of the war.

NOT FAR FROM LANGELINIE, A BALDING, MIDDLE-AGED CASH REGISTER salesman, working for the American company, National Cash Register, felt a similar frustration to Jacobsen and Kieler as he pedaled along a street in the city. Jens Lillelund, who was generally as mild-mannered as he looked, came upon a company of Wehrmacht soldiers singing a patriotic German song from the First World War, "*Wir fahren gegen Engeland*" ("We sail to take on England") and lost his temper at their arrogance. He made the mistake of spitting into their midst and was immediately collared by the Germans and hauled off to a Copenhagen police station for a six-hour cuffing and interrogation session.

A Danish police officer eventually took pity on him and showed him a back exit from the lockup, advising Lillelund not to be so stupid around the Germans the next time. Lillelund took the advice to heart and determined that if and when he was next arrested by the Germans, it would be for something that hurt them as much as it hurt himself. That didn't prevent him from spending many an evening over the next few months slashing the tires of German automobiles on nighttime wanderings through the streets of Copenhagen.[5] It also didn't stop him from beginning to take lessons in elementary bomb-making chemistry when a pharmacist friend advised him that calcium chlorate, granulated sugar, and acid, mixed in the proper proportions, made a fine incendiary bomb.[6]

OUT IN THE NORTHERN TIP OF JUTLAND, NOT FAR FROM AALBORG, IN THE village of Bronderslev, a group of schoolboys on recess witnessed the coming German attack on Norway as waves of Messerschmitt fighters buzzed overhead. They were alarmed, but confused—what were these planes doing in the sky overhead? Back inside the schoolhouse, they sang hymns in an assembly and learned from their teachers of the king's and prime minister's addresses advising the people of Denmark of what had happened. They were warned not to make trouble with the occupiers.

Later that day, however, two brothers, at home and beyond the watchful eyes of their teachers, fashioned a launching pad from a length of wood and a makeshift fulcrum found in the yard. They began to propel some wet snowballs into the air toward the passing planes. Of course, none of their missiles even left the yard, let alone reached their distant, speeding targets, but it felt good to be launching something at someone.[7]

A DANISH SCHOOLTEACHER EMPLOYED AT A SCHOOL IN NORTHERN SWEDEN on April 9 had a more complex reaction to what was happening in his home country as he read about the occupation from across the Oresund. Watching the events in Denmark with concern, Aage Bertelsen couldn't help but feel that Denmark's freedom meant less to him than did his hope that his friends and loved ones back in Denmark would be kept safe and sound during the invasion. Ashamed by his own sensibility, he nonetheless couldn't help but feel hope that his fellow Danes would surrender to the Germans rather than face the onslaught of a futile fight against the powerful Reich. His thoughts drifted to a future in which he could return to a

Denmark left unscathed by the destruction of a massive German assault.

In the weeks and months that followed, even through his return to Denmark and finding an ever-growing resistance movement in his country, Aage would remain an adherent of the Danish government's cooperative policies as they related to Germany. All the way up to the moment when Germany decided something must be done about the Jewish population of Denmark, three years hence. That was the step too far, the point from which there would be no turning back.[8]

EIGHTEEN-YEAR-OLD HENNY SINDING WAS DREAMING OF THE UPCOMING sailing season in April 1940 when the Germans burst into Denmark. The daughter of a Danish Navy officer who commanded the Danish Lighthouse and Buoy Service in Copenhagen, Henny had grown up on the waters of the harbor and continued to live in housing provided to her father and his family by the Danish Navy in the enclave of Nyboder, which sat on the Christianshavn Kanal just across a narrow stretch of water from the old city in Copenhagen. The distinctive naval housing, bright-yellow-painted row houses that lined the canal, was a landmark for sailors and visitors to the city alike.

The canal ran parallel to Copenhagen's inner harbor, which flowed from the Oresund down into the city. Here was Henny's avenue to peace and contentment out on the water. She skillfully raced sailboats for a sailing club docked just north of the city. She handled dinghies, cutters, sloops, and eventually Olympic-style sloops, gaining an intimate knowledge of the sound in the process. Joined with her already existing knowledge of the docks and canals on which she was growing up, even as a teenager she was developing skills that would soon prove vital to the resistance and the rescue of Denmark's Jewish population.

Of course, all of this was still well in the future. That April morning, Henny had just begun working under her father for the Danish Navy's lighthouse service. Her office was down at the Royal Dockyards, and one of her principal assignments was to keep supplies flowing to the Drogden Lighthouse, which sat at the southern end of the Oresund off the village of Dragor, south of Copenhagen.

The means of getting provisions to this station was a forty-foot boat built of oak and pine about twenty-five years prior to the occupation and operated by a four-man crew. Called the *Gerda III* because it was the third generation of workboats manning these duties from the harbor, the vessel was used to not only provision the lighthouse but also maintain the buoys that marked safe passage through the sound. It was a steady workhorse of a ship, and each morning, it shipped out from the dock in front of Henny's office and each evening it returned to the same berth, ready to continue its assignment the next day. Even as the occupation of Denmark took place and the streets of Copenhagen filled with German soldiers, Henny and the others working for the Lighthouse and Buoy Service understood that their work was still governed by Danish command, so there would be little or no change to their duties until they heard otherwise from the Danish naval command. And on the day of, and in the days after, no word from on high came down to suggest that their work and duties would be measurably changed. [9]

Which turned out to be true for most of the Danish population in the immediate aftermath of the occupation.

NOT SO FOR A SMALL GROUP OF OFFICERS WHO WORKED IN THE INTELLI-gence section of the general staff of the Danish military. With emotions ranging from appalled to deeply disappointed in their own commanders' response to the occupation, they began to formulate a surreptitious response. The officers represented a range of sectors within the military, including the cavalry and the Danish Navy. The officers were soon collecting information about German positions and movements in Denmark, with an eye toward passing their intelligence on to the Allies in London.

The group, unofficially labelled the Princes, knew that Great Britain was establishing an organization to aid and assist with resistance groups in occupied countries called the Special Operations Executive (SOE). The Princes began searching for a means to make contact with the SOE when one of the group's members, an officer from the Danish Intelligence service named Volmer Gyth, was introduced to a newspaper correspondent named Ebbe Munck by Munck's sister-in-law, Jutta Graae, who was a friend of Gyth's.

Graae worked for a bank in Copenhagen and had many connections both in the city and Great Britain, and Munck was a well-known reporter for one of the largest daily newspapers in the city, *Berlingske Tidende*. He had been posted to Berlin, London, Spain during the civil war there, and Finland to cover the fighting that broke out there in 1939 and 1940.[10] He had also made several expeditionary trips to Greenland, where among other feats he became the first Dane to climb Greenland's tallest mountain. What was most pertinent in this resume to Gyth in 1940, however, was the fact that when Gyth met Munck, the reporter had just got himself appointed as his newspaper's correspondent in Stockholm. While these connections, Gyth to Graae to Munck, were newborn in the spring of 1940, they would soon grow into a vital link between the Danish resistance and the Allied cause and, in time, directly to the SOE.

Gyth, and others among the Princes, sent their gathered information via messages that were put on microfilm and smuggled across the Oresund, usually by Danish businessmen holding Swedish passports. They were carried in shaving kits, hairbrushes, and hidden in small containers that could be anally inserted then passed to Munck, who relayed them to a British SOE officer serving in Stockholm. The system would continue through the course of the war, providing the Allies with invaluable information about the political state of Denmark and the German military over the years to come.

Slowly but surely, like-minded Danes were making connections and asking each other questions about what could be done to counter the forces of the occupation.

LEO BESEKOW, A TAILOR IN COPENHAGEN AND THE FATHER OF A WELL-known Danish actor named Sam Besekow, had his own ideas about how to protect himself and his family from what portents this incursion on Danish society might bring. A Jew from Czarist Russia, Leo Besekow had fled that country many years before in the midst of a horrific pogrom. He had no illusions about what horrors an autocratic government could inflict upon its people, particularly its Jews. On the same day that the Germans swept into Denmark, Leo went out and bought a brand-new gold cigarette case, which he then presented to his son, Sam. "If ever we must flee again," he said to Sam, "take this and sell it somewhere so as to get a start!"[11]

CHAPTER 3

The Jews of Denmark

NOT FAR FROM LANGELINIE, THE MERMAID STATUE, AND THE GERMANS pouring from the decks of the troop ship docked there; not far from Henny Sinding and the Royal Dockyards; not far from King Christian X and the ministers at the Amalienborg Castle; and even closer to two other royal homes in Copenhagen, the Christianborg Palace, which held both the Danish Parliament and the king's residence, as well as the Rosenborg Castle, yet another royal home in the area; just down the street from the famed round tower in Copenhagen built by King Christian IV in the seventeenth century as an astronomical tower; and not far from the University of Copenhagen, Hans Christian Andersen Boulevard, and Tivoli Gardens, the well-known Danish amusement park in the heart of the city; indeed, nestled right in the bosom of all of these Danish institutions sat the Great Synagogue of Copenhagen, built by the Jewish community of the city in 1833.

The Jews of Denmark, just under eight thousand people in 1940, had a fairly long and consequential history. Unlike in other European countries, there was no history of Jewish ghettos, no enforced Jewish isolation or pogroms of any sort. Antisemitism existed, but it tended to be incidental to daily life in Denmark, and Jews were fairly well integrated into the business community of Denmark. In fact, many of the first and longest-patriated Jews in Denmark were Sephardic Jews who came from families that had been invited into the country by King Christian IV in the seventeenth century in order to boost the trade capabilities of the nation. In exchange, they were promised freedom to practice their religion. In 1814, yet another king granted them the full rights of Danish citizenship. In time, they became so well accustomed to Danish society that they began to think of themselves as Viking Jews. Until the German occupation, the greatest threat to their community was that they would be assimilated out of existence through intermarriage and conversion.

The early years of the twentieth century brought a further influx of Jewish immigrants from Eastern Europe, primarily from Russia. These were generally people fleeing pogroms and persecution, or they were young Jewish men escaping conscription in the Czarist Army, which filled its ranks with peasants dragged from the villages of Russia and thrust into the military service for a mandatory twenty-five years.

Two additional surges of Jewish refugees added to the population in the years before occupation. The first group came primarily from Germany in the years after Hitler's rise in 1933 and after Kristallnacht in 1938. These were political refugees, many of them children, who were brought out of Germany by sympathetic organizations in Denmark, like the Danish Women's League for Peace and Freedom and the Society of Jewish Women. Their ultimate goal was to see that these young people would one day find a home in a new Jewish state in Palestine.

Similarly, a second substantial group of young Jews arrived in the early 1930s from various European countries with the same intent of ultimately landing in the Middle East. These nearly 1,500 young Zionists came to Denmark from various European countries to learn the ins and outs of Danish agriculture. The goal was to take that knowledge with them to Palestine, where they would pioneer in a new Jewish state and make the desert bloom.

Anti-Semitism existed in Denmark, as it did elsewhere in Europe, but it never reached the fervor that could be found just across the border in Germany, and the numbers of Danes who enlisted in the Nazi movement were limited. Indeed, in the same year that Hitler rose to power in Germany, 1933, the year the Great Synagogue of Copenhagen celebrated its one-hundredth anniversary, it received the full blessing of King Christian, who not only came to a ceremony to mark the occasion but also participated in the special service. What other national leader in Western Europe would have provided a similar blessing in the lead-up to Hitler's Nazi assaults on the Jews and the continent?

For all this, Denmark maintained very strict entry and residence regulations for German Jews trying to flee Nazi Germany just prior to the war. Danish politicians and leaders were content to suggest that the country was satisfied with its attitude toward the nation's Jews, meaning they were satisfied to accept their own population of Jews as full-fledged citizens of Denmark, but, please, no more.

For their part, Danish Jews felt as secure in their homeland of Denmark as they could anywhere in Europe. Jews in Copenhagen were, of course, well aware of the virulent anti-Semitism of Hitler and the Nazis. Kristallnacht was a recent and vivid memory of the terrors being inflicted on the Jews of Germany, but Danish Jews maintained a faith in the Danish system of government and its insistence that all its people would have the full rights of citizenship, even during the occupation.

Part of this attitude toward the occupation, with its reliance on the protections of Danish traditions and governance, was forced upon them. What other choice did the Jews of Denmark have but to put in their lot with the Danish government as it acquiesced to German control? It wasn't as if the eight thousand or so Jewish souls in the country had any means to resist in the face of the overwhelming power of the Reich.

Remember, too, that Denmark was the first country in Western Europe to be occupied by the Germans. The years of the "Final Solution," the years of sweeping up the Jews of the Netherlands, the Jews of France, the Jews of Norway, of Italy, of Hungary, of Czechoslovakia, of Yugoslavia, of Greece, were yet to come. The death camps were yet to come.

Even after the German occupation and all the uncertainties entailed in being sucked up by the tentacles of the Third Reich, the Jewish population, in general, felt as certain as most other Danes in the hope that the country's culture, its democratic traditions, its king, and its economic importance to Germany would save it from the usual depredations visited on Germany's own Jews and the Jews of Eastern Europe. If they just kept their heads down; if they stayed as invisible as possible, they might make it through.

As Marcus Melchior, Ph.D., the second-ranking rabbi at the Great Synagogue of Copenhagen, put it soon after the occupation, "I was not only Danish. I was Jewish. What was going to happen to us now? But regardless of this special fear, the predominant emotion in me, as in Danish Jews in general on this April 9th, was this: What about Denmark? What about our small, decent, delicate, gentle, quietly happy fatherland? What about the King? . . . We turned to the day's tasks stunned and dulled, but compelled to pretend that the world was still standing."[1]

To confirm his sensibility, the rabbi turned to C. B. Henriques, an esteemed lawyer in Copenhagen and chairman of the Danish-Jewish Council in the city. When Melchior ran into Henriques that fateful morning of the occupation, the first words from Henriques's mouth also reflected the deeper concern at the moment. "They are taking our lovely country," the lawyer said.[2]

Ten-year-old Leo Goldberger was the son of the chief cantor at the Great Synagogue. The family had moved to Copenhagen in 1934 from Moravia in Czechoslovakia, when his father, beginning to sense a deepening anti-Semitism in their Moravian surroundings, decided to move the family to safer grounds in Denmark.

Then the day of the occupation came, and suddenly the skies above their new home were darkened by waves of German planes flying above. Leo would later remember finding one of the green leaflets dropped by the planes. He read it and snickered at the "broken Danish" he saw there. The Germans urged Danes to remain calm. The Wehrmacht had "no aggressive intentions, they only wanted to protect Danes from the evil designs of the Allies." The Danes were told to go about their business as usual, simply continue with their daily routines as if nothing untoward had happened, and in fact, to a great extent, Danes, including Jewish Danes, did exactly that. The Tivoli Gardens remained open, the king was soon resuming his daily rides from the royal stables through the streets of Copenhagen. The government reopened to business, the police remained in place, businesses opened their doors, farmers continued to milk their cows, even the Danish armed forces were left in place. The only real difference, Goldberger noted years later, was that the streets were full of German troops and SS officers.

Even the Jewish community returned to its usual daily life. The Jewish school Leo attended, the Jewish clubs, the Great Synagogue itself, all remained open and active, and while the young Goldberger noted an occasional feeling of tense and ominous anticipation, he saw that anxiety principally among those Danes who had arrived in the country from areas that had experienced the horrors of pogroms and anti-Semitism prior to their arrival in Copenhagen.[3]

To Bent Melchior, the teenage son of Rabbi Melchior, it was unthinkable that people should be persecuted because of their religious beliefs in Denmark. No Danish government could survive, he'd grown up believing, that accepted or remained passive to such a position.

However, the Jewish community of Denmark was not of one mind in 1940. The Viking Jews tended to have the deepest faith in the Danish government to protect their interests—the new immigrants, less. The members of the Jewish community in 1940 Copenhagen were like Jews throughout Western Europe in the 1930s, according to Melchior. Subdued. Unobtrusive. Trying to keep a low profile. "Don't let the Nazis know that you are here. Be quiet. My father was told on several occasions that he was speaking too loudly against what was happening. We were not suffering more than others in the country. We should not complain more than others. In the years of cooperation this tendency became even more pronounced. Nobody should say we provoked the Germans."

There was a pretty constant comparison to what was happening in Norway, according to Melchior. But there was a faith that Denmark was different and would remain different. "We were reminded that in Norway, they ended up with the Quisling government. In Denmark we kept a democratic government which was certainly more hostile to the Germans than what was happening in Norway."[4]

In Denmark, the government would strike a deal with Germany to make sure the rights of its citizens remained protected against any depredations advanced by the Nazis. This was Denmark, and it had been so for hundreds of years.

CHAPTER 4

Christian X Goes for a Ride

ON SEPTEMBER 29, 1940, KING CHRISTIAN X CELEBRATED HIS SEVEN-tieth birthday with a ride from Amalienborg Castle through the streets of Copenhagen. To honor the occasion, thousands of citizens came out to cheer his journey with countless Danish flags and thick throngs in the streets of the center city. He wore a full military uniform and cap and rode his favorite horse, Rolf. Offering frequent salutes to the cheering crowds, he slowly circled the cobblestone streets before winding up back at Amalienborg, where he and Queen Alexandrine stood on the balcony and continued to greet the adoring citizens of the city.[1]

The celebration stemmed from a sense of pride that Denmark still stood in one piece. After almost half a year of occupation, the country was essentially functioning as it had before the Germans came pouring over the border. There was no destruction to speak of; the country's Jewish population had been thus far unscathed by the German occupiers. There were rumors that the Germans had been prevented from ordering Danish Jews to wear yellow stars only by the intercession of the king, who was said to have insisted that if his Jewish population was forced to wear yellow stars, he would, too. But they were only rumors. No such demand was ever made of the Danish Jews, and no such statement from the king was ever made or penned.[2]

There were blackouts and rationing and isolated Allied bombing raids, but as Jorgen Kieler noted many years later, not many Danes suffered materially at the time. Instead, and what was in some sense worse, Danes felt like "we were living with a bad conscience." While the rest of Europe was feeling the full weight of German oppression, from the bombing raids in Rotterdam, to the Blitz raining down in London, to the puppet regimes installed in France and Norway, Denmark was doing quite well by comparison. But a feeling of uncertainty and paralysis gripped much of the nation, as did questions about whether or not this policy of cooperation with the German occupiers was what patriotic Danes ought to be doing.[3]

Denmark was a country long accustomed to peace. Not only had the nation not been involved in the First World War, it also hadn't been a part of any war since the mid-1800s. Not only that, but culturally, it was a nation far different than its neighbor to the south. Danes had a rich and proud history of democracy that advocated for the rights of the country's citizens, even the small number of Jews who had lived for many years within its borders, mostly in the city of Copenhagen. Now for the first time in nine hundred years, the destiny of the country had been handed over to Hitler's Nazi Germany without a fight. Denmark would serve not only as a buffer for Germany against the Allies but also as an avenue to Norway and as the grocery store for its citizenry, providing German families and the country's armed forces with all the butter, cheese, hogs, and beef they needed to counteract any wartime shortages that might arise in the Fatherland.

The German ambassador to Denmark swore that his country would not interfere in Denmark's internal affairs, and to some extent this seemed to be the case in the early months of the occupation. The Gestapo had a limited role in maintaining police control in the country, which was left primarily in the hands of the local police. The Danish Army remained intact after being forced to give up some of its artillery and other weaponry. The Danish Navy was allowed to continue to train officers and carry out maneuvers. The Germans even set up an employment bureau in Copenhagen, ostensibly to ease the severe unemployment problems still ravaging Denmark in the wake of the Great Depression. Of course, the jobs being offered Danes were in Germany and were either directly or indirectly intended to further the war efforts of the Third Reich, but they were jobs.

The Danes had few illusions about whether Nazi anti-Semitism would at some point rear its ugly head in Denmark; there was just too much evidence elsewhere in Europe to feel sanguine that it wouldn't. At least initially, however, there were no overt threats against the Jewish population of the nation. Those working in the Danish government, along with the Jews themselves, wanted to believe that Germany would honor its hands-off policy regarding the country's Jews.

With what was called "a policy of negotiation and cooperation" between the two countries, life in Denmark continued largely as it had before the occupation. Schools remained open, businesses continued to operate as they had, and King Christian X continued to take his morning ride, greeting his citizens as he clopped through the cobblestone streets of Copenhagen. The fact that those streets also contained large numbers of German soldiers gawking at a king, who continued to take his daily ride without a heavily armed security guard accompanying him, suggested a huge difference in the Copenhagen before April 9 and this new one.

The king served as the chief totem of the idea that Denmark remained a proud and independent nation, even in the midst of its occupation. It was said that he never returned the salutes of the German soldiers who greeted him as he made his morning rides through Copenhagen, but instead pointedly and graciously acknowledged the greetings of his own citizenry. And countless Danes would claim later that they were often asked by those same German soldiers how the king of Denmark could ride safely through the streets unaccompanied by guards, to which they would reply that Christian rode accompanied, just as he was on his birthday in Copenhagen, by all the people of Denmark.[4]

This same patriotic fervor had perhaps its most widespread expression in a nationwide fad called *alsang*, which began in early July 1940 in Aalborg. There, on the fourth, an all-singing event was staged at a public park. The public was invited to sing along with a local chorus to a number of patriotic Danish songs, including "I Am Born in Denmark," "The Danish Song," and "I Love the Green Groves"—all immensely popular and well-known Danish tunes. About 1,500 people attended the first gathering, and subsequent events brought even larger crowds. Newspaper coverage of the festivities and then radio broadcasts elicited even more enthusiasm for the gatherings, and soon they were happening all over Denmark. In September, a nationwide alsang convention in Copenhagen drew a remarkable 150,000 people to the sing-along. Even more listened and sang along on their radios at home. An estimated 720,000 Danes took part nationwide, and a songbook was published in the king's name to honor him on his seventieth birthday.[5]

Regarding King Christian's faithful allegiance to Denmark's Jewish citizens, aside from the apocryphal legend that he volunteered to wear a yellow star if Jews in his nation were forced to wear them, he was also credited with responding to a German diplomat who questioned him about what he would ultimately have to do about "the Jewish question" in Denmark by saying "There is no Jewish question in the country. There is only my people."[6] Similarly, when another German official reproached him for "negligence of the Jewish problem," he answered by saying, "We have never considered ourselves inferior to the Jews. We have no such problem here."[7]

For all that, Jorgen Kieler remembered the summer of 1940 "as a grim period of my life." He recalled that, along with the alsang festivals, there were collective hiking trips called alsang trips organized within communities. They were also meant to foster and demonstrate national unity. While he took part in some of the activities, Kieler quickly realized that they would not lead to the sort of active resistance to the occupation that he was beginning to see was necessary to effect change.[8]

When he and his siblings—Jorgen and Elsebet were now joined in their studies in Copenhagen by Flemming and Bente—all four bicycled back to the city that fall from the summer holidays in Horsens to continue their education (a trip of 155 miles), they quickly realized that they needed a new flat to accommodate all of them. They found a place on Raadhusstraede, in the heart of the city, just a stone's throw from the university, the canals, and the seat of government at Christianborg.

The sisters shared the large living room in the flat, while the brothers took the two smaller rooms in the back of the accommodations. Living on a tight budget, the siblings ate jointly, usually carrots and stews, or at the nearby student cafeteria (nicknamed "Cannibals' Kitchen") at the university. As the eldest, Elsebet was the boss of the household, which didn't prevent Jorgen from complaining at the never-ending carrots that were served. As the two oldest siblings, their rivalry in the apartment would remain loving but persistent over the coming months.

That fall, they settled into a students' existence, with Jorgen beginning his medical studies at the University of Copenhagen with a particularly challenging class in anatomy taught by Professor H. R. Hou-Jensen. He became friends with fellow students Cato Bakman, Holger Larsen, and Niels Hjorth, who in the months to come would become integral fellows in resistance activities.

A shocking incident in October of that year helped nudge all of them closer to the movement. A German soldier was visiting a housemaid at the institute where their professor lived and worked. Something happened between them, and Hou-Jensen felt obliged to throw the German soldier out of the residence. A fight ensued, and Hou-Jensen was thrown down a flight of stairs and died. "Our anger knew no bounds," Kieler later wrote. But, of course, in a country occupied and controlled by the Germans, it had no place to be vented.[9]

THE INTRUSION OF THE OCCUPATION ON DANISH LIFE CONTINUED through a long, cold winter. There were distant indications that not all Danes were satisfied with the cooperation policy agreed to by the Danish government. The Danish ambassador to the United States, Henrik Kaufmann, was the most public dissenter from his government's new order. Just a day after the occupation, Kauffmann announced in Washington that he would no longer accept or act upon orders from the new government in Copenhagen. Ties were temporarily cut between his office in Washington and the Danish government. Kauffman remained in Washington, where he essentially ignored Copenhagen, while Copenhagen ignored him. But more trouble cropped up between them in a year's time, when, essentially of his own volition, Kauffmann signed over to the Americans the right to establish military bases in Greenland in order to defend that Danish territory from German attack. The Danish government in Copenhagen tried to void the agreement and charged Kauffmann with treason, but Kauffmann declared that the government in Denmark was acting under the auspices of a hostile power in Germany, and he ignored their orders to rectify matters. The White House said thank you very much and began to plan to establish bases in the icy north.[10]

Expatriate Danes living in London formed a group called the Danish Council during the Blitz to show solidarity with the Brits during the relentless bombings that fall. At the same time, Winston Churchill was setting up his SOE, the secretive organization designed to aid resistance movements and sabotage efforts against Germany throughout the occupied nations.

One of the primary movers in the creation of the SOE, a London banker named Sir Charles Hambro, had many connections to Denmark, including with the Danish Princes—the military officers who, as noted, had already been discreetly gathering information on Germany's defenses in Denmark as well as the shipping that was passing through Danish waters. They had already sent their first reports on these matters along to their man in Stockholm, the journalist Ebbe Munck, who had just started his new job as a correspondent at *Berlingske Tidende*. Hambro made a trip to Sweden in the early fall of 1940 to establish a working connection with Munck and, through him, to those supplying intelligence from Copenhagen. All of this intrigue would soon prove essential for British intelligence gatherers in the SOE.

In these early stages of the resistance, there was no attempt by anyone in the nascent movement to directly attack the German occupiers through sabotage. For a variety of reasons, the time was not yet ripe. First off, direct action would have been pointless in the face of Germany's overwhelming power. Second, there was a concern among those army officers supplying intelligence to the SOE that their own Danish military would be demobilized if the Nazis suspected intrigue within its officer ranks, thus ending the Princes' ability to gather information. Third, the SOE was not yet set up to train and supply would-be Danish saboteurs in the art of underground war. Finally, there were already plenty for resisters to do to counter Nazi propaganda and press censorship, with efforts at creating an underground press and creating access to the free press, including BBC reporting from London.[11]

The year 1941 began on a sour note for those looking for a change in the cooperative policy within the Danish government. First, it disassociated itself from the efforts of the Danish Council in London at the behest of German demands, then it acquiesced to German demands when Hitler began his Operation Barbarossa, the massive German effort to subjugate the Soviet Union as it had Western Europe. Danes were immediately suspicious of what these efforts would cost their own country. Germany had already begun to squeeze Denmark to supply more of the agricultural and industrial goods needed to help feed and supply its army and citizenry, so what would it demand now? Might it even insist that Danes, particularly those of German origin in southern Jutland, be conscripted to wage war along with the Wehrmacht in the Soviet Union? And what of the small but vocal group of Danish Communists living as citizens of Denmark? Would the Danish government insist on their protection as Danish citizens when the German SS demanded their arrest, as they did soon after the invasion of the Soviet Union?

The answer to that last question was *no*, and it came quickly in the late summer of 1941, when Danish Communists were rounded up and taken to a Danish internment camp, Horserod, in August. Soon after, the Danish Ministry of Justice drafted a law making any Communist activities and organizations illegal in Denmark.

That fall, matters became even more serious as the Wehrmacht moved deeper into the Soviet Union and pressured Denmark to join the Third Reich, Japan, and Italy in the Anti-Comintern Pact, which aligned the countries within the pact against international communism, in particular.

Danish Communists had not been particularly popular among liberal-minded Danes in the recent past, particularly after they supported the Soviet Union in its invasion of Finland two years earlier. But the Kielers, no Communist sympathizers themselves, were nonetheless appalled by the acquiescence of the Danish foreign minister, Erik Scavenius, to this German demand, as well as the general treatment of Communists in the nation.

When fellow students decided to stage demonstrations against Denmark's signing of the pact in Copenhagen late in November, the Kielers joined the crowd. Gathering at the popular eating hall, Cannibals' Kitchen at the University of Copenhagen, the students began a march along the cobblestone streets toward Amalienborg Palace in "a mood of revolt," Kieler recalled.[12] What was supposed to have been a peaceful protest soon turned ugly when Danish police got involved and unlimbered their billy clubs. Among those whose heads were cracked open was Jorgen Kieler, a fact that he would not soon forget.[13]

Afterward, students involved in the demonstration fully expected university authorities to take measures against the protesters, including possible expulsion, but just days after the Comintern excitement, the world was stunned by news of the surprise attack at Pearl Harbor and the entry of the United States into the conflict. Even in the flat on Raadhusstraede, far from what was happening in the Pacific, it became hard to focus on the events on campus and in Denmark. This was now a world war.

CHAPTER 5

Movement

T HE HISTORY OF DENMARK SUGGESTED WHY BOTH THE COOPERATIVE response of the Danish government and the angry protests of Jorgen Kieler and his fellow students were not unexpected in Copenhagen. In the first instance, the nation had a recent history of steering clear of European entanglements, especially those that involved its powerful neighbor to south. In the second case, Danish citizens had long prided themselves on their independence, dedication to democracy, and willingness to fight to protect these elements of their national identity.

The geography of the country linked it tightly to the commerce of northern Europe and Germany. The narrow body of water that connected the North Sea and the Baltic, called the Kattegat, flowed between Norway and Denmark around the Jutland peninsula. Between Denmark and Sweden, to the east, the water narrowed into a strait called the Oresund, which had long been a crucial component of Danish nationhood. In the late sixteenth century, King Frederick of Denmark built a castle at the narrowest point between the two countries at a village called Helsingor, which would soon become known as Elsinore in the world of William Shakespeare's *Hamlet*. The newly built castle, called Kronborg, was opened in 1574[1] and soon contained a bristling thicket of cannons along its parapets. With these guns aimed out over the sound, Danish royalty soon began to "pull over" commercial ships from around the world to tax these vessels, whose owners were trying to do business between Western Europe and the Germanic city-states on the Baltic, as well as those in Poland, Finland, and the Baltic states.

The funds collected there were substantial and helped build Denmark into a modern nation. However, in the same era as Kronborg was built, Denmark and Sweden, who had been allied, along with Norway, in a union of Scandinavian nations, began to squabble. A series of sixteenth- and seventeenth-century wars between the two neighbors resulted in a peace that was decided in favor of Sweden, which won land concessions from Denmark on the eastern side of the sound. A final series of battles, during which the two countries found themselves allied with opposite sides in the Napoleonic wars of the first decades of the nineteenth century, was the culmination of the Scandinavian warfare. Unfortunately for Denmark, it was tied to the French in these last fights, one of which featured a fleet of British ships helmed by Admiral Horatio Nelson defeating a Danish fleet boxed into the Copenhagen harbor.

As a result of these last defeats to the Royal Navy, Denmark retreated into an extended period of peace and neutrality, which came to an abrupt end in the middle of the nineteenth century when the budding power of a unified Germany, under the leadership of Otto von Bismarck, began to assert itself on the continent. Germany cast a covetous eye toward the provinces of Schleswig and Holstein, which rested on the Jutland peninsula between Germany and Denmark. Though the land was then under Danish control, ethnically, the population was largely German and German-speaking. The population there was inclined to side with the nation to the south, particularly since Germany was, at the time, enacting liberal political reforms that appealed to the general populace. In 1864, Bismarck used this dissension as an excuse for sending troops into Jutland, where they quickly drove Danish armed forces out of both provinces, cutting the territory of the Danish portion of Jutland by almost half in the process.[2]

For years afterward, Danes dreamed of one day regaining this territory, but the fact is the current boundaries between Germany and Denmark were settled by this first invasion by Germany during the American Civil War. One inadvertent effect of the invasion and the new boundary was that the lines of the new Denmark denoted the extent of Danish speakers in the country, making an already homogenous country even more Danish than it had been before.

Another effect was to make Denmark even more chary of international conflicts, especially those where Germany had a contravening interest. This reluctance to be involved was reflected in the fact that the country was about to enter a long period of neutrality that would extend through the First World War. Aside from mobilizing about fifty thousand reserve troops who would never see action during the war, the country's single defensive measure was to mine its territorial waters, including the Great Belt, the body of water on the western side of Zealand between it and the island of Fyn. This was undertaken as a means of keeping Allied navies from infiltrating Danish waters from the North Sea to the Baltic. It was also a concession to Germany, whose Baltic waters were now largely protected from the north by this Danish measure.

On the opposite side of Zealand, on its eastern front, facing Sweden, the castle at Helsingor continued to stand as a symbol of Denmark's pride, history, and sense of independence. With Sweden just a stone's throw away across the Oresund, this Renaissance castle stood as it had since the sixteenth century, as a symbolic bastion of Danish nationhood.

A 1907 addition to the mythology of Kronborg was made present in the dark casements of the castle. Sculptor Hans Peder Pedersen-Dan was commissioned by a local hotel in Helsingor to create a bronze sculpture depicting the legendary figure Holger Danske, whose name (Olger, the Dane) and links to Arthurian legend made him a nationwide hero.

His heroic roots stretched back to medieval France, where his acumen in battle, innate chivalry, and connection to Denmark lifted him to folk hero status in the eyes of Danes. In the story, Olger saved Charlemagne from the Saracens and wound up retiring to his homeland in Scandinavia, where he rested until the day he was needed once again to protect Denmark. Known throughout Denmark, Holger Danske was celebrated in a famed eighteenth-century opera, numerous stories and poems, and a Hans Christian Andersen fairy tale. In the castle sculpture, Holger was depicted as a hero at rest, seated in a chair with his crossed arms resting on a sword won in battle with the Saracens. Wearing a long beard and helmet that hooded his brow, with a shield beside his chair, and his eyes shut in tentative slumber, Holger waited for the moment when he would be called into action.

The hotel placed the original bronze statue in front of its own doors when it was unveiled in 1907, but a larger plaster model of the sculpture was designated to occupy a shadowy nook just off the entrance to Kronborg. There, it served as a symbol of the peaceful yet wary nation of Denmark.

That was exactly how millions of Danes viewed themselves in 1940 when war, rooted once again in Germany's expansionist impulses and this time laced with the fascist authoritarianism of Adolph Hitler and the Nazi Party, came bursting through its door.

Resistance, like the national icon, Holger Danske, was a dormant figure in Denmark in the early stages of the occupation; it was about to be roused.

ABOUT THE SAME TIME AS THE DEMONSTRATIONS WERE HAPPENING IN Copenhagen, a pair of teenage brothers, recently moved from Odense to Aalborg in northern Jutland, were trying to form a new club at the school. Their father was a pastor who had been transferred to the new post and settled his family, including his boys, Jens and Knud Petersen, into their new home. The brothers arrived with an already established admiration for the resistance efforts being undertaken across the North Sea by Norwegian fighters as well as the British Royal Air Force. In Odense, before the move, they had formed something they called the RAF Club to honor British pilots fighting the German Luftwaffe. Now, in Aalborg, in their new school, they formed a new group that they called the Churchill Club and called themselves the Churchill Boys, in honor of Great Britain's wartime leader.

Enlisting a handful of like-minded students at their school, the brothers and the club members began to pursue trouble in the form of small acts of defiance and sabotage against the Germans stationed in the Aalborg area. They created an anti-Nazi sign, a takeoff on the swastika, with arrowheads punctuating the tips of each arm of the symbol, and they painted it all over town. Unfortunately, its mocking tone was lost on most townspeople, who simply didn't know what it meant.

They graffiti-ed the words WAR PROFITEER on the businesses and homes of people who had dealt with the Nazis and wrecked the vehicles of German officers by dropping lit matches into gas tanks or by smashing car radiators. They stole weapons from German soldiers, including grenades. Getting their hands on these was "no trick at all," according to the recollection of one member of the Churchill Boys, who said that "the Germans were incredibly careless with their weapons," leaving them lying around outside their barracks or propped against walls in local restaurants.[3]

As the weeks passed in early 1942, the boys of the Churchill Club grew increasingly bold in their sabotage, culminating in the burning of a freight train loaded with war supplies, including one car loaded with airplane wings. They also set fire to a truck with another load of war materials covered in straw. The boys simply set the hay on fire and slipped away as the lorry drove down the street in a blaze whose origins no one could figure out.

In May, they were fingered by a coatcheck girl at a restaurant who saw Knud Petersen lingering around the establishment on the same evening weapons went missing. The girl pointed out Knud to the police, who grabbed him, interrogated him, and soon had the names of his accomplices. All wound up in the local jail and subsequently received prison sentences of one to three years for their activities.[4]

By this time, the resistance was whirring on several fronts. In December 1941, the British SOE made its first tentative foray into dropping agents into Denmark at the behest of the Danish Princes, who wanted to establish a radio transmission-and-receiving station so that Denmark resisters could send and receive messages with the SOE free of going constantly through Ebbe Munck in Sweden. The SOE dropped two parachutists over southern Zealand with orders to contact resistance forces and establish radio connection to England through a transmitter that was dropped with them. Unfortunately, the parachute of one of the operatives failed to open and he died in the fall. The other jumper, a Danish man named Mogens Hammer, survived the drop and went on to help organize the first SOE team in the country. Still, it would be many months before a well-established line of personnel, munitions, and weaponry could be set up between the British operatives and Danish resistance fighters.

Meanwhile, since the April 9 occupation, control of radio services and newspaper publications had fallen under the purview of the government's foreign ministry. The ministry, of course, had German bureaucrats breathing heavily on their necks to make sure no anti-German news was featured. For skeptical Danes being fed a diet of happy journalism about Hitler and the Third Reich, an unencumbered press was considered an absolute necessity. People could listen to the BBC on the radio, and Swedish newspapers were pretty easily smuggled into the country. Now, underground papers began to appear as well, and in a short time they would become immensely popular.

Land og Folk (Country and People) appeared monthly beginning in October 1941. It was soon followed in December by *De Frie Danske* (the Free Danes), which began its publishing history with a scathing editorial rebuke of foreign minister Erik Scavenius, the man behind Denmark's acquiescence to the Anti-Comintern Pact.

In April 1942, the journal *Frit Danmark* (Free Denmark) joined the parade of underground newspapers with an editorial board whose members stretched across the Danish political spectrum, from the chairman of the Communist Party in Denmark to Christmas Moller, leader of the Conservative Party. He had been a member of the Danish cabinet in early 1940 but was forced out of the government a year later because he was considered too negative by the Germans. Moller and his family escaped to England in 1942, where he began to write for *Frit Danmark* as well as becoming a voice for Danish resistance on the BBC.[5,6] His criticisms on the radio of the Danish government's continuing cooperation policy made him a thorn in the side of both Danish and German leaders, but he was popular with the Danish population as a whole.

Both individual circulation for the papers and the number of journals published increased at a remarkable pace through 1942, so that by the end of the year there were an estimated forty-nine papers being published, with a combined circulation of more than three hundred thousand.[7]

As the year progressed, the "Jewish problem" in Denmark was largely subsumed by Germany's continued "problem" with European Jewry in general. Roundups of Jewish populations began in earnest throughout the summer, and reports of atrocities against Jews in occupied countries filtered through the press in neutral Switzerland. Stories of Jews being swept up from Austria, Poland, Hungary, Ukraine, and Czechoslovakia as well as in the Netherlands, Belgium, and France were hard to fathom. Rumors of extermination camps were just beginning, but few gave credence to the idea that any civilized nation could be so vicious.

A group of physicians at Bispebjerg Hospital in Copenhagen, led by a surgeon named Dr. Karl Koster, responded to these reports by creating a petition that stated the doctors would continue to support the Danish government in its cooperation policy only if the government continued to prevent any persecution of its Jewish citizens.

Meanwhile, the Jewish population itself was caught in the extremely hard spot between trying to avoid attention and trouble by keeping their heads down yet quietly cheering every German setback in the worldwide conflict. Under the circumstances, they could hardly stand publicly in support of the efforts of the small resistance movement. Herbert Pundik, the fifteen-year-old grandson of a Russian hatmaking immigrant and the son of a man who was trying to hoist himself into the middle class in Copenhagen, was a member of the Great Synagogue congregation. He would later remember being severely scolded by the chief rabbi when his parents discovered that he was involved in distributing anti-Nazi newspapers around town and asked the rabbi to mete out a stern warning.[8]

The Danish government, with the notable exception of the already expelled Christmas Moller, remained staunch in its defense of the cooperative policy. In early September 1942, the Danish prime minister, a social democrat, broadcast a nationwide address to the people in which he chided those in the population "who have acted without understanding or have made statements in words and in writing that are in conflict with the policy pursued by the government and the views held by the sober majority of the population with regard to the attitude we should adopt under the prevailing conditions." That meant those who were opposed to the policy of cooperation.

"There have been, in particular, in recent times," he went on, "cases of sabotage against the German armed forces in this country, and it is these deplorable cases which give me reason to say here some serious words for reflection." Not only were the Danish police committed to assisting the Germans in preventing and prosecuting these crimes, he said, but Danish citizens should as well do their utmost to point out and prevent the same. "Help make it clear to everyone, and especially to the young, that anyone who commits sabotage or assists in it or withholds knowledge of sabotage plans from the authorities or fails to contribute to the investigation of sabotage, is acting against the interests of his country." It seemed to many like a license to snitch on their neighbors, a very un-Danish act.[9]

For its part, Germany continued to refrain from twisting the arm of Denmark regarding its Jewish problem. German diplomats in Denmark advised Berlin that the public sentiment among the Danish people was so peculiarly democratic that any movement against its citizenry would cause more internal trouble than it was worth and that it was good to remember that the Danish people were supplying Germany with a good deal of their food as well as industrial production.

AND SO THE COOPERATIVE POLICY BETWEEN THE TWO NATIONS CONTINUED until the king's birthday in September 1942. For the occasion, Hitler sent a telegram "effusive with greetings and congratulations,"[10] as one historian described it. King Christian X was far less expressive in his reply, writing simply, "My best thanks, Christian Rex."[11]

To Hitler, the terse reply sounded like a brush-off. As with all autocrats, a slight like that could not be tolerated. It was said that Hitler flew into an immediate fury, and the fury evolved into a heated simmer characterized by a note sent to the Danish foreign minister at the order of Joachim von Ribbentrop, Germany's foreign minister, suggesting that perhaps the king had "misunderstood entirely the greetings from the Fuhrer."

It should have been interpreted as a "special honor." As for the king, in the future, "all ways and means possible [should] be employed to prevent a recurrence of such behavior."[12]

What might have been a mere kerfuffle if Hitler had not been so thin-skinned quickly evolved into a serious problem, dubbed the Telegram Crisis, which would not only jeopardize the whole cooperation agreement but would also lead in just a month's time to Berlin sending two new leaders to Denmark to administer German policy in the country. On the military side of the German occupation, General Hermann von Hanneken was chosen to take command of Wehrmacht forces in Denmark. Von Hanneken was brought on board to see that Denmark's western coastline was strengthened against possible Allied attack, a matter that had become of much graver concern since the United States had joined the war with the United Kingdom. He was also expected to supply the stick to the Danish people, if they, their king, or their parliament showed any inclination toward defiance of their German partners in cooperation.

Since von Hanneken had little experience in political matters, Berlin also sent an SS officer named Werner Best, who had a background working with civilians in occupied territories. Best had previously served in occupied France, where he had worked on creating a new vision of Europe that would divide the conquered territories into regions based on racial principles formulated by theorists in the Nazi Party. His role in the German administration was to make sure the Danish government stayed both cooperative with the wishes of the Reich and appreciative of the special privileges it was granting the Danes vis-a-vis its Jewish citizens.

CHAPTER 6

1943

ALL OF THIS HUBBUB HEIGHTENED A SENSE OF PRECARIOUSNESS AND anxiety among Danes in general and Jewish Danes in particular. It raised levels of uncertainty about the future of the cooperation policy among those who had already begun thinking that resistance would ultimately be the only tenable position toward the occupation. All of which was heightened in November of 1942, when Germany began arresting Norwegian Jews and sending them to the camps. Of the approximately 1,700 Jews in Norway, around 530 were detained and shipped south, stopping at the Port of Aarhus in Denmark on their way, ultimately, to Auschwitz. The human cargo was identified by the Danish police, but no attempt was made to rescue them.

The humiliation inflicted upon the Danish government by the Telegram Crisis convinced Jorgen Kieler and his siblings that there would be little that it could do to prevent Germany and the Nazi Party from doing whatever they wanted to do in Denmark. Given what was happening all over Europe at the time, and right then, right across the sound in Norway, that meant that eventually, and despite the much-vaunted protections guaranteed by the Danish government, Hitler and company would one day focus on the Jewish problem in Denmark and begin the eradication of Danish Jews. Under the circumstances, what should the Jews of Denmark do? What should Danes in general do?

Sweden, just a few miles across the Oresund from Denmark, seemed the most likely place of refuge for Danish Jews, but it was far too early for most of Denmark's Jews to even consider uprooting their still stable lives in Copenhagen to make the drastic move to a new nation. The material lives of Danes, unlike those of people in the rest of Western Europe, had barely been affected by the war. In fact, agricultural production in Denmark had increased over the first years of the war as more Germans were fed with Danish beef, pork, and butter in 1943 than 1942.[1] That is to say nothing of the fact that Sweden didn't seem particularly interested in accepting an influx of refugees from across the border in Norway, let alone across the sound from Denmark. Their economic ties to Germany were at least as strong as Denmark's, and they had little interest in poking the Third Reich bear with such an open defiance of its well-known interests.

At the apartment on Raadhusstraede, what to do under these circumstances became a debate of deep moral magnitude. The siblings felt that simply pretending that all would be well with Denmark if they did nothing was the sort of head-in-the-sand posture that they simply couldn't countenance in themselves. Something had to be done. A budding philosophical debate between Jorgen and Elsebet was also brewing. An avowed pacifist, Elsebet was fearful of where a full-fledged commitment to resistance might take them. Both she and Jorgen sensed that it might ultimately lead them to acts of violence and that acts of violence might have consequences beyond their control, including death. A thought that Elsebet did not want to entertain.

It was almost a relief, then, when Jorgen was approached, just before the Christmas holidays, by a fellow medical student with a request that he and his brother and sisters distribute a letter from an underground member of the movement, and he jumped at the opportunity. The fellow student was a young man named Niels Hjorth, and the letter was written by Mogens Fog, a professor of neurology at the University of Copenhagen, a founder of the Free Denmark movement, and someone who had gone underground when the Communist Party had been outlawed in the country.

Fog's missive was essentially a call to action for students at the university. Personal responsibility against the occupation and those acquiescing to it needed to be taken by everyone. "Only a drop in the ocean, that's what they say. Well now, the ocean consists of drops."[2]

As a follow-up, Hjorth asked if the siblings might be willing to help print *Frit Danmark*, the paper that they had already been distributing, at the flat on Raadhusstraede. Jorgen, Elsebet, Flemming, and Bente agreed to do so, and soon enough a duplicating machine occupied a space in the living room of the apartment. The Kieler siblings became full-fledged members of the Free Denmark movement. To be fully committed to the cause of the resistance brought a sense of peace to the Kielers. "Two and a half years wandering in the wilderness were over" is how Jorgen summarized his feelings.[3]

They were not alone in feeling as if a corner had been turned. Jens Lillelund, the cash register salesmen who had been apprehended for spitting on a group of German soldiers soon after the April 9 occupation, had tried to keep a hand in early resistance efforts. Jens continued to employ his rudimentary bomb-making skills assembling small but pretty effective incendiary devices. With the help of his wife, Ena, who bought the bomb materials and served as a lookout, Lillelund was soon placing his makeshift explosives beneath a few German cars and running for dear life after the fuse was lit.

But being a member of the resistance was a pretty lonely position for many months in Denmark during the first couple of years of the occupation, Jens discovered, and his efforts served to no great effect. He soon realized that if progress was to be made in the fight against the occupiers, it would need to be through collective action, which was why Lillelund was happy to make the acquaintance of Josef "Tom" Sondergaard in the fall of 1942.

Sondergaard was the co-owner of the Stjerne Radio shop on busy Istegade Street in central Copenhagen. Lillellund, whose job with the National Cash Register company first brought him in contact with the radio shop, discovered that Sondergaard and he shared similar ideas about the German occupation and what might be done about it. Neither was an obvious saboteur. Middle-aged businessmen of the day, both were given to wearing fedoras and jackets. Lillelund was fair-haired and balding; Sondergaard was swarthy, with a thick brow and a heavy, though close-shaven beard. Neither Lillelund nor Sondergaard, or the shop itself, were exactly what they seemed. The radio shop crew included not only Sondergaard but also Carl Munck, the other co-owner of Stjerne, who employed a pair of his brothers at the shop, as well.

The group was linked not only by its hatred of the occupiers but also by the fact that all were involved in the writing, editing, and distribution of an illegal anti-German magazine called *De Frie Danske* (as opposed to *Frit Danmark*, which the Kielers were involved with in their own sphere), which was being printed in the back room of the radio shop, right there in the heart of Copenhagen. The Muncks and Sondergaard had been practicing their own brand of agitprop in the streets in front of the shop by playing American and British tunes from loudspeakers onto bustling Istegade Street when German troops were nearby. Songs like "It's a Long, Long Way to Tipperary" as well as the Sunday news broadcasts from the BBC.[4] On a more dangerous level, the group had, as well, made a few preliminary attempts at bomb-making.[5]

Lillelund quickly became a regular at the radio shop, but he knew, as did the others, that as bold as they might be, their work wasn't as effective against the Nazi takeover as it could be. They needed assistance to really show the people of Denmark that a resistance was active and fighting to rid the country of the Germans. They needed weapons and bomb-making supplies as well as training and intelligence on the sorts of targets that would do the most damage to the occupying force.

They got some assistance in these areas from the earliest resistance group to organize in Denmark at the time: BOPA (Borgerlige Partisaner, or Civil Partisans) was the nickname for the first centrally organized sabotage organization in the country. It was composed of a small group of Communist partisans who formed after they were forced to go underground when the party was banned in 1941. The organization's first acts of sabotage were carried out during the summer of 1942 by around fifteen Communists, which included Mogens Fog, the university professor who penned the letter that the Kielers helped distribute over the Christmas holidays.[6]

To arm their group, BOPA members stole weapons and munitions from the German and Danish Armies. Many of their early members were veterans of the International Brigade, which had fought in Spain during the civil war there in the late 1930s; they had some training in the tactics of sabotage and war.[7] They supplied the group at the Stjerne shop with weapons when they could, but both BOPA and the radio shop group soon realized that it would be most effective for them to work directly with the SOE. However, making that connection was not as easy as looking for a phone number in a Copenhagen directory.

AFTER ITS INITIAL PARACHUTE DROP, WHERE IT LOST ONE OF ITS TWO agents, the SOE reassessed its plans and paused until the spring of 1942 before resuming the drops. The results remained mixed. Of the first three parachutists to drop in Denmark that spring, two were killed while being arrested by Danish police.

In October 1942, Mogens Hammer, the original parachutist who survived the jump that killed his partner, made back and forth trips after that first one. After trying to set up a consistent radio transmission system in Denmark, he went back to England and then returned to Denmark. The purpose of this second drop was for him to establish and maintain a network of contacts so that the work of supplying the Danish resistance could begin in earnest. Hammer made some important connections, including with Mogens Fog and BOPA.

The following spring, the SOE also connected with a group centered around an inn (or *kro* in Danish) in northern Jutland. The owner of the establishment was a man named Marius Fiil. He, his family, and a handful of neighbors and close acquaintances became known in resistance circles as the Hvidsten group.

Fiil helped identify a good place in the region to serve as a drop zone, on the edge of a forest near the kro. Beginning in March and into April and May, the group became the primary receptacle for airdrops from the SOE, which included voluminous amounts of weapons and munitions as well as additional SOE agents. Fiil, his wife, and their two daughters and two sons-in-law, along with their closemouthed friends, who included a local veterinarian, a truck driver, a miller, and a carriage maker, collected and stored the munitions that were dropped near the inn. In addition, they hid the agents who landed near the Hvidsten kro drop zone.

The home of one of the daughters, Kirstine, nicknamed "Tulle," and her husband, Peter Sorensen, became the center of the group's activities. Not only did they house the SOE parachutists who dropped into their world, but Tulle and her sister also served as couriers for the group, helping to establish and keep open lines of communication between the newly arrived agents and the established Danish resisters. Tulle and her husband also helped plan and execute the highly successful drops. There were just four drops that spring, but in them the Hvidsten group was able to receive and deploy seven agents and over fifty containers of weapons and explosives, making it one of the most successful SOE drop zones in all of Europe.[8,9]

CHAPTER 7

Bohr

A T LEAST ONE MORE SOE ACTION NEEDS MENTIONING: IN MARCH, THE SOE enlisted Volmer Gyth, the prince who had helped establish the link between his group of military intelligence officers and Ebbe Munck in Stockholm, to help establish another vital conduit for the Allied effort in Denmark.

When the German Wehrmacht marched into Denmark and usurped the freedom of the Danish people, they also ensnared Denmark's most renowned and respected citizen, the world-famous physicist Niels Bohr. Gyth first contacted Bohr in early 1943 at the request of the SOE, who were relaying an inquiry from British scientists: Would Bohr be willing, the scientists wanted to know, to come to Britain to work with physicists on a most-important project for the Allies? The Danish physicist had previously expressed a deep disdain for Nazi ideology, and it was assumed by the British that if he had allegiances in the war, they would incline toward the Allied side of the conflict.

Bohr had worked or studied with every leading physicist in the world by the time World War II began. His ascendence in the realm of the science began soon after he began studies in England in 1912 to do postdoctoral research on an emerging idea. He began to focus on what came to be called quantum physics, which was essentially the study and description of the mechanics of how atomic particles interact with one another. His ideas were new and radical and were met with resistance from older physicists and excitement by his own younger generation of scientists.

Over the next decade and a half, Bohr's models for the behavior of the cloud of electron particles whizzing around an atomic nucleus proved accurate in experiments time and again, and his work was lauded and gradually gained acceptance as groundbreaking in the world of physics. In 1916, the University of Copenhagen awarded him with a new professorship, which was soon followed by his being named the head of a newly created Institute of Theoretical Physics in Copenhagen. In 1922, he won a Nobel Prize for his work and his institute quickly became known as a hub for the best and brightest of Europe's young physicists, including the Hungarian scientist Georg Hevesy and the brilliant young German Werner Heisenberg, who arrived in Copenhagen in 1926 to serve as Bohr's assistant and polish his own theories of quantum mechanics.

Along with his friend and colleague, Albert Einstein, Bohr was widely regarded as one of the world's most brilliant physicists, and he was a dyed-in-the-wool Dane. He came from a well-known family in Copenhagen. His father was a highly regarded member of the faculty, a professor of physiology at the University of Copenhagen, and along with his younger brother, Harald, also a budding scholar, Niels had been a standout football player on the Danish national team in their youth.

Niels lived with his family in a mansion in Copenhagen, right next to the famed Carlsberg beer company, which had, in fact, gifted the opulent residence to Bohr as a gesture honoring "a man or woman deserving of esteem from the community by reason of services to science, literature, or the arts." His brother, a mathematician of renown and prestige, was also on the faculty at the University of Copenhagen.[1]

One other important biographical fact was that Niels Bohr's mother came from one of the leading Jewish families of Copenhagen. Ellen Adler was the daughter of a well-known banker who had served in the Danish Parliament and who sent Ellen off to the university, where she met and fell in love with Niels's father. Though Ellen had sublimated most ties to her religious background through the marriage, and Niels himself was not an active participant in the faith, his links to Judaism remained an important component in his life, as would soon be made evident.[2]

Bohr's accomplishments in the world of physics occurred at an hour when the science of physics was taking on an importance on the world stage that it had never known before. The mysteries and latent power of a potential atom bomb were being explored at a head-spinning rate in Great Britain, the United States, and Germany, and the Allied request of Bohr as expressed through Gyth, that he come to London to work with British scientists, was also an expression of their desire that he not be cornered by the Germans and coerced into working on their nuclear project. In short, Bohr was wanted by the Allies to work on their own vital and top secret atomic bomb project, which British and American scientists hoped might bring an end to the war.

So it was that Gyth paid a visit to Bohr at his mansion at the Institute of Theoretical Physics on the grounds of the Carlsberg company in Copenhagen in March 1943. But Bohr immediately rejected the offer to come to Great Britain without some written confirmation of its legitimacy. It was too early for him to consider uprooting his family on the basis of a visit from a young officer like Gyth.

Gyth dutifully relayed this answer back to London via the mail through Stockholm, which involved, in this case, hiding the microfilm response beneath postage stamps. The SOE's response was to send Gyth back to Bohr with the request that he impress upon the physicist the deep Allied concerns that Germany would complete its atomic work before it could be finished by the United States and Great Britain.

Yet again, Bohr put the brakes on his removal. He was just not convinced that it was feasible that anyone could harness nuclear power in the form of a bomb at this point in the work. At any rate, he could keep a closer eye on Germany's progress in the matter in Denmark, where German scientists continued to use his laboratories at the institute and where he could keep tabs on what they were doing far better than he could in London or the United States.

Gyth once again passed the message on to the SOE, and this time they got back to him through Jutta Graae, Munck's collaborator in Copenhagen. Incoming from London was a direct appeal to Bohr from one of his closest colleagues in Great Britain, Professor James Chadwick, a physicist at Liverpool University. This time the subterfuge to get the message to Bohr was even more elaborate than hiding microfilm beneath postage stamps. Graae contacted Gyth to tell him that a set of keys had arrived from Sweden with a message embedded in them for Bohr. To extract the message from the keys, Gyth would need to file down the keys to a depth of four millimeters, where the spies at the SOE had embedded a tiny piece of microfilm containing the message from Chadwick. The speck of microfilm then needed to be floated out of its hidey-hole with a syringe, placed on a slide, and viewed through a microscope.

Chadwick's message assured Bohr that he would be welcome in England with open arms and that he could continue the work that he was pursuing in Copenhagen in Great Britain, but that he might be asked to advise on "certain special problems on which his cooperation would be of the greatest value."[3]

Once again, Bohr refused the invitation. He still felt the need to stay in Denmark to fulfill his "duty in our desperate situation to help resist the threats to our free institutions and to protect the refugee scientists who have sought sanctuary here."[4]

There remained, too, his ongoing skepticism about the possibility of creating a bomb. "However, neither such duties nor the danger of reprisals against my colleagues and relatives would weigh sufficiently to keep me here if I felt I could be of real help in other ways, but that is scarcely likely. Especially I feel convinced that regardless of what the future may hold, immediate use of the latest wonderful discoveries in atomic physics is scarcely possible."

CHAPTER 8

August 1943

EVENTS ON THE WORLD STAGE WERE FELT IN DENMARK IN THE SUM-mer of 1943. Not only had the German advance in the Soviet Union stalled at Stalingrad, but the Allies also were now fully invested in the war effort. They'd pushed Rommel out of North Africa and were advancing up the boot of Italy and had driven Mussolini out of office. It seemed to many in Denmark and elsewhere that the tide had turned in the war and that it was only a matter of time before the Allies, bolstered by the presence of American armed forces in the battle, would soon set their sights on the liberation of Western Europe.

Encouraged by these sensibilities and now with the help of munition supplies from the SOE, Danish partisans began to nip at the heels of the German occupiers with an increased level of sabotage. Beginning in July, attacks against companies doing business with Germany as well as the railways on which supplies headed to Germany were carried began in earnest. Most of the activity was initially centered in Jutland, in Esbjerg on the west coast, where a fish warehouse that had been supplying its catch to Germany was blown up by resisters. The subsequent fire precipitated fighting between Germans, who blamed locals for the fire, and the citizens of Esbjerg, who objected to the rough treatment. Meanwhile, at the shipyard in Odense, a German minesweeper was bombed by saboteurs, which led to the deployment of a German security force at the harbor. The increased presence of German authorities prompted a strike by 3,500 Danish workers at the shipyard.[1] Issues were finally settled only after the German Navy agreed to haul the damaged minesweeper away from Odense. It was a victory for the resisters, but it was hard to say, at this early stage of the struggle with Germany, whether it was pyrrhic. [2]

All of this activity didn't go unnoticed at the Stjerne Radio shop in Copenhagen, which was still blaring its BBC broadcasts and "Long Way to Tipperary" style song selections from its storefront loudspeakers. Sondergaard, Lillelund, and the Muncks had used their connections to BOPA to garner some explosives with which they did some damage to local factories. But increasingly, they felt the need to work directly with the principal source of munitions in Denmark, the SOE, in order to get the amount of explosives they needed to do real damage to the German occupiers. Under the circumstances, however, in which resistance figures were multiplying daily and the dangers of undercover agents from the Danish police or the Gestapo posing as resistance fighters were ever-present, it wasn't a simple proposition to safely contact the SOE. It was also no easy task to get supplies from Jutland to Copenhagen, particularly because the Great Belt—the waterway separating the islands of Zealand and Fyn from the Jutland peninsula—was well guarded by the Germans. Finally, for the small group of would-be saboteurs in the radio shop, why would the British trust them, a group of middle-aged men hanging around a store, with their precious bomb-making equipment?

CHAPTER 9

Holger Danske 1

In order to project a more concrete image of themselves as a group of resistance fighters, Sondergaard, Lillelund, and the Muncks decided to give their little organization a name that would resonate with their fellow Danes. They chose to call their group Holger Danske, after the legendary Danish hero who was said to have saved Denmark in past times of crisis to the nation. The ferocious knight, having served in the employ of Charlemagne, was called home to Denmark at a moment of peril for the monarchy. He now occupied a chair in the king's castle and sat, with his helmet on, his shield at his side, and a sword across his lap, waiting for the enemy to arrive—a symbol of the peaceful, yet wary, and fully prepared nation of Denmark.[1]

Here was an icon Danes could quickly associate with the current crisis. Not only was Hans Christian Andersen's story about him still taught in schools, but the eighteenth-century opera about Holger Danske was being restaged for large audiences during the war, a must-have ticket for Copenhagen theatergoers. And of course, one of the most famous sculptures in the country still sat at the Kronborg castle, memorializing the figure of Holger Danske at Shakespeare's Elsinore, at the narrowest point of the Oresund.

The seemingly intractable difficulties of connecting with the SOE for the newly christened Holger Danske resistance group were finally overcome in late July 1943, when Tom Sondergaard was arrested by the Danish police and thrown into jail. There, he was rescued by a pair of resisters, who took him to a safehouse, where he met Poul Hansen, one of the SOE parachutists. In this roundabout fashion, Holger Danske made the connection not simply to the SOE but also to the cache of munitions they would need to set off the sort of explosion that would catch the attention of the German occupiers. In fact, when Lillelund saw the amount of incendiary bombs and explosives available to the group via the SOE, he would later tell an interviewer, "It was like the first time I saw a Christmas tree."[2]

They soon settled on a target substantial enough that it would no doubt grab the attention of all of the Germans and all of Denmark and remind the entire country of the legend of Holger Danske. If they could pull it off. The largest exhibition hall in all of Copenhagen, indeed, in all of Scandinavia, was a structure in the district of Frederiksburg, just on the edge of the center city called the Forum. Built in the 1920s as a venue for bicycle racing, auto shows, and industrial exhibits, it was an unusual structure for the time. It had a concrete block foundation and was encased in glass on its upper floors; framed by steel girders, it was large enough to cover most of a single city block. The Germans had recently announced that they were usurping the building for use as a barracks for their burgeoning army forces based in the country.

The thinking among the Holger Danske group, was fairly simple. They assumed that a successful attack on the Forum, along with the other attacks occurring that summer, would so enrage the Germans that the Reich would eventually place intolerable demands on the Danish government and jeopardize the cooperative policy between the two nations. They were hoping to achieve what were called "Norwegian conditions," under which there would be no cooperation at all between Germany and Denmark. The thinking was that as things stood now, Germany was controlling the ways and means of Danish governance, anyway. So it was better to have a complete break now than be forced into whatever future measures the Germans might impose, including the roundup of Denmark's Jewish citizens and arm-twisting recruitment efforts aimed at sending Danes to the Eastern Front.

All of which might explain the reluctance of large segments of the

Jewish population in the country to fully embrace the resistance movement. Jews in Denmark remained reluctant to bring attention to their plight for fear that a focus on them would simply remind the Nazis of the unresolved Jewish problem in Denmark and suggest that something needed to be done soon about their presence in a country controlled by the Third Reich and Adolph Hitler.

To the resisters, however, there could be no comfort in continuing with the status quo. Denmark and its Jews could never be safe or free with Germany as its occupier. Which is why on August 24, 1943, a handful of Holger Danske saboteurs descended upon the Forum with a destructive intent.

Work on the renovation of the Forum was ongoing that day when the resisters began to arrive around noon. Indeed, the time of the attack was intended to coincide with the daily lunch break of the work crews. The saboteurs wanted to be certain that no Danish lives would be lost or put at risk in the attack. One of the group, a man named Max Baeklund, rode an elongated bicycle with a carrier on its underside, a style of bike known locally as a Long John.[3] Suspended in the rack was what appeared to be a case of Tuborg beer, the famed local Copenhagen brew. Hidden under the bottles were twenty-eight kilos of plastic explosives.

Baeklund got off his bike near the south entrance to the hall, while Lillelund leaned against his own bicycle near the same entrance, reading a newspaper. A taxi driven by a third member of the group was parked outside the Forum. In the back seat sat another member of Holger Danske, with the cell's only submachine gun, a recent acquisition from the SOE, straddled across his lap. Sondergaard and the final member of the group, a man Ewald Moesgaard, arrived, both wearing workmen's overalls. They moved directly into the building to help Baeklund carry and place the explosives inside. Lillelund, the taxi driver, and Bob Jarset, who held the submachine gun, stood watch outside.

Once inside, the trio with the faux case of Tuborg scanned the building. They hustled a work foreman and guard outside with a wave of pistols that they'd brought along for just such a purpose. The case of explosives was placed in the center of the hall by Baeklund, and the three saboteurs were just getting set to light the fuse on the bomb and run when yet another Danish worker appeared and pleaded with Sondergaard: Could he please be allowed to grab his bicycle before it was blown to smithereens by the coming blast? In wartime Copenhagen, bicycles were worth their weight in gold, and he would need it for future work. Sondergaard took pity on the man and told him to go fetch his bicycle and then decided to do a final check in the building for stragglers. It was that last search by Sondergaard that turned out to be one too many.

Baeklund lit the fuse with Tom Sondergaard still inside, and the blast came in a matter of seconds. It was loud enough to be heard all the way to the harbor in downtown Copenhagen and powerful enough to shake buildings throughout Frederiksburg. Debris rained down outside, mainly glass, and concrete turned to a dense powder that filled the air and covered those standing around outside the Forum, including the members of Holger Danske. As sirens begun to wail around them, a headcount revealed that one of them was missing. A split second later, Lillelund saw Sondergaard crawling from the wreckage of the building, bleeding heavily. The other Holger Danske members lifted Sondergaard into the waiting taxi, and the driver sped off to a nearby safehouse, where Baeklund's brother, a doctor, tended to Sondergaard's wounds.[4]

The hall was left a skeleton of its former self. All of the glass was gone, and most of the concrete was pulverized. Oddly, no flames accompanied the blast, because there was little in the structure that was flammable. What stood were the girders that had framed the building, now suggesting the ghostly presence of what had been largest exhibition hall in all of Scandinavia. Hundreds of Danes gathered about the rubble, mouths agape, wondering who was responsible.[5]

The explosion resonated beyond the confines of Copenhagen. Word of the bombing filtered out to Jutland in Esbjerg and Aalborg and in Fyn at Odense. In conjunction with the turmoil from earlier in the summer and ongoing incidents in the provinces, it added to a sense of upheaval and chaos in the country as a whole. The death of a young resistance fighter in a clash with Germans in Aalborg and more strikes and work stoppages added more fire to the flames. Which prompted the German military leader in Denmark, General von Hanneken, to send tanks into Aalborg, further enflaming the situation. Seven Danes were killed during the unrest, and Germany declared a state of emergency in the city.[6]

On the day of the exhibition hall bombing, Berlin ordered Werner Best, who was overseeing the cooperative policy in Denmark for the Germans, to come home immediately to explain to Hitler what was happening in the country. When he got to Germany, Best tried to explain the difficulties of occupying Denmark to his spluttering Fuhrer. Best, who had seen firsthand the seriousness of the Danish sensibility about the nation's Jewish citizens—and knew that any attempt to round up or ghettoize Jews would be met with staunch resistance in Denmark—tried once again to impress this fact upon the Fuhrer, but Hitler was having none of it. He said bluntly that what was happening, or not happening, with the Jews of Denmark was "loathsome."[7] Change was needed in Copenhagen, and it was needed immediately. If Best couldn't put his foot down on the unrest in Denmark, General Hermann von Hanneken, who was Best's archrival for the role of plenipotentiary in Copenhagen, certainly could.

CHAPTER 10

Jorgen and Elsebet

E VEN AS THE ACTS OF SABOTAGE GREW MORE FREQUENT IN DENMARK, culminating in the increase of bombings and strikes in August, back at their flat in Copenhagen, the Kielers and the coterie of like-minded students who were printing and distributing *Frit Danmark* argued over how best to continue their activities in the resistance. In the spring of 1943, the sentiment of the majority of the dozen or so students in the Raadhusstraede circle was that sabotage was still premature. For some members of the group, particularly Elsebet Kieler, the difficulty with the violent route was philosophical and religious. A confirmed pacifist, she knew that the bomb-making and carrying of guns involved with the work of a saboteur would inevitably lead to acts that would most likely be murderous. She couldn't justify the use of deadly weapons in her mind when the Christian commandment, "Thou shalt not kill," was a simple tenet of her life.

Others in the group were deterred from the sabotage route by more practical considerations. The feeling among them was that as students, they should leave sabotage to resisters with more knowledge of the tools and skills necessary to carry out the deeds. People who worked in factories, working men and women in general, were more apt to know and have the special skills needed to infiltrate industrial settings where their bombs could do the most damage. Beyond the Kielers, the group was composed of med students like Jorgen and Flemming, including Niels Hjorth,

Holger Larsen, and Cato Bakman; two pairs of siblings, Hanne and Hans Moller and the Lund sisters, Ebba and Ulla; and a trio of law students, Jette Stamp, Helge Jensen, and Jorgen Jacobsen.[1]

Jorgen was among the group of students who felt that it was not right for resisters like himself to assert the need for sabotage without being willing to risk all the dangers incumbent in performing the role of a saboteur. Jorgen had also been influenced by the effects of a British bombing raid in Copenhagen in January 1943. The RAF had struck a shipbuilding yard in the heart of the city and wound up killing a handful of Danish workers while inflicting virtually no damage on the yard. To Jorgen, it seemed obvious that a Danish sabotage team could do a far better and more effective job than planes dropping bombs from above.[2]

His sisters, Elsebet and Bente, remained firm in their commitment to nonviolent protest, but they were troubled enough by the ethical questions involved to seek counsel on the matter. Elsebet wrote to a well-known Danish poet and spiritual leader in the movement named Kaj Munk, who was both a resistance leader and a clergyman, to ask his advice on what path she should pursue. His reply was unequivocal: "Burn all your literature on this topic," he wrote, "at the present moment it is not relevant, or is simply a millstone round your neck—and learn how to use a machine gun."[3]

It would take some time for Elsebet to take this advice to heart. Not so for Jorgen. He went back to Horsens that summer and almost immediately hooked up with an old schoolmate there named Peer Borup, and they began plotting means to bring sabotage to Horsens, just as it was being done in nearby Esbjerg and Odense. Like the members of Holger Danske, they had a rather grandiose vision of what was to come with their actions. They imagined that their sabotage would foment general rebellion in the Horsens area, which would prompt German reprisals, which would initiate strikes, street disturbances, a state of emergency, and ultimately a breakdown of German-Danish relations. Their ultimate hope was for the Allies to acknowledge Denmark "as one of them in the struggle against Hitler."[4]

Kieler, his friend Borup, and his fellow med student from Copenhagen, Niels Hjorth, who was spending the summer working at a hospital in Jutland, were spurred into action by circumstances in the city of Aalborg, where a German patrol took two resistance members prisoner. Rumors quickly flew that they would soon be put to death. Kieler and Borup hoped to instigate a strike in Horsens by simple persuasion in order to distract the Germans from their plans, but they had only limited success in getting the shops in the city to close their doors, and no factories were shut down. Some stronger tactic was needed. And the two settled on a large act of sabotage as their best means to impress themselves on the situation.

There were two parallel railways that ran along the eastern seaboard of Jutland between Aarhus to the north and Horsens in the south. The route had grown vital to the Germans since Sweden had recently revoked a transit agreement with the Reich, which pushed all transit coming from German-occupied Norway through Danish Jutland and down to Germany rather than through Sweden. Saboteurs had already noted the importance of these lines and the increased usage and had caused disruptions on one of them, but resisters had not yet struck at the other line, where a railroad bridge that stretched over Stensballe Sound just outside of Horsens made for a strategic target. Kieler and Borup marked it with an *X*.

Like Holger Danske, however, they had the initial problem of finding the explosives necessary to carry out the sabotage. They also had the same problem with the SOE—there were no connections that they were familiar with in the Horsens area to call upon. So Borup went to local BOPA resisters in the area, who offered some modest instruction on how to use the explosives and steered him to a shoemaker's shop in Horsens where he would find the bombs needed and get additional advice on their use.

There were two bombs in the package. Though Kieler and Borup knew or understood little of the munitions they would be planting, they later learned that one of them was a British-manufactured plastic explosive and the other was what was known as a termite bomb—a firebomb with a smaller explosive element; it, too, was of British design and make. Each had detonators that allowed the saboteurs an hour's escape time from the moment the fuse was lit to the bombs' explosions.

The bicycle ride to the sound was pedaled in a steady rain that added to their nervousness. They were fearful that any accident, any bad jolt in their ride, might cause the explosives to detonate. They got to the bridge safely and scoped it out, noting that it was constructed of iron and that a pair of sleeper cars were perched on its bed. They decided to put the more powerful bomb, the one with the plastic explosives, at the intersection of two load-bearing girders. The firebomb was attached to one of the sleepers. Working through the rain to the best of their knowledge and capabilities, Jorgen and Borup placed the bombs, lit the fuses, and pedaled for home.

Back in Horsens, Jorgen listened for the explosions emanating from the bridge. He worried about the windows in the homes surrounding the structure, that the blast would shatter glass and disrupt innocent lives. As it turned out, his fears were misplaced. He thought he heard just one small explosion in the night, but hardly the boom he'd expected.

In the morning, his apprehensions were confirmed—he and Borup cycled back to the bridge and saw that it was still standing. The only damage was a small hole blasted in the center of the structure, along with some fire damage to the sleeper. No windows in the nearby homes were shattered; no girders were crumpled into the water.

Kieler and Borup were failed saboteurs but were safe and sound and undaunted. They decided it was time to head back to Copenhagen to continue their resistance work from the flat on Raadhusstraede.

That night, after a good-bye to their parents, Jorgen and his sister Bente took the last train out of Horsens and returned to a drastically changed city. [5]

CHAPTER 11

State of Emergency

W ERNER BEST RETURNED TO DENMARK FROM BERLIN IN THE DOG-
house. Not only had he failed to do anything to dampen the increasing levels of sabotage in Denmark, but the ongoing "loathsome" Jewish problem in the country also remained as it had been since Germany
had occupied Denmark, which is to say, nothing had been done to resolve
the nagging matter of the Jews' continued presence there.

To begin to rectify issues in Copenhagen, Berlin decided to replace
Best as its principal policy advocate in Denmark with von Hanneken, the
military leader, who was given a list of specific demands for the Danish
government, dictated by German leadership in Berlin, and to be presented to the Danish Parliament. On the morning of August 29, the Danish
Government was ordered to declare an immediate state of emergency in
the nation. Public gatherings of more than five people were outlawed, as
were strikes and any kind of financial support for strikers; curfews would
be imposed at eight-thirty in the evening, with no exceptions; and all fire-
arms that had not been confiscated already were to be turned in by September 1. In addition, special tribunals were to be established to deal with
any infringements upon the special dictates of the emergency acts, and
sabotage or any attacks on Wehrmacht units or members of the military
or possession of weapons or explosives were punishable by death.

The Danish Parliament and cabinet of ministries barely mulled them
over. They simply could not accept the German demands and still call

themselves a proud nation. The government flatly rejected the stipulations and shut down its functions and offices. King Christian not only applauded the decision of his parliament but also actually declared himself a prisoner of war. The Danish government, cooperative or otherwise, was essentially over.

All the dictates rejected by the Danish Parliament were thereby imposed by fiat and enforced by the Wehrmacht. The next day, the citizens of Copenhagen awoke to find German troops swarming everywhere in the city, guarding and occupying all government buildings. In addition, von Hanneken ordered the roundup of hundreds of Danish leaders, including military figures, intellectual and political leaders, and, for the first time, leaders of the Jewish community.

Best, now second-in-command in the German hierarchy in Denmark but still trying to curry favor in Berlin, gathered a group of Danish editors around him and lectured them as if they were children: "In this ridiculous little country, the press has inoculated the people with the idea that Germany is weak. . . . The proclamation [of von Hanneken] is our answer."[1]

The Copenhagen that the Kielers returned to from their summer in Horsens was already altered by the time they arrived. The government of Denmark, having rejected the German ultimatums, felt it had no alternative but to resign, which it did with the king's acceptance. Telephone and postal services were suspended. Germany flooded Denmark with a surge of army troops and proceeded to disarm the Danish military. German police arrived to bolster the Danish gendarmerie. The cooperative regime was over.

Some, like Jorgen Kieler, had hoped that the members of the Danish government might have escaped to Sweden or somehow to Great Britain to form a government-in-exile that could align itself with the Allied war effort, but it didn't happen. Instead, government operations were turned over to the Danish civil service, which functioned at a bureaucratic level, providing day-to-day civic services and functions. The Danish police and judicial system remained, but with an overbearing German presence constantly looking over their shoulders.

The question of what was to happen next buzzed over the city of Copenhagen like those low-flying German bombers that had flown over Denmark on April 9, three years earlier. Gone to Sweden for the most part, at least temporarily, was the resistance movement, at least in its Holger Danske manifestation. In the wake of the grand explosion at the exhibition hall, HD 1 was able to transport the wounded Tom Sondergaard across the Oresund to Sweden, and most of the rest of the group followed him over the water as the state of emergency took effect. Only Jens Lillelund remained behind to maintain some semblance of the organization, but for all intents and purposes, Holger Danske was over.

After the resignation of the parliament, von Hanneken and the Wehrmacht quickly moved against the Danish military, beginning with the army. There was some fighting in the process as the Germans assaulted and disarmed a number of Danish garrisons. When the dust had settled, over six thousand Danish soldiers had been taken into custody and fourteen killed in the skirmishing.

The Danish Navy put up a fight at the Copenhagen Navy Yard, lobbing grenades and firing machine guns as the German Navy swept into the harbor. The Danes delayed the inevitable just long enough for the Danish admiral commanding the fleet to run up a flag signaling to his vessels that they should scuttle their ships or make a dash for Sweden. Within a matter of minutes, much of the Danish Navy was either headed to the bottom of the Kattegat or the Oresund or on its way to Sweden. Of the nearly fifty ships in the fleet, only six wound up in the hands of the Germans. At any rate, and despite the last second heroics, the Danish Navy ceased to exist.[2]A cousin of the Kieler siblings was a naval cadet on a Danish ship sailing in the Great Belt between Jutland and Fyn on its way to Sweden when it was boarded by sailors from a German vessel. The Danish captain, however, had already placed a bomb in the lower decks of his own ship, and he called his crew together and told them to put on lifejackets, that the ship would soon be going down. Indeed, that's what happened, and the cousin, Svend Kieler, along with a buddy of his named Erik Koch Michelsen (nicknamed Mix), soon found themselves floating in the sound as they watched their ship sink to the bottom. The two, along with the rest of the crew, were soon picked up by the same Germans who had apprehended their ship in the first place. They would ultimately wind up being held as prisoners for a brief time. Mix was incarcerated at a Danish Navy lighthouse off the southern coast of Zealand at Drogden, where he made the acquaintance of the crew of the lighthouse supply ship, the *Gerda III*, as well as the young woman, Henny Sinding, who handled the boat's scheduling. All of these—Henny, Mix, Svend, and the *Gerda III*—would soon be part of the life of the Kieler siblings in Copenhagen.

IN ADDITION TO THE ATTACKS AGAINST THE DANISH MILITARY, THE GER-mans began to round up citizens suspected of being involved in the resistance. Included in this initial sweep were educators, journalists, artists, and intellectuals, along with many of the leading figures in the Jewish community in Copenhagen, including Max Friediger, chief rabbi of the Great Synagogue; C. B. Henriques, head of the temple's Jewish Community Council; and Axel Margolinsky, a leader in the life of the synagogue and the Jewish community in Copenhagen. All were rounded up and detained at Horserod, the Danish detention camp in northern Zealand.

The arrest of the chief rabbi caused a deep unrest to settle over the Jewish community in Copenhagen, with reverberations that swept through other rabbinical offices. The chief cantor at the synagogue, Eugene Goldberger, and his family, including fifteen-year-old son Leo, had a terrifying three-o'clock-in-the-morning visit from the police. The cops pounded on the front door of the house with rifle butts, waking up the neighbors, and called out for the "Goldbergers" to come out. The cantor went to Leo's bedroom, where Leo and a brother were hiding, to implore them to remain quiet. The pounding continued, as did the shouting for the "Goldbergers." Only when the neighbors called out, saying the family had left Copenhagen for a summer cottage in the north, did the Germans go away. It was a partial truth. Leo's mother and a baby were, in fact, at a cottage on the north end of the island near Helsingor. That's where Eugene and his two older boys went surreptitiously the following morning to escape the growing tension of Copenhagen.

Two days later, there was a break-in at the law office of Arthur Henriques, brother of C. B., during which armed assailants took the syna-gogue's community files in what appeared to be an obvious attempt to collect names and addresses of members of the community. An ominous occurrence. The theft was brought to the attention of a Danish minister who, in the absence of a cabinet and government, was managing the for-eign office in Copenhagen. A protest was also sent to Werner Best, who was still acting as plenipotentiary for the German government in Den-mark, despite the fact that his authority in that position had just been compromised by General von Hanneken's state of emergency decree.

Best did nothing about the break-in, which alarmed many Jews in Copenhagen but still prompted no immediate response. The Jewish com-munity still held out hope that Denmark would somehow reinstitute its government and once again return to the status quo, the cooperative agreement, that had pertained for the past few years.[3]

As the level of resistance rose in 1943, there had been a slight increase in Jewish efforts to leave Denmark. A group of Zionists from Eastern Eu-rope who had come to Denmark prior to the war to study Danish agricul-tural techniques pioneered some possible escape routes. Some explored the possibility of fleeing by means of continental railroad transportation headed toward the Middle East. A group of five hid in large crates shipping to Turkey, but they were caught in Hamburg and would ultimately wind up in Auschwitz.

Another group of agricultural trainees learned how to sail a fishing boat and pilfered one from a Danish village for a midnight voyage to Swe-den. The trio involved was successful in their escape, proving the feasibili-ty of the route. Any other attempts of this sort, however, were discouraged by the fact that Sweden offered no sense that its arms were open to a mass migration of Danish Jews. It was also assumed that the German Navy and Denmark's own Coast Guard were thick in the Oresund, watching for and ready to apprehend any would-be refugees escaping Denmark for Sweden. In addition, the more established Jewish community in Copenhagen still felt that escape attempts were premature and ill-considered in light of on-going circumstances.[4] The leaders of the community still didn't want to rock the boat for fear that overt dissent and resistance would bring the wrath of the Reich down upon them and wreck what was, if not an ideal, at least a workable set of circumstances for the Jews of Denmark.

They would have been far less sanguine if they had known what Best was doing behind the scenes. In an effort to regain favor with the powers in Berlin, head of the SS Heinrich Himmler and German Minister of Foreign Affairs Joachim von Ribbentrop, Best began to shift his thinking in regard to his long-standing certainty that inflicting the Reich's usual remedy for dealing with the Jewish problem in its occupied lands—round-ups and camps—would only aggravate the Danish people and cause more troubles than it was worth. There was no Danish government now to protest German policies. Why not give Hitler what he wanted? What was standing in his way?

In a telegram sent to Ribbentrop soon after the state of emergency was declared, Best requested that the increased numbers of German police coming to Denmark to supplement the Danish police be placed under his purview, as well as the special court system that would deal with matters pertaining to the resistance. Ribbentrop's response was noncommittal. In a follow-up telegram on September 8, Best sent a fateful note to the foreign ministry reinforcing his earlier telegram and going a step further. Now he recommended that the time had come for the arrest and deportation of all of Denmark's Jews, to be carried out by the newly reinforced police presence that he'd requested in his earlier telegram and which would be serving under his authority rather than his rival von Hanneken's.

The new message and request thrilled its most important recipient in Berlin. In fact, Adolph Hitler was so delighted to hear that the time was ripe for action against the Danish Jews that he immediately reversed his recent decision to elevate von Hanneken and restored Best as Germany's plenipotentiary in Denmark. It was precisely the effect that Best had hoped for.

Of course, none of these exchanges were known to the people in Denmark, with the exception of Best's staff in Copenhagen, who would be involved in carrying out the plan. One of these, a German diplomat named Georg Duckwitz who headed German shipping operations in Denmark, was aghast at the plan. He had lived in Copenhagen for many years and was a close friend and confidante of Best. He was also tight with a number of Danish political figures, including leaders of the Danish Social Democrats, one of the two major political parties in Denmark.

Duckwitz had a deep understanding of Danish concerns and attitudes, especially as they pertained to feelings about the German occupation. He knew that the moves against the Jews outlined in Best's telegram would enflame public opinion against the occupation in Denmark and would ultimately be a cauldron of trouble for Germany. Duckwitz not only said as much to Best, he also headed off to the foreign ministry in Berlin in a futile attempt to see if he could do anything to offset the influence of Best's telegram.

He soon learned that Ribbentrop had passed Best's telegram on to Hitler, who, as noted, was more than happy to see it. The Fuhrer passed to Himmler the responsibility of providing Best with all means necessary to solve the technical issues of a roundup, which included providing the trucks and ships necessary to arrest the Jewish population and put them on transport to be sent to Theresienstadt, a concentration camp near Prague in Czechoslovakia. The enthusiasm of Hitler for his Final Solution was not easily contained. The wheels for the gathering of the Jewish population of Denmark were turning, and there was nothing that Duckwitz could do about it in Berlin.

As it turned out, Duckwitz was not through in his attempt at thwarting the full impact of the decision.[5]

CHAPTER 12

Duckwitz

ON SEPTEMBER 17, THE DANISH FOREIGN MINISTER, NILS SVEN-ningsen, visited Best in his office to pass along a new complaint about another German burglary. This time it was at the Jewish community center in Copenhagen, where offices had been broken into by Germans wearing civilian clothing. They had been driven to the center in a German police car, detained the Jewish librarian and archivist who ran the offices, and impounded books and archival records. More names and addresses of members of the Jewish community were stolen, again with obvious intent. This time, Best admitted knowledge of the affair, but he brushed it off as small potatoes, an attempt by German authorities to find and arrest people working in the resistance.[1]

Duckwitz, who was privy to the meeting between Best and Svenningsen, quizzed Best afterward about what was really happening. Best confessed to him that the raid had, in fact, been preparatory to a coming roundup of Jews, to which Duckwitz asked that he be kept in the loop regarding the timing of events, a necessity in his role as director of shipping in Denmark. The next day, Best informed Duckwitz that two transport ships needed by the Germans for moving the Jews of the city out of Denmark would be pulling into the Copenhagen harbor on September 29. The same day as this conversation, September 18, a contingent of SS commandos arrived in Denmark to help facilitate the *aktion* to come.[2]

Duckwitz felt it was time for him to take more immediate action. He traveled to Stockholm to tell the Swedish prime minister about the impending roundup of the Jews of Denmark and to encourage him to open Sweden's ports to Danish Jewish immigrants. The Swedish prime minister, Per Hansson, told Duckwitz that he couldn't speak for the entire Swedish government. That he couldn't supply an immediate answer, and even if he could, he would have to let Berlin know if, indeed, Stockholm decided to let the Jews come into Sweden.

It was obviously not the answer Duckwitz was hoping to hear. Duckwitz left Sweden to head back to Copenhagen, where, Hansson told him, the Swedish embassy in Denmark would keep him posted on Berlin's reply to the idea of allowing the Danish Jews into the country. Duckwitz was fearful that he already knew what that answer would be.

IN THE MEANTIME, WORD HAD REACHED NIELS BOHR AT HIS INSTITUTE AT the University of Copenhagen that action would soon be taken against him and his institute colleagues, many of whom were Jewish and already refugees of German oppression. The rumor was that a Gestapo agent had been assigned the task of arresting Bohr a few weeks earlier, during the emergency roundup at the end of August, but the agent had held off when it was decided that the apprehension of Denmark's most famous scientist was certain to garner negative worldwide attention and that the arrest would receive far less publicity if done during the coming general roundup of Jews.[3]

Bohr had also grown nervous over other rumors that he'd heard about the Germans' advances on their development of atomic weaponry, namely, that they were ramping up production of uranium and heavy water, elements crucial to their development of a nuclear bomb. He wrote a letter to his friend Professor Chadwick, confiding his concerns about the development of the German bomb, and he contacted Gyth to get the missive sent to England via Sweden. This flurry of action made the extraction of Bohr from Denmark an even greater concern in the eyes of the Allies, and they quickly responded to Bohr's expression of growing urgency.

In addition, Bohr soon learned from the Swedish ambassador to Copenhagen that a Jewish émigré scientist and collaborator at the institute named Stefan Rozental was about to be arrested by the Gestapo. Bohr contacted the underground, and arrangements were made to get Rozental out of Denmark to Sweden. The escape took place by means of a nine-hour voyage in a rowboat pilfered from a city park in Copenhagen. As it turned out, the trip was a portent of escapes to come.[4]

A few days later, Bohr once again got together with the Swedish ambassador, who this time hinted that it was Bohr's turn to be arrested by the Gestapo. His brother, Harald, confirmed the rumor the next morning when he told Niels that an anti-Nazi German woman who worked at Gestapo headquarters in Copenhagen had passed along word to him that she had seen papers straight from Berlin, ordering the arrest of both Niels and Harald.[5]

The Bohrs decided to leave immediately. Niels and his wife, Margrethe, and Harald, with his wife, made hurried preparations to get out of Copenhagen. Niels and Margrethe left behind two sons after making arrangements to have them brought over later under less fraught circumstances. The two couples walked through Copenhagen to an area on the southern edge of the city where all the streets were named for famous composers. They were guided to a crowded gardener's shed on Mozartsvej, where another group of refugees were huddled, waiting for the signal that it was time to go. When the moment arrived, all were herded through dark alleys beneath a night sky to a motorboat docked on a quay on the inky water.

Bohr was given space in the cramped boat's cabin, while others squeezed among herring boxes on the deck. The vessel's engine coughed awake, and with its pistons sputtering, it headed into the sound on its way to Limhamn, a village near Malmo in Sweden.[6]

SOON AFTER HIS RETURN TO COPENHAGEN, DUCKWITZ VISITED BEST AND learned with finality that there was no German plan to pull back: the pogrom was going to happen. It would take place to coincide with the arrival of the transport ship in the Copenhagen harbor on October 1. The roundup of Danish Jews would begin on the first day of Rosh Hashanah.

Duckwitz was convinced that the movement against the Danish Jews was a grave mistake by the Reich, an unforced error that would eventually have dire consequences for the Germans. He was also convinced that Best, at bottom, agreed with him, that removing the Jewish population by force was an unnecessary measure that would ultimately simply enflame the rest of the Danish population against the Germans.[7] Duckwitz continued to feel as if it was his duty to inform the Danes of what was coming, and he felt that he had, if not the full blessing of Best in this task, at least an implicit understanding that he could go ahead and do so.

On September 28, Duckwitz hustled over to a meeting of the Social Democrats at a workers assembly hall in Copenhagen, where he knew that he would find not just sympathetic listeners to the news he had but also listeners who could pass the importance of its meaning to the appropriate ears in the city's Jewish community.

Despite all the inklings that had been taking place in the country, despite the emergency measures, the martial law, the ruination of the Danish government, and the earlier arrests of Jewish leaders, it was still not a message that was certain to be immediately acted upon. Jews were still being told by the remnants of the Danish foreign ministry that the Germans had no plans to take action against them. Because of his connections to the Danish government as the former leader of the country's Social Democrat party and because of his connections to the leaders of the Jewish community, Duckwitz felt certain that Hans Hedtoft was the best man to approach with his warning. His words to Hedtoft painted a stark picture of what was to come: German ships will soon anchor in the Copenhagen harbor. Those of your Jewish countrymen who get caught by the Gestapo will forcibly be brought on board the ships and transported to an unknown fate.[8]

For his part, Hedtoft described himself as speechless with rage, listening to Duckwitz and realizing what was to come. All he could manage to say to the German was "Thank you for telling me," then Duckwitz was gone and Hedtoft was left to pass the word on to the Jewish community.

Knowing of Duckwitz's closeness to Best, who would have been the source for this information, and knowing that the German shipping expert had no ulterior motive for misleading him on this crucial matter, Hedtoft felt certain of its authenticity. It was now up to him to convince the Jews of Copenhagen that after all the warnings and cautionary notes that had come their way over the past months, that this was the warning that had to be heeded.

He drove to the office of C. B. Henriques, the esteemed attorney and president of the Jewish Community Council, and asked to speak to him in private. Nervous and uncertain at what was to come, Hedtoft told Henriques that a terrible disaster was about to take place. "The action against the Jews which we have feared is about to be carried out," Hedtoft said. He told Henriques that on October 1 and 2, the Gestapo was coming to all Jewish homes in the city to detain and march the Jews of Copenhagen to ships in the harbor, there to be transported to camps in Germany and parts east. "You will have to warn every single Jew in this town," Hedtoft continued. "We are ready to give you all the assistance we can."[9]

Henriques's response was quick and unequivocal: "You're lying," the lawyer said.

Henriques had just talked with Acting Chief Rabbi Marcus Melchior, who'd met with five members of the foreign ministry the day before. There had been rumors the Friday before that an action was coming, but they'd been dampened over the weekend when the nation had once again celebrated a birthday of King Christian, his seventy-third. Melchior was reassured by the secretaries with whom he'd met: if anything was going to happen, the Jews of Copenhagen would be properly warned.

But the reason the Danish foreign ministers had nothing to tell Melchior, argued Hedtoft, was simple: it was because the Germans had told them nothing. The Jews would be at their most pliable if they suspected nothing. His warning of impending disaster, on the other hand, was coming from Duckwitz, the one member of the German plenipotentiary staff who could be trusted to tell the Danes the truth about what was to come.

It took endless minutes for Hedtoft to convince Henriques of the pending danger. Finally, the true nature of the crisis sank in. Henriques was convinced and promised to go directly to the Jewish congregations through its rabbis. It was September 28. The week of Rosh Hashana, the Jewish New Year.

CHAPTER 13

Time to Act

Leo Goldberger, the son of the great synagogue's cantor, was annoyed by the fact that his father was making him go to the earliest service on the day before Rosh Hashanah. There didn't promise to be a whole lot of attendees at the temple that early, and a *minyan*, a quorum of ten adult males, was needed in order to have a public service. Leo had gone through his bar mitzvah just a year earlier, so he qualified now as an adult and was needed for the head count.

Leo felt further put out as he and his father walked into the synagogue and saw probably seventy-five or eighty people in attendance. His presence hadn't been needed after all. But as the service began, he quickly understood that something different, something serious and important, was going on there. Still vivid in his mind was the night just a few weeks earlier when the Gestapo had pounded on the family's front door, calling for the "Goldbergers."

A renewed sense of dread settled within him as he watched Rabbi Melchior approach his father on the altar during the service with a worried look on his face. The rabbi whispered something to the cantor soon after Leo's father had begun the singing. Now the same concerned expression that the rabbi wore was passed to Leo's father and subsequently to faces all over the synagogue. A moment later, the rabbi raised his hands and the singing stopped. He stepped forward to address the congregation. It is time for us all to go home, the rabbi announced. The service was over.

It was time to prepare to leave the country. The Nazis are coming. Let others know

There were moments of stunned inaction until Rabbi Melchior repeated what he had just told them, this time as a shout. Quickly, the members gathered their coats and belongings. They paused only briefly for hugs, kisses, pats on the back. The touch of hands and exchange of fearful looks. Be strong, be brave. It cannot be as awful as you think.

The synagogue was closed the next morning. Leo Goldberger, his father, and his brother were out of Copenhagen, back in hiding once more, with his mother and little brother at their summer cottage north of the city. Scores of other Danish Jews had likewise headed to whatever safe houses they could find.[1]

THAT SAME MORNING AT A PUBLIC SCHOOL IN NORTH COPENHAGEN, SIX-teen-year-old Herbert Pundik was summoned from a French class by the school's headmaster along with a couple of classmates and the teacher. In the hall outside the classroom, they were told bluntly, "The persecution of the Jews will soon begin. You had better hurry home. The Germans may be here at any moment."[2]

Pundik was the grandson of Russian Jewish immigrants to Denmark who had escaped a pogrom in their native land in the early years of the century. The grandfather was a hatmaker, and Pundik's own father had sold his father's hats to dockworkers in the Copenhagen harbor in the early years of his career. He'd since become a successful businessman, affording his family a nice apartment in East Copenhagen.

After receiving the headmaster's warning, Herbert ran back into the classroom to retrieve his schoolbag. The classmates still inside vaguely understood what was happening; an ominous sense of dread hung in the air in Copenhagen at that moment, and Herbert's sixteen-year-old friends were old enough to sense it. A close chum of Pundik's handed his Jewish classmate his own Boy Scout compass as a going-away present to Herbert for an uncertain future.

Herbert headed for home, crossing the bridge over the Langelinie harbor toward East Copenhagen. He took a streetcar to Fridtjof Square, where he hopped off and, to his own mind inexplicably, stopped at a newspaper vendor's stand to pick up a paper. As if he needed to read about the pressing news that the Germans were coming for him and his family and all the other Jews of the city.

By the time he got home, his whole family was dressed and ready to go, wearing winter clothes and carrying a bare minimum of luggage. It turned out that his father had received a call at his office from a friend who had attended the morning service at the synagogue. Pundik's father called his own father and brothers, and so the word had spread through the Jewish community in Copenhagen.

Though the Pundiks had been alerted to the impending *aktion*, there was still a great deal that they didn't know, beginning with the fact that two German transport ships were on their way to the Langelinie pier in the Copenhagen harbor, preparing to be loaded with the Jews of the city in order to ship them to Germany and on to the camps. Though they were packed and ready to go, the Pundiks didn't know where they were to go for the night, let alone for the days and weeks to come. If it was to Sweden, how would they get there? Who would transport them? How could they avoid the Gestapo patrol boats cruising in the Oresund? Would Sweden let them in? How would they pay for their journey?[3]

There was one other thing they'd heard rumors of but didn't know with absolute certainty. Those concentration camps that the Germans were planning to ship them to were not just labor camps but rather killing grounds. Jews were being slaughtered all over Europe. And now the Nazis had come to Denmark, the one country on the continent where they thought they were safe.

GERMAN SPIES WERE THICK IN MALMO, THE SWEDISH CITY DIRECTLY across the sound from Copenhagen. It was where Niels Bohr and his family landed after their flight from Denmark. Volmer Gyth, Bohr's contact with the resistance and the SOE, was already in Sweden—in Stockholm— and was well-aware of both the scientist's exodus and the fact that he was in immediate danger of being swept up in Malmo by Nazi agents who were embarrassed by the physicist's escape.

Bohr's escape was not complete. The British had hoped to whisk Bohr quickly out of Sweden to get him to London as soon as possible. The problem was that Bohr had learned from the party leader, Hedtoft, just as he was leaving Denmark, of the Nazi's plan for a nationwide sweep of all the Jews of Denmark, beginning that weekend. He felt an immediate obligation to do what he could to help prevent the mass detention of the would-be refugees. The answer seemed to him that he should try to make sure Sweden opened its arms to anyone wishing to escape from Denmark. He asked to go to Stockholm, where he thought he could use his influence and reputation to convince the Swedish foreign ministry to announce to the Danish people that refugees would be welcome.

Getting Bohr safely to Stockholm was itself a problem. Gyth had been in touch with a Swedish police official whom he'd warned of the dangers facing Bohr in Sweden, The official had blithely responded that Malmo was not Chicago, the American city with its famous gangster reputation. Gyth had responded that under the current circumstances, something far more dangerous than Chicago was on the other side of the Oresund in Denmark. Gyth took it upon himself to head to Malmo to escort the scientist to the capital city.

Under Gyth's watchful eye, Bohr made it safely to Stockholm and asked to talk with the Swedish undersecretary of foreign affairs to request that a Swedish protest of the German action be made public. The subsequent publicity, Bohr believed, would pressure the Nazis to desist with their roundup of the Danish Jews and encourage Sweden to allow Danes to come to its shores. But Bohr got nowhere with the undersecretary.[4]

He then decided to go directly to Gustav, the king of Sweden, who happened to be married to the sister of the Danish king. Christian's sympathies for the Danish Jews were well-known. However, Gustav had his own government to deal with, and despite the dire circumstances and the sympathies of his brother-in-law, there remained opposition to letting the Danes into Sweden.

From the beginning of the war, European Jewish refugees had sought and been denied temporary refuge in Sweden. A small shift in this obstinance began when Norway had been occupied by the Nazis. Sweden allowed about half of that country's Jews, around nine hundred in total, to take refuge in Sweden. Sweden had also been allowing small groups of Jews and other refugees into the country for some time, but the large exodus envisioned for Denmark's Jews was still hard for the Swedish government to countenance or encourage, despite the growing acceptance of the fact that a Nazi *aktion* was coming.

News of this eventuality had even reached the United States, where the independent Danish ambassador, Henrik Kauffman, now no longer officially representing Denmark but still with influence on Danish funds in the United States, offered to help fund Jewish refugees who landed in Sweden. Danish assets in America were frozen at the time, with control of these funds in the hands of the American president, Franklin Delano Roosevelt, with whom Kauffmann had a friendly relationship. Kauffmann's generosity two years earlier in signing over the rights for an Allied military base on Greenland was still received gratefully at the White House. Also to consider was the fact that the Danish Merchant Navy had continued to supply vital transportation needs to the Allies through the first years of the war despite, its burdensome relationship with Germany.

On the other hand, Denmark itself had a somewhat compromised reputation in the United States because of the cooperative policy with the Reich. The feeling was that not only had Denmark not put up a proper fight before it was occupied but also that the relationship that evolved between Denmark and Germany after the occupation was a little too comfortable for the Danes, in Allied opinions, especially considering the devastation in other parts of Europe.[5]

Ultimately, the Swedes turned down Kauffmann's offer, anyway. As it turned out, the argument that ultimately swayed them was similar to what had galvanized the increased pace of resistance in Denmark. It was the pretty sure knowledge that Germany was beginning to lose the war. Like everyone else, the Swedes could see what was happening in Africa, in Sicily, in Italy, and all along the Eastern Front.

Bohr left his meeting with the king pleased about the discussion but not absolutely certain of its outcome. He had apparently set the wheels in motion, however. Still, he wasn't ready to be flown to Great Britain.

BACK IN COPENHAGEN, HERBERT PUNDIK'S FATHER CALLED FOR A TAXI TO facilitate the family's departure. Herbert threw together a small bag of clothing, leaving behind his most precious possessions: a stamp collection, a collection of postcards that he'd gathered from uncles who had traveled in India and Africa, and a small library of favorite books, including *Tarzan* and the collected comedies of the Danish writer Ludvig Holberg.

His mother gave the apartment key to a neighbor, and everyone clamored down the stairs. Herbert stifled an impulse to knock on the door of a girl on the first floor, the object of a deep crush. The family climbed into the cab and headed toward Lyngby, a northern suburb of the city, where Herbert's father had a business associate who was willing to take the Pundiks in for a night.

The next day, the Germans came to the vacated apartment and rang the bell. And rang it again. And again. Until the neighbor lady came out to tell them that the Pundiks had left. Finally, the Germans gave up, a scenario that was repeated often in those first two days of October 1943 in Denmark. The Jews had gone underground.[6]

CHAPTER 14

The Germans Move Against the Jews

FROM THE GREAT SYNAGOGUE OF COPENHAGEN, WORD OF THE IMPEND-
ing roundup spread like wildfire throughout the city and out into the
countryside, but there was no central means for Jews in Denmark to communicate with one another, and shortly after 9:30 on the evening of Friday,
October 1, 1943, phone service across the country was abruptly cut. How
was word to get out?

Earlier that evening, at eight o'clock, the German *aktion* began when
twenty large trucks in a convoy left the port of Copenhagen filled with
green-uniformed members of the German Wehrmacht, grinding through
the heart of the city. Also occupied by the soldiers was the one active news
bureau in the city, to make sure no teletype could be sent out to tell the
outside world of the raid. By eleven-thirty that evening, thirty more trucks
had joined the first twenty, and all exit roads from the heart of the city had
been blocked.

German soldiers, along with Danish police, began scouring the streets,
looking for Jewish names on doorplates in the city. Others consulted the
directories that the Gestapo had swiped earlier from local synagogue
offices in preparation for this day. They smashed in apartment doors to
cross-examine the occupants about whether they were Jewish. In some
cases, they were able to collect keys from apartment building custodians
and were thus able to obviate the need for kicking in doorjambs. Whole
families were dragged away, including the elderly and at least one baby,

only two months old. They were bullied toward the dock, where one of two large steamships, which had just arrived in the Copenhagen harbor, was ready to transport them out of the country.[1]

Some Jews found shelter with non-Jewish Danes; some hid in the parks and wooded areas around Copenhagen; many sought shelter at city hospitals, especially Bispebjerg Hospital, which rested on a hill overlooking downtown Copenhagen and served as a teaching hospital for the university. It had expansive green lawns on the property and an extensive underground tunnel system connecting its various wings and pavilions.

At an old-age home near a Copenhagen synagogue, 150 German policemen invaded the premises and marched away all its residents, aged sixty to ninety. Here were some of the most brutal assaults. A bedridden woman, paralyzed for over ten years, was dragged into the nearby synagogue, interrogated, and beaten when she couldn't name any leaders of the resistance. The Germans stole everything they could get their hands on and pissed in the synagogue for good measure.[2]

Early in the morning on October 2, a group of Danish Communists who had previously been detained at Horserod, the Danish detention camp in northern Zealand, were marched to the Langelinie dock to be loaded on the second of the steamships. They were lined up on the promenade and watched in horror as the elderly Jewish prisoners from the home were forced with whips and kicks onto one of the ships while the Communists were being prodded onto the other. Both ships began to steam away between ten and noon.

That night, a little more than two hundred Jews were rounded up in Copenhagen and an additional eighty-two were grabbed in the western provinces of the country to be transported later, but fortunately, hundreds of Jews had already left their homes to look for hiding places before the roundup could reach full scale.

Quite a number of Jews quickly found their way to the coastal villages and towns of Zealand, including Helsingor, with its looming castle fronting the shore overlooking Sweden. Here was the inviting narrowest stretch of waterway on the Oresund. But almost every town on the coast suddenly looked like a means of escape to the would-be refugees, from Gilleleje at the very top of Zealand down all the way to Dragor, south of Copenhagen, with its half-timbered cottages and winding village streets all seeming to lead down to its docks and quays.

The taxis arrived from the city with their desperate passengers looking to find fishermen willing to transport them across the sound to safety in Sweden. But with no entrée to the community of fishermen and no contacts to facilitate or organize the connections, it was not an easy path to follow. Money was needed to pay first for the transport to these coastal departure points and then to pay the fishermen for the means to cross to Sweden. For those who considered finding a rowboat to paddle themselves across the sound, the Germans had imposed, just a few weeks earlier, a rule prohibiting anyone but a licensed fisherman from keeping a vessel on the water. All other boats needed to be hauled at least one thousand feet inland.

There were numerous other obstacles for individuals and families making the journey. Rabbi Melchior of the Great Synagogue of Copenhagen used a connection with a Lutheran pastor in Orslev in southern Zealand, near the island of Falster, to arrange passage with a young fisherman who promised to take him and his family, along with thirteen other refugees, to Sweden. They left that evening on what was promised to be a six-hour voyage. The only problem was that six hours soon turned into twelve hours, and when dawn appeared the next morning, the fisherman could see land off the bow of the boat and soon recognized that what he was looking at was not Sweden, but another Danish village on Falster. He admitted to his passengers that he had lost his way and had been obviously sailing in circles. He suggested that they go back to where they'd begun and try again when the German ships patrolling the waters of the Oresund were less thick. But everyone on board protested that there was no going back now. It was only after Melchior forcefully took the rudder from the young sailor's hands that the Melchior family, along with the other refugees, headed toward Sweden.[3]

Still, the roads to the coast were quickly crowded with taxis loaded with families desperate to find a way out of Denmark.[4]

KING CHRISTIAN X OF DENMARK ISSUED AN OFFICIAL PROTEST TO BEST ON the first day of the roundup. Best passed the message on to Berlin, but the day was nearly ended and the action in full fury before the German plenipotentiary deigned to speak directly with anyone from the Danish government. He told the director-general of the Danish foreign ministry, Nils Svenningsen, that "elements hostile to the Reich" were being arrested and would be transported to camps in Germany on the two large ships now anchored in the Copenhagen harbor. Svenningsen presented a letter to Best imploring the German to send those being detained to camps in Denmark, where they would be overseen by Danish authority. Best said that he could not make that decision on his own, but he would pass it on to Berlin, knowing full well that the answer would be silence. The Danish Jews and Communists were irrevocably on their way to German concentration camps.

IN JORGEN KIELER'S GROUP ON RAADHUSSTRAEDE, THE DEBATE BETWEEN pacifism and activism had long since ended. The roundup of Danish Jews was not just imminent; it was here. With more and more German soldiers appearing in the streets of the city, the threat was apparent and immediate. All agreed that a line had been crossed and that action of any means, violent or otherwise, was necessary to stop what they were beginning to see was the inevitable expulsion of the Jews. In discussions among themselves, it was understood that they needed to plan for the coming pogrom and implement their actions *now*, if they were to stay ahead of the Germans. Kieler listed five things that they all agreed were needed: (1) weapons, (2) money, (3) boats, (4) accommodations for the refugees, both in preparation for leaving and once they arrived in Sweden, and (5) Jews.

Like the Nazis looking for the Jews of Denmark in order to ship them off to the camps, the Danes who wanted to help were themselves uncertain about where to find them. It would be the hardest of their tasks, and the group on Raadhusstraede postponed it while they divvied up and set out to do the other assignments.

Jorgen went with his medical school friend Niels Hjorth to scrounge for pistols from a sympathetic police force that they'd heard about in a northern city. The guns they were seeking were the same ones that had recently been confiscated by the police after the end of the August crackdown. Acting on a tip that the police in Varde would be amenable to their request, Jorgen and Hvorth took the train west and were able to collect seven guns with ammunition.

Jorgen and the group already had a few weapons on hand. They came to Copenhagen via the Kielers' cousin, Svend, the Danish Navy cadet who had been dunked along with his friend and fellow cadet Mix in the waters of the Great Belt just a few weeks earlier. While Mix had been interned at Drogden Lighthouse, Svend had been loosely jailed at the navy base in Copenhagen, where he and his fellow interns were frequently allowed passes to go wherever they cared to in the city. As it turned out, Svend took the opportunity to visit his cousins at the apartment on Raadhusstraede, where he brought along Mix. Both Svend and Mix expressed an interest in getting involved with the resistance group working out of the apartment.

The two Danish Navy cadets also happened to have access to a number of weapons stored at the armory at the naval station where Svend was currently being held. Would it be possible to hide them at the apartment? Jorgen Kieler quickly agreed to the proposal, though he had one condition: that he and his other resistance fighters be allowed to use them for their own purposes in the struggle. All was soon agreed to, and one item on the needs doing list was checked off.

Jorgen's sister, Elsebet, was given charge of another. She went with another member of the group, Klaus Ronholt, to find the means to afford transport for the refugees. Ronholt was the son of a large landowner outside of the city and was well-connected to other estate owners with substantial holdings in the rural areas of Zealand, north and west of Copenhagen. These lands had done well under the occupation, in part by providing the foods that were shipped to Germany to feed the families of the occupiers. Though these large estates were on the wane in twentieth-century Denmark, they were still present in the Danish countryside, and a typical Danish manor could rival the baronial homes dotting the

English countryside, with their sweeping landscapes and luxurious homes straight out of Jane Austen or *Downton Abbey*.

Under the guise of being a newly affianced couple looking for gifts, Elsebet and Klaus secured invitations to the parlors of numerous country manors. Once there, they fessed up to be looking for donations to help finance the boats that would be needed to ferry Jews across the Oresund.

Klaus knew the milieu well, understood that to get the largest donations, they would need to act as if they were a part of this upper crust. Though Elsebet considered it a costly and unnecessary means of transportation, Klaus said they should take a taxi from estate to estate, suggesting that it would give him and Elsebet the appropriate air of class to meet the landed gentry. He also chided her for wearing plain clothing—thick, warm stockings rather than chic nylons.

His father greeted them like a lord of the manor, wearing riding boots with a brace of hounds in tow. Without bothering to ascertain the truth of the matter, he assumed Elsebet was "herself a Jewess, you can see that clear enough."[5]

At one of the manors that they visited, Klaus and Elsebet found themselves in the midst of an elegant dinner party, where Kieler's plain dress style turned out to be "the sensation of the evening," according to Elsebet's later account. It disarmed the partygoers, who considered them "*die kleinen Idealisten*" (the little idealists) and subsequently opened their coffers for the cause.

In the end, they managed to collect one million kroner, an enormous sum at a time when what was known as a "Jewish ticket"—the approximate price for a passage on a fishing boat to Sweden—cost around 1,000 kroner. By way of another illustration, Elsebet kept the money collected for Jewish transportation in one envelope in a dresser drawer at the apartment, right next to an envelope that held her monthly allowance from her parents for living expenses in Copenhagen. The money from her parents totaled 20 kroner.[6]

The sisters Ulla and Ebba Lund were given the assignment of finding boats for the transport of refugees. The daughters of an upper-middle-class engineer in Copenhagen, Ebba and Ulla, like almost everyone else in the group, were students at the university. The family had a cottage on the island of Christianso, just off the coast of Zealand, and through their frequent visits there, they knew the son of a fisherman, who steered them toward a mysterious figure known simply as "the American." The American lived beneath an upturned boat near the Copenhagen harbor. A quay there served as a dock for a whole row of fishing boats, and fishermen used the area near the American's lean-to boat to dry their catch. The American knew all the crews and made introductions between them and the sisters, who let it be known that they were looking for transport for Jewish refugees and had cash to pay the fishermen for the dangers they would face from the Germans and other inherent troubles of the task. In a matter of just a few days, the Lund sisters had arranged for seven to ten boats to serve as ferries for the refugees between Copenhagen and Barseback, just across the sound in Sweden. In fact, they soon had more boats than they could fill. What was needed now was to find Jews to fill them, as well as places to house the refugees before they were loaded into the fishing boats.

Jorgen contacted his parents and his friend Peer Borup in Horsens. The Kielers sent a pair of Czech Jews down to Copenhagen. They had crossed three national borders to get to Horsens and were now about to cross a fourth. In their exhaustion and bedraggled countenances, Ulla thought them "walking caricatures" of the refugee Jew. The refugees got on well with the American and were deeply grateful for the help in Copenhagen. They turned out to be the first two people for whom Ulla arranged transportation.[7]

JORGEN WAS ATTENDING A MEETING OF UNIVERSITY STUDENTS AT THE Rockefeller Institute on campus when his fellow med student Cato Bakman burst into the auditorium. Bakman breathlessly announced to the assembly that he was bringing "greetings from Niels Bohr in Sweden." According to Bakman, Bohr had spoken with the Swedish prime minister: Sweden was receptive to receiving the refugees. To all those gathered in the auditorium, it was the first signal that Sweden would accept Denmark's Jews.

Even as the members of the group went about their business, there was uncertainty about what had just transpired. But soon, Swedish radio began broadcasting notification that the shores of the country were now open to Danish refugees. And at Niels Bohr's request, the Swedish foreign ministry continued to broadcast the notice, even as Swedish newspapers printed the announcement on front pages across Scandinavia. It was unmistakable: the message was crossing the Oresund again and again, and soon, God willing, refugees would be doing the same.

His sense of duty to the Jews of Denmark complete, Bohr himself would soon be on his way to England, though even that journey would turn out to be fraught with unforeseen and unanticipated danger.

PART 2

Exodus

CHAPTER 15

Finding a Way Out

MOST OF THE JEWS TRAVELING FROM THE CITY IN THE FIRST COUPLE of days after the Swedish announcement headed toward the coastal towns, particularly toward the narrowest points of the Oresund, near Helsingor and Snekkersten, to the north of Copenhagen, which were only two and a half miles from Sweden. Others went toward Dragor in the south, just outside of Copenhagen. Their thinking was that, in a pinch, they might be able to find a rowboat and paddle themselves to Sweden if needed. Lucky for them, given the cold and choppy waters of the sound, few resorted to this option.

The initial flight from the city was chaotic and frightening. Cabs were loaded with what belongings individuals and families felt they could bring on boat rides that were not booked and unpaid for while they were headed to a destiny that was still vaguely considered to be "the shores of Sweden." No one was organizing the escape; there were no services provided beyond the assistance of the volunteer helpers who were trying desperately to locate Jews whom they could steer toward safe passages.

Yet up and down the coast of Denmark, groups of Danes stepped forward. Many hotel owners and private homeowners provided shelter to the travelers as they looked for boats to take them over the sound. One innkeeper in the town of Rodvig gave his entire occupancy over to refugees and then steered others to homeowners willing to take more Jews.[1]

The taxi drivers taking the Jewish families to the coast did not do so for free; the drivers were risking fines and loss of their cabs if they were discovered helping Jews escape. Few begrudged them the cost of the ride, even if some of the fees seemed inordinately high. Yet, the fares were coming from the pockets of already strapped Jewish families.

Both German Wehrmacht troops and the Gestapo were out in force, though the sense was that the ordinary German soldiers, the green-uniformed Wehrmacht troops, were far less diligent in corralling refugees than the Gestapo. Many considered the idea of rounding up and arresting Jews as not part of the duties that they had signed up for when joining the army.

In the suburban city of Lyngby, Aage Bertelsen (the Danish schoolteacher who had watched the occupation of Denmark three years earlier with mixed emotions while teaching in Sweden at the start of the occupation) began to organize a rescue effort for the Jews of the region based out of his home and school. Bertelsen had been happy to see that his country had not been decimated by the German assault in April 1940, yet he was torn by the fact that the long years of occupation had left Denmark in a compromised position with its oppressive occupier. Now, in the face of this unprecedented assault on the Jews of his nation, he and other faculty members at his school in Lyngby started to organize a rescue effort. Aage and his wife were quickly stunned and overwhelmed by the numbers of Jew who needed help in the area.

Many of these refugees were brought to the Lyngby group by a Jewish student in Copenhagen who was studying veterinary surgery at the university. David Sompolinsky was a devout Orthodox Jew from a large family whose patriarch had arrived in Denmark from Poland by way of Malmo in Sweden in the 1910s. They were members of an ultra-Orthodox synagogue in Copenhagen.

On the brink of the Jewish New Year, even before the announcement of the pending purge, young Sompolinsky had begun to contact his fellow congregation members to warn them of the coming crisis and to urge them to seek refuge. In the process, Sompolinsky contacted some of his old teachers at his former high school in Copenhagen, looking for places where his fellow Jews might hide. Those teachers in turn steered him to the faculty in Lyngby, and the connection of rescue efforts between city and suburb was made. Sompolinsky came to visit the Lyngby group for the first time the Sunday following the initial raid, and he was immediately welcomed as a conduit to the Jewish community they were trying to assist.[2]

Sompolinsky turned out to be a dynamo of aid and usefulness to the efforts of the cohort. Disregarding the personal dangers of what he was doing by contacting his co-religionists in Copenhagen, Sompolinsky wandered the streets, knocked on doors, made phone calls, and brought refugees to the Lyngby group for transport to Sweden. In the first week after the initial raid, Bertelsen estimated that largely through Sompolinsky's efforts the Lyngby group helped four to five hundred people find assistance in their efforts to escape Denmark.

Sompolinsky and his family had been warned before the outset of the assault by a teenage acquaintance, the son of a tailor who was doing what Sompolinsky himself would soon begin doing: knocking on the doors of Jewish families in the city to spread the word. The young man had been sent by the Social Democrat Party to get the news out, but the Sompolinskys had a hard time believing it. There had been so many rumors and alarms before, why should they believe this one now? But something in his friend's delivery of the news struck the Sompolinsky family as sincere and believable, and suddenly, they realized they had to act, especially David.[3]

During his tireless work, Sompolinsky would end many of his evenings camped out on the couch in Bertelsen's living room in Lyngby. The mix of cultures was a learning experience for both the Bertelsens and Sompolinsky. Because he was a devout Orthodox Jew who kept strict kosher dietary habits, feeding Sompolinsky was no easy matter for Bertelsen's wife. Even more vexing for some in the Lyngby group was the fact that he refused to shave his beard without the use of his own electric razor, which was back in his apartment in Copenhagen. As a consequence, his beard had grown into a thick, dark tangle that in the minds of his Danish compatriots served as a neon sign proclaiming "I am a Jew" to everyone, Gestapo agents and collaborationists alike, who saw him wandering the streets. Bertelsen was given the assignment of telling Sompolinsky that he couldn't go out anymore to look for refugees. It would put the whole group in danger if he was discovered.

Sompolinsky's response was to say that he would simply go to his apartment in the city and pick up his electric razor and trim his beard, but that was quickly deemed too dangerous by the group. What if he was caught? Was it really necessary to have an electric razor? they asked. Yes, Sompolinsky explained: it was one of the tenets of his Orthodoxy. Moses had commanded that it was fine for men to trim a beard, but not to shave it with a blade. His particular sect of the faith allowed for the use of an electric razor, but a straight razor and even trimming with a scissors were taboo.

Someone said that they should just find an electric razor in Lyngby as a substitute, but the relatively newfangled invention turned out to be as rare as hen's teeth in the town. In fact, Bertelsen had never seen one in his life.

At last, someone heard of an electric razor owned by someone outside the cohort in Lyngby. The razor was borrowed for Sompolinsky, and in a matter of minutes, he emerged from the bathroom with a beard trimmed down to a manageable stubble. He soon began his crucial work once again.[4]

In a brief period of time, Sompolinsky and Bertelsen became fast friends and taught each other the ins and outs of their respective religions and cultures, even as they organized the refugees and looked for means to get them out of Denmark.

BACK IN THE CITY, MESSENGERS MOBILIZED BY THE RESISTANCE JOINED the Jewish community in going door-to-door in search of Jewish families. Some Jews took refuge with Gentile friends, Catholic churches, and Protestant ministers. Some found shelter in hotels, cellars, and warehouses. Some hid in the woods outside of Copenhagen, which prompted university students and members of the resistance to organize search parties to scour the forests, looking for Jews.

Others came themselves to the resistance movement as well as to the hospitals in the city, which were turning out to be one of the great avenues for escape. Led by the young surgeon Dr. Karl Koster, the entire staff of Bispebjerg Hospital prepared to receive and hide Jewish refugees from searching members of the Gestapo. At first, a plan was devised to register the Jews under Danish names like Hansen, Jensen, or Petersen and house them in underground corridors, as well as in the 130 apartments in the complex reserved for nurses, who volunteered their residences for the Jewish families. Jews who happened to be in the hospital at the time of the action were immediately discharged and reregistered with Danish names.[5]

Jorgen's friend and fellow med student Cato Bakman knew Dr. Koster and other staff members at Bispebjerg, and he helped coordinate efforts to get Jews from the hospital to the docks for the transport to Sweden.

The Kieler group sent out Elsebet and Bente, who seemed to have the best luck looking for Jews, hunting in the city center for refugees from Poland and Czechoslovakia. With the help of a local art dealer named Carlo Madsen, who knew the city like the back of his hand, they looked in backyards and alleys and the dark corners of Copenhagen. Some Jews continued to resist the notion that the persecution was beginning, particularly the Viking Jews. One story made the rounds of an elderly pair of sisters in Copenhagen who, when told that the police were looking for Jews, decided, because they were good law-abiding citizens of Denmark, to make things easier for the gendarmes by turning themselves in at Gestapo headquarters.

There were times when negotiating skills had to be employed to convince reluctant refugees that it was time to flee. Jorgen visited an actress named Illona Wieselmann from the Royal Danish Theater, who was represented by her attorney, who asked some questions on her behalf: What guarantees could be offered to people being transported? What sort of security would be given, and what would be the arrangements once she got to Sweden? Of course, Jorgen could supply no answers to these questions. When Elsebet came to collect her the next day to begin the journey, her suitcases were open and she was still uncertain, saying that she wasn't even sure she was Jewish. She'd come to Copenhagen from Vienna years before and knew nothing of her ancestry. Wieselmann eventually agreed to go with Elsebet and ultimately made her way to Stockholm, where she would once again pursue her acting career on the Swedish stage.[6]

At the start of the escape, individuals were paying between 500 and 3,000 kroner for passage with the fishermen. It seemed like an exorbitant sum to many, but it was also understood that the fishermen were not only risking capture by the Gestapo for their pains, they were also subject to losing their boats and thus their livelihoods if they were waylaid. Out on the sound, the waters were assumed to be thick with both German and Danish patrol boats, though it became quickly noted that the Danish Coast Guard was far less diligent in its patrols than were the Germans.

Kieler's group sent its transports over to Barseback in Sweden, which was directly across the Oresund from Copenhagen. Because of a nighttime curfew in the Danish city, transports were loaded and sailed in daylight hours, often dodging German dockside patrols. The members of the group never used their real names and never took any refugees to the apartment on Raadhusstraede. Typically, the Jewish individuals or families would take taxis to the port area of the city, always careful to be dropped off shy of their ultimate destination on the docks so as not to reveal the helpers working there to guide them or the boats involved in the transport.

One of the great sources for refugees turned out to be another publisher in the underground press whom the Kielers had come to know through their own publishing efforts. Mogens Staffeldt owned the Nordic Bookstore in Copenhagen, and through word of mouth in the underground, its back room soon became a gathering place for refugees looking for a passage to Sweden. The fact that the store was right across the street from Gestapo headquarters in Copenhagen did not deter Staffeldt or his younger brother Jorgen; a lawyer named Sven Truelsen, and Jens Lillelund, the Holger Danske saboteur, who knew Mogens Staffeldt from resistance circles in the city were also integral to the effort. In the wake of the explosion at the Forum in Copenhagen, Lillelund had become the only Holger Danske member to stay in the city. The wounded Tom Sondegaard was still recuperating in Sweden, while the other members of the group had considered it too "hot" to stay in Copenhagen through the crackdown that followed.

Lillelund remained a steady presence and now turned his efforts toward the evacuation by serving in the back room of Staffeldt's bookstore.

In fact, he brought one of the first groups of refugees to the store in the early days of the escape.

There were about twenty Jews in the contingent, and at least half of them were children, who became frightened and loudly tearful in the process of being transferred to the fishing boats. The disturbance became so troubling to the Staffeldts and Lillelund that they decided the kids would have to be sedated for the length of the process. A sympathetic doctor was summoned, and he proceeded to give the kids, one by one, a sedative to put them to sleep for both the loading and the trip across the water. After the experience, sedation became a standard procedure for young children being ferried to Sweden.[7]

The first transport from the Kieler group left on Monday, October 4, on a ship arranged by the American. These were the Jews from Horsens brought to Copenhagen by way of the Kieler family and Peer Borup, who would continue to funnel refugees from Jutland to Copenhagen throughout the evacuation. He also provided Jorgen with intelligence regarding at least one informer in Horsens, a photographer who had supplied the names of most of the Jews in the city to the German commandant there. Already among the resistance, there was a growing sense that a price would be paid by collaborators for their aid to the Gestapo.[8]

Meanwhile, the American continued to find transport for evacuees, including room on fishing boats for another thirty refugees the following day. They had been sheltered at Ebba's parents' house near the port at Nordhavnen in Copenhagen until the boats were ready for them down at the harbor. Ebba began to take responsibility for guiding refugees onto the boats at the dock. To help signify her role to the Jews who were leaving, she took to wearing a red hat to give the escapees a marker for their exit. She would soon be joined on the docks by another young woman, Henny Sinding, who would also wear a red hat and guide groups of Jewish refugees to her own boat at the dock near Christianshavn, which was south of Ebba's port.

THE CREW OF THE GERDA III, THE FISHING BOAT THAT SAILED REGULARLY between the Drogden Lighthouse and Henny's dock in Christianshavn in

Copenhagen, contacted Henny, the daughter of the Lighthouse and Buoy Service manager, soon after the escape began. They asked her to come to a meeting on their boat.

The Lighthouse and Buoy Service was a part of the Royal Danish Navy, and Henny Sinding's father, Paul, was the officer who oversaw the comings and goings of vessels from the Royal Dockyards, where the *Gerda III* was berthed. Henny Sinding, the teenage champion sailboat racer at the Copenhagen yacht club who'd been looking forward to a summer of racing in the sound prior to the occupation three years earlier, was a familiar figure at the dock and well-known to *Gerda*'s crew.

She, her father, mother, and two siblings lived in housing provided by the Danish Navy down at the same Royal Navy docks. These were the distinctive string of row houses, a landmark in the city, painted a bright yellow and topped with red tile roofs. Called Nyboder, or New Barracks, by the citizens of Copenhagen, the housing had been constructed in the seventeenth century, with additions built in the nineteenth. Their color scheme matched that of the Royal Dockyards directly across the harbor. Henny had been working under her father in the service for the past three years, and the crew thought she would be an ideal person to talk with about a pressing concern that had been brewing.

Surreptitiously, just talking among themselves, the crew had not only expressed their sympathies for the plight of the Jews but also concluded that the *Gerda III* would be an ideal boat to transport refugees from Copenhagen to Sweden, with its well-concealed quarters below deck that offered room for at least half a dozen passengers. In normal times, the *Gerda III* had served as the supply boat for the Drogden Lighthouse, which rested in the Oresund just outside of Dragor. Indeed, the crew was largely composed of Dragor men, and the lighthouse was operated by Ejler Haubirk Sr., who was known to be sympathetic to the resistance. In fact, Haubirk's son, Ejler Haubirk Jr., was a well-known resistance operative in the area and would continue in that role for the rest of the occupation.[9]

Dragor was an archetypical Danish fishing village, tightly packed around the harbor, with winding cobblestone streets spreading out from the docks. The lanes were lined by simple cottages sheltered by tile and grass-covered roofs. The Haubirks had helped color the perspective of the village as a whole, including the crew of the *Gilda III*. It was a community inclined toward resistance long before the opportunity for overt action presented itself.

When Sven Kieler's navy buddy, Mix, was interned at the lighthouse for a time after his capture by the Germans in the Great Belt, he became friends with both the crew of the *Gerda III* and Henny Sinding, the young blonde sun-kissed champion sailor who brought supplies to the lighthouse on a regular basis. When the crew brought Henny into their discussions about using the *Gerda III* to ferry refugees to Sweden, they asked a couple of things of her: Could she convince her father to look the other way for a few weeks while the *Gerda III* deviated from its usual course in the Oresund out to the Drogden Lighthouse and back so they could run Jews to Sweden? And could he find a different berth for the *Gerda III* back in Copenhagen? It was currently berthed on Christianshavn Kanal across from Wilder Square at the Royal Dockyards, on a pier teeming with Gestapo. They needed space to keep the operations safe from prying and dangerous eyes.

Because she was the daughter of a patriotic Dane, the crew suspected that Henny had the same sympathies that they did, but in these uncertain times, who could be 100 percent certain of such things? As it turned out, they needn't have worried. Not only did she fulfill the *Gerda III* crew's requests with her father, she also would soon become, along with Ulla Lund, a legendary figure on the docks of Copenhagen. Wearing her own red knit cap to identify herself to dozens of escaping refugees, she darted from the warehouses down by the Copenhagen docks to the waiting *Gerda III*.

Like everyone else in those frantic early days of escape, the well-intentioned crew of the *Gerda III*, who had both the will and the means to help in the crisis, now needed the most vital part of the mission: the human cargo that needed to be rescued. As it happened, the connection to a source of Jewish refugees had already presented itself to Henny and the crew in the person of Mix.

Even as he was being held at the lighthouse under loose restrictions that allowed him frequent visits to Copenhagen, Mix was helping Svend Kieler smuggle weapons to Jorgen Kieler and his friends at Raadhusstraede. Mix and Svend also served as recruiters for Jorgen and the other Kielers, bringing a number of sailors who, with Svend, had been interned at the naval yard in Copenhagen into the group centered out of Jorgen's apartment.

All of these connections naturally aided the effectiveness of efforts to funnel Jews to the docks and to subsequently ship them to Sweden. Mix soon developed a tight and trusted relationship with Jorgen Kieler, and he introduced Jorgen to Henny. Through Henny, Jorgen got to know the crew of the *Gerda III* and Henny got hooked into Jorgen's connections to the refugees being organized in the back of Mogens Staffeldt's bookshop and at various hospitals in the city, including Bispebjerg. There his brother, Flemming Kieler, Cato Bakman, and other medical students/resistance figures helped link the refugees being spirited out of Denmark through the hospital to a means to get to Sweden through those providing transit. Thus a steady stream of refugees began appearing at the docks to be whisked out of Denmark and off to Sweden on fishing boats rounded up by Ebba and Ulla Lund with the help of the American, as well as the *Gerda III* crew and Henny Sinding. Something resembling an organized escape was being formed.

CHAPTER 16

Bispebjerg

AT BISPEBJERG, VIRTUALLY THE WHOLE STAFF OF THE HOSPITAL, FROM nurses to ambulance drivers to doctors and aides, became part of the rescue operation. Jews were admitted, as mentioned earlier, under Danish-sounding names with imaginary diagnoses, then hospitalized in various wards or, if the wards were filled, in the extensive nurses' quarters. More than 130 of these apartments existed in the extensive underground corridors beneath the grounds of the hospital; all were given over by the staff for the crisis.[1]

Finding funds for the transport was undertaken primarily by the doctors, who tapped resources like the Danish Physicians Movement as well as private citizens with the means to contribute. Jewish "patients" would be transported from the hospital to the docks by means of ambulances or taxis.

Dr. Koster had been a stalwart in these operations from long before the Nazi action against the Jews. As far back as early 1942, a Danish resistance saboteur had been shot by German soldiers during an attempt at bombing a factory. He came knocking at Koster's apartment door, bleeding profusely and looking for help. Koster called for an ambulance and arranged for an operating theater at Bispebjerg to be readied for the wounded man. He followed the saboteur to the hospital, where he removed one bullet from the man's stomach and one from his liver. He then, so as not to draw adverse attention to the wound, had the man admitted to the hospital with a perforated ulcer. A technically correct diagnosis, but one that failed to mention the perforation had been caused by German bullets.[2]

Early in the second week of the evacuation that October, a medical student named Ole Secher came to Dr. Koster at the hospital with a dire situation. He and other students had discovered forty Jews hiding in the woods outside of Copenhagen. To get them from the woods to the hospital, Secher had come up with an ingenious idea. He would disguise them by pretending they were mourners in a funeral party. The refugees, dressed all in black and carrying flowers, would pretend to be a large party grieving a loved one, wind their way through the streets of Copenhagen, and head toward a burial on the hospital grounds. Trucks would then come to pick them up at the ceremony to take them to the harbor.

Koster quickly invested in the ruse but suggested that it needed revision. There were often Gestapo on the hospital grounds, and a large group gathered in the open-air cemetery would draw too much attention to what was going on. He suggested instead that he find space for them in the hospital chapel, where they would be less conspicuous and could be loaded in increments into the waiting trucks for the final leg of their trip to the boats.[3]

One major hiccup in the plan landed in Koster's lap the morning it was to be enacted. Instead of forty Jews, Secher wound up bringing 140 to the hospital, explaining to Koster that the extra refugees just joined the group when word spread of the funeral procession throughout the community. Despite this huge addition to the outline of the plan, just one truck turned up to get the would-be escapees to the docks for transport.

Again, the hospital had to quickly revise the idea as it was impossible to leave that number of refugees in the chapel until they could all be hauled away. By hiding families in the chapel, the nurses' quarters, and every other nook and cranny available, somehow Koster and the staff at Bispebjerg found a way to accommodate all the refugees and spirit them away to the docks in single-one truck-sized increments.

After word of the bold escape hit the streets, Jewish refugees began flooding Bispebjerg. The head nurse gave Dr. Koster an extra set of keys for the nurses' quarters to help accommodate the influx. Ambulance and taxi drivers made countless trips from the hospital to the docks. On occasion, fire trucks were used to transport the travelers.[4,5]

The money to pay the cab drivers and for the passage over the sound was normally paid through donations made to the hospital, but in one remarkable case, expenses came from the highest source in the land. During a particularly busy moment at the height of the evacuation, Dr. Koster found the coffers bare just as group of Jews were being prepared for transport. In searching around for some source of emergency funds, he remembered that King Christian was being held under house arrest in nearby Sorgenfri Palace. In a move that was considered as audacious as it was necessary for the rescue of the refugees, Koster sent two of his most trusted nurses to the king to ask for his charity. According to Koster's own account of the incident, "They were not disappointed."[6]

Bispebjerg was not the only Copenhagen hospital involved in rescue efforts. The municipal hospital of Copenhagen helped coordinate activities at a number of hospitals. Beginning soon after rumors of the coming *aktion* became loud and persistent in the city, doctors at the hospital, led by ophthalmologist Dr. Steffen Lund, began to meet daily in the hospital library, where they organized and gathered information in order to set up a communications network with area practitioners, who were advised to pass on solid information about avenues of escape to their Jewish patients. It was through this word of mouth that reports of Jewish families hiding in the woods came to light.[7]

Another group of rescuers was centered at the Rockefeller Institute at the University of Copenhagen. Professors Richard Ege and Poul Brandt-Rehberg from the institute's biology wing helped guide a number of Jews as well as resistance fighters and downed pilots out of Denmark to Sweden.[8]

EVERYONE IN THE JEWISH FAMILIES WHO FLED, EACH INDIVIDUAL, HAD A tale of uncertainty and fear that would last a lifetime. Some tales were more fraught than others, some ended in tragedy, but all were undertaken under the specter of menace and a haunting urgency.

The escape of Leo Goldberger, the fifteen-year-old-son of the Copenhagen cantor, began with a simple journey to a suburb north of Copenhagen, where Leo's father thought he had secured a means of exit with a wealthy Jewish family who had a home on the coast. The homeowner had arranged for a Chris-Craft boat to take himself and his family to Sweden, and he offered passage to the Goldberger family, as well. Unfortunately, the price for passage was far too steep for Leo's father to pay. He simply didn't have the money, and his host was not going to pay for Goldberger and his family's trip.

Obviously terrified of the pending circumstances, Leo's father decided to head back into the city to look for some means to find the cash to afford a passage to Sweden. He took a train to the city the next day with the idea of somehow finding the money to pay for his family's voyage— maybe getting an advance on his cantor's salary. As luck would have it, there was a Christian woman riding on the same train whom the cantor knew. She was a member of the Women's International League for Peace and Freedom, a relief organization that Goldberger had done some work for in the past. She wondered about his obviously agitated state, and when he explained, she said immediately that she would take care of everything. They arranged to meet later that day, at which time she presented Leo's father with a loan from a Lutheran pastor named Henry Rasmussen who was associated with Copenhagen's Israel Mission. The loan amounted to 20,000 kroner, an enormous sum in Goldberger's world and more than enough for him to pay the passage fee for everyone in the family.[9]

Leo's father was given the address of a house on the coast south of Copenhagen near Dragor, and after making a quick return trip to the family's Copenhagen apartment to grab a very few items, including Leo's newly acquired flashlight, he headed back to his family and then shepherded them south to their departure point.

It was a cold night, and the family huddled together on a beach outside of Dragor, looking out over the black sound, listening to the lapping waves, and waiting for a signal light to tell them their ship was coming in. Leo's youngest brother, three years old, had already been given a sedative for the trip. His mother stood by, holding a bag of threadbare socks—her mending, which for inexplicable but somehow calmingly domestic reasons, she had thought to bring. When they finally saw the flashing light, they waded 100 feet out into the surf, up to their chests, with Leo's father carrying the youngerboys, Leo clutching his flashlight, and his mother holding tight to her bag of socks until they finally reached the boat.

They were hoisted aboard the fishing boat and eased down into the cargo hold, where they were directed to lie down, joining about twenty other Jews in the darkness. They were concealed by fish-fouled canvases, then the crew set sail. After a time on the open water, the family was let out of the hold and Leo's father began using his cantor's voice to softly sing a prayer from the Psalms as they huddled on deck; a few hours later they could see the bright lights of the Swedish coastline drawing near.[10]

LYNGBY, WHERE THE PUNDIK FAMILY HAD SPENT ITS FIRST NIGHT OF EScape, offered just a brief moment of respite. Herbert's father had hoped to find a means across the Oresund in this suburb, but he had no connections to the resistance movement and thus no connections to a means of escape. What he did have was a contact with a fisherman in the coastal village of Sletten, just south of Helsingor. The family had spent summer vacations at the man's cottage in years past, and he agreed to help.

The Pundik family took a taxi to Sletten and once there were steered to a villa on a bluff overlooking the coast. They were directed to a spacious living room and told to wait for the arrival of the fishing boat that would take them to Sweden. Hope beckoned just beyond the Danish shore.

The villa was soon filled with other refugees who were also looking for those same fishing boats. Most of the newcomers were delivered in ambulances from Copenhagen hospitals. The going price for passage to Sweden from the villa was 2,000 kroner.

Late in the morning after their arrival at the villa, the Pundik family was told to get ready to leave. They were sent down the beach to a pier where a dinghy would take them out to a fishing boat waiting 100 meters out into the sound. The family saw the little sailboat approaching the dock to ferry them out to the fishing boat, but it cruised right on by to another landing down the sound. The Pundiks were left without a means to get to the fishing boat.

They later learned that a number of fishing boats in the Sletten area had been detained by German patrol boats at that same location, with the occupants, both refugees and crew, sent to the Horserod detention camp. Of course, they couldn't be certain that any of those boats were the one that they had been destined to take, but in the end, they would consider themselves lucky to have missed this first chance at escape.

The Pundiks wound up back at the fisherman's cottage in Sletten, and they stayed there two more nights before a good deed helped them across the sound. A business acquaintance of Herbert's father had heard from the man in Lyngby who had put the family up the first night that the Pundiks had not made it out of Denmark and were now trapped somewhere along the coast in one of many possible cottages between Sletten and Helsingor. The man, named Nicolaisen, took it upon himself to knock on every door that he could find in that ten kilometers distance to see if the Pundik family had lighted within.

When he finally found the right fisherman's cottage and knocked on the door, the fisherman, who'd been selflessly sheltering the family for a few days now, actually said "No" when asked by Nicolaisen if the Pundik family was inside. He was so fearful of informers and the Gestapo lurking along the coast that he wasn't willing to trust a stranger with the Pundiks whereabouts.

Thankfully, Pundik's father was close enough to the front door to recognize his business partner's voice, and he stuck his head out to alert the fisherman that this was his friend. Nicolaisen had finally found the right house.

Soon, a car arrived to transport the Pundiks to yet another coastal village, this one north of Helsingor, and the very next day, Nicolaisen found a fishing boat to take them across the Oresund. They were in Malmo in Sweden four days after they'd first set out from Copenhagen.

CHAPTER 17

Gerda III

WHEN HENNY FOUND A NEW BERTH IN COPENHAGEN FOR THE *GERDA III*, it was right in the heart of the city's harbor on the northern end of Christianshavn Kanal, near a warehouse called Justensen's Storage, which would turn out to be an ideal location for hiding away refugees just prior to their evacuation. On the shore side of the warehouse, there was an entrance door into which Jews could surreptitiously enter; on the quay side of the building, there was a gate that could be opened for quick access to the *Gerda III*.[1]

Henny's job was to meet the refugees at a location agreed upon by one of the groups funneling Jews out of the city—the Kielers, the hospitals, Mogens Staffeldt's bookstore helpers, and others—and guide them to the warehouse, where they might have to stay for days at a time to wait for the trip to Sweden. Henny and the crew members preferred to take married couples, with each parent handling one child because each child had to be accompanied by an adult. All the loading of boats, most dangerously but necessarily, was done during the daytime. She would begin her rounds at one in the morning, tiptoeing past her sleeping mother before heading down to the docks and guiding the refugees to the warehouse, where they would hide until daylight when the sailing could be done. Any nighttime activity drew immediate suspicion, not only because of the curfew in the city but also because all the departures had to be done during work hours, when the fishing boats were going about their daily business.[2]

The waiting in the warehouse could seem interminable, and like other transport helpers, Henny and the *Gerda III* crew kept a supply of sleeping pills handy to keep anxious children from getting overly excited. Any luggage allowed would be taken to the warehouse and stored during the course of the day. There was typically some food and drink available for the refugees in the holding area, but appetites were rarely sharp.[3]

The *Gerda III* could handle up to fifteen refugees per trip. The biggest worry in the process involved two German guards who daily patrolled the pier running along the canal. They would walk along the cobblestone for about one hundred meters on each of their patrols, meet right in front of the *Gerda III*, then turn, face each other, and head back in the other direction. It was immediately after they faced each other and turned that Henny would signal for the refugees to scoot, one at a time, from the warehouse, through the gate, and onto the boat, where the crew would stow them in the hold. It was always a moment of terror for Henny. She would signal the adults to come first, followed by the children, holding her breath until all were on board.

When the ship was loaded and ready to set sail, the crew would turn over the engine, a loud process with a sputtering, coughing echo that could be heard up and down the canal. It would prompt an immediate appearance from the German guards, who needed to do a final check before they could allow the *Gerda III* to head out into the sound. The refugees, stowed in the hold with the supplies for the Drogden Lighthouse and covered with canvas, could have been quickly discovered if the guards looked thoroughly. But the crew had developed a rapport with them, and the Germans were typically more interested in the bottles of Carlsberg the crew offered the guards each morning than climbing down into the dank and smelly hold. They would usually just open the hatch and peek inside, then give the go-ahead for the boat to head out into the strait on its daily run to the lighthouse.

The *Gerda III* would make its crossing to Sweden to drop off its refugees before its scheduled delivery to the Drogden Lighthouse. There were German lookouts placed at the lighthouse, and the *Gerda III* crew felt it would be tempting fate to first make the delivery, opening the hatches to drop off supplies and possibly exposing the refugees to German eyes in the process. Of course, going all the way to Sweden in the first leg of the trip and then stopping for the lighthouse delivery on the way back raised all sorts of questions about just what the *Gerda III* had been doing and why it took so long to make its rounds.

Thankfully, the boat was given a certain amount of leeway in its operations, and there were numerous destinations in Sweden to which it could go without raising questions. If the boat headed north from Christianshavn, it might go to Malmo, Barseback, or all the way up to Helsingor; if it went south from its harbor, destinations were typically Limhamn, Klagshamn, and Skanor to the far south on the Swedish coast.

The boat was stopped by German patrol boats several times during its rescue missions, but the captain of the *Gerda III*, a man named Einer Tonnesen, was able to avoid inspection by shouting an explanation of its supply duties to the patrol boats as the two vessels rocked in the pounding waves in the middle of the Oresund. Everyone aboard worried about what might happen if they were ever stopped going or coming from a trip to Skanor, well to the south of the route to the Drogden Lighthouse. But it never happened for the *Gerda III* when its hold was full of Jews.

Though the distance to Sweden was never terribly long in nautical miles, for the refugees, the trip could feel like forever and was always unnerving. In the first week of October 1943, winds on the sound ranged from twenty-five to thirty-eight miles per hour,[4] as recorded by the Drogden Lighthouse. These winds raised waves four to six meters high, which left waters in the Oresund a soaking froth of whitecaps and spray and rocked the passengers below in a stomach-churning wooden tub smelling of fish and brine.

German efforts to curtail the rescue were hampered by a variety of factors. The first was the difficulty of policing the coast of a multiple-island nation with a coastal geography as varied and long as a South Sea archipelago. The German Navy simply didn't have enough vessels to cover all the bays, inlets, and fishing villages from which refugees could embark for a quick sail to Sweden. The original plan of the Germans was to rely on a close relationship with the Danish Coast Guard to help keep matters under control in the eventuality that refugees would start to flee Denmark. Of course, the close relationship quickly disintegrated when the Danish government collapsed, and the Danes were left to figure out what their role should be in the roundup.

In addition, the German Navy was itself strapped with other matters in the North Sea. The primary concern of larger ships in the German Navy was guarding the shipping of raw materials and manufactured goods from Sweden and Norway to ports in Germany, most particularly the iron ore coming from mines in Norway and heading to smelters in the Ruhr of Germany. At the time of the exodus, there were only six Danish Coast Guard cutters, manned by German seamen, operating in the Oresund out of the harbor in Helsingor.[5] And according to George Duckwitz, the effectiveness of these boats was compromised by the fact that their German commander had responded to Duckwitz's appeal to his conscience about what was happening to the Danish Jews, and he essentially took them out of commission for a period during the height of the rescue.[6]

There were other matters hampering the German efforts. The sheer number of Jews who rushed to the coast necessitated policing activity on shore that limited the sea search. To find Jews and limit their escape, the Gestapo and the Danish Coast Guard (which was quickly proving unenthused by its role in the roundup effort) had to divide their resources, which led to fewer arrests and apprehensions on the water.

The rescue efforts also happened to coincide that October with the height of the herring season in Denmark. That meant the waters off the Danish coast were thick with the 1,300 or so licensed fishing vessels plying the waters along the Zealand coast.[7] Discerning which boat was full of refugees and which was full of herring was no easy task for German patrol boats plying the choppy seas of the Oresund.

Finally, the Swedish government had given leave for its own coast guard to assist in the rescue of the refugees. So those crews were greeting many of the boats in the middle of the sound to take on passengers and see them safely to the Swedish coast.

CHAPTER 18

Bohr Makes It to Scotland

B Y OCTOBER 6, WITH DANISH JEWS NOW STREAMING INTO SWEDEN AND his sense of duty at least partially fulfilled, Niels Bohr finally felt comfortable enough to leave Scandinavia for England. In Stockholm, he accepted an invitation from Lord Cherwell, a British physicist and one of Churchill's principal scientific advisors, to fly to England.

Leaving his wife, son, and brother in Stockholm, Bohr was taken to an airfield where a British Mosquito bomber awaited to fly him west. The Mosquito was a lightweight, twin-engine plane designed to fly fast at high altitudes to avoid the antiaircraft batteries that were bristling along the coast of Norway. Aside from the pilot, the plane could hold only one passenger, strapped into the aircraft's bomb bay, behind the pilot so it could maintain its altitude and escape any flak coming up from below.

Wearing a flight helmet and suit, Bohr was buckled into the back of the aircraft with instructions on the use and location of an oxygen hookup in case they had to fly so high his oxygen became limited. His helmet had earphones connected to the pilot, who was supposed to tell Bohr when the oxygen would be necessary. But unfortunately, the helmet was tight on Bohr's head, and when the plane took off, he tried to adjust it and somehow lost his intercom connection with the pilot. Soon after they took off and began their ascent, the lack of oxygen overcame Bohr, and he passed out on the way over Norway. The pilot had no means to connect with his passenger, so Bohr spent the length of the journey unconscious in the back seat of the plane. It was only after they landed in Scotland, that he came to again.[1]

Fortunately, Bohr woke up none the worse for wear. For the next few weeks, he toured British research facilities and learned of the great progress that had been made by the Allies toward harnessing the enormous energies of nuclear power into a weapon that would change the outcome of the war and forever change the world. His skepticism about the possibilities of such an advance began to disappear. And by early December, he would prepare for a trip to the United States, to a desert facility in New Mexico headed by the American physicist J. Robert Oppenheimer. Los Alamos, Bohr now learned, was the center for these advances and the epicenter of Allied efforts to construct an atomic bomb.[2]

CHAPTER 19

Gestapo Juhl, Gilleleje, and the Elsinore Sewing Club

ORGANIZED EFFORTS TO ESCAPE DENMARK TOOK PLACE FROM DOZENS of locations north and south across Zealand. From the many coastal villages that lined the Oresund to whatever reedy harbor, rickety dock, or dilapidated pier sagged out into the water, a launch site was born. All that was needed was a means of transportation, and ad hoc escape attempts were undertaken.

Along with the highly successful efforts in and near Copenhagen, one of the best-known locales for escape was centered around Helsingor, where the Kronborg castle loomed over the narrowest stretch of water on the Oresund. This is where, in Shakespeare's imagination, Hamlet's tortured soul haunted the grounds and where in the dark recesses of a basement nook a giant statue of the mythical Danish hero Holger Danske dozed with his broadsword across his lap, waiting for the call to rescue the Danish people from those who had occupied these Nordic lands. The narrowness of the distance between Sweden and Denmark at Helsingor— the fact that from the parapets on top of Kronborg, Sweden looked close enough to a reach with a long, cold swim—made the locale as inviting as any on the sound for would-be refugees.

For all the helpers, resisters, and ordinary Danes searching for Jews to assist across the sound, the Jewish refugees themselves remained through-out the escape the best source for finding and alerting their fellow Jews.

Community connections, word of mouth, telephone calls, looking out for one another—these were the best means for spreading the word. But often, in the early days, they steered one another to the same locations for escape. Which was why so many were soon taking the twenty-five-mile train ride north from the city and getting off at the Helsingor station, which was located a short distance from the harbor and the castle. The depot was soon periodically crowded with swarming refugees looking for a vessel to take them to Sweden. The danger of having this concentration of people looking to flee was obvious, and it was no surprise that also centered at Helsingor was a contingent of Gestapo that would prove to be the most active of all the security forces employed by Germany in the roundup.

Still, the allure of the area was great. A number of ill-prepared and ill-considered crossings were attempted, too often with tragic outcomes. Rowing across the narrow strait tempted a number of refugees, but the great majority of these efforts, undertaken by voyagers with little or no experience in the stresses, physical demands, and rough seas of the process, soon failed. The refugees either turned back or found themselves thrashing in the choppy seas.

On the night of October 5, close to the shores of Sweden, a rowboat with eight people aboard capsized. The refugees had engaged a blacksmith from Espergaerde, a town just south of Snekkersten, to row them across, but he failed to get them to safety. Just three of the escapees were saved by the Swedish Coast Guard, and all of these lost other family members in the tragedy.[1]

Another rowboat, filled with ten refugees, began to take on water in the sound and capsized, sending a father and his eldest son to the bottom, while four more of the man's children clung to the boat and were ultimately rescued, only to discover later that their father and oldest brother had drowned.

In yet another dire circumstance, seven people drowned in the chilly water when a Swedish vessel hit their motorboat in the sound. One family on board, non-Jewish refugees who were fleeing Denmark because of their resistance activities, had sedated one of their young boys, and they couldn't awaken him when their boat was struck. He drowned in the ferment that followed the collision.[2]

As Helsingor became overrun with refugees, the number of boats available for transport was simply not great enough to accommodate all who wanted to go. Some organization was needed to make sure boats and willing fishermen could be provided for the fleeing refugees as well as to find shelter for those who came to town to looking for a means to escape.

Five men, solid middle-class citizens of the community, including a police detective, a physician, a bookkeeper, a reporter for the local paper, and a bookbinder, had all come to the movement at the beginning of the exodus, when one of the five, Berge Ronne, the newspaper correspondent, had happened upon a scene in the middle of Helsingor. Ten strangers were being dropped off in the center of the town, and they immediately started racing to and disappearing within a garage attached to a nearby house. When he asked another witness for an explanation of what he'd just seen, he was told that he'd just witnessed a group of Jews in the process of escaping the roundup in Copenhagen. Ronne didn't even know the roundup had begun.

He contacted his friend Erling Kiaer, the bookbinder. Neither had any sympathies for the Nazis and both felt the occupation had gone on far too long. They also felt a moral responsibility to do something about this purging of Denmark's Jewish citizenry.

Soon, they gathered three more like-minded citizens—a doctor, a police officer, and a bookkeeper—and together they created a group that they dubbed the Elsinore Sewing Club to hide the true intentions of their mission. At first, they simply helped refugees find places to stay while awaiting boats. A local innkeeper in nearby Snekkersten was extremely helpful, offering his hotel accommodations to Jews. They were also able to find summer and private homes for overflow.

The doctor in the group, Dr. Jorgen Gersfelt, turned out to be a great help. He provided the sedatives for the children traveling over the sound, which by now was a standard procedure in rescue operations; he also served as a driver to get the refugees to various hiding locations and to

the boats that would take them over the water. As a physician, he was al-
lotted extra gasoline coupons in the existing ration system and thus had
the means to use his car.[3] Because of his status as the town doctor, he had
also been entrusted with the keys to the summer homes of a number of
part-time residents of nearby Snekkersten. He freely used these homes as
hiding places for refugees on the run.

To help deal with the overflow of refugees, the Elsinore Sewing Club
devised a plan to take refugees across to Sweden without overburdening the
fishing boats in the area. German railroad trains made the crossing on large
ferries stationed at Elsinore. They would come from Sweden to Denmark
filled with iron ore for trips south to Germany, but heading back to Sweden,
they would be empty. The cars would be locked when empty, but the stay in
Elsinore before they were shipped back to Sweden was long enough for the
Elsinore Sewing Club to jimmy the locks open and hide Jews inside. Once
they had been ferried over the sound, arrangements were made for them to
be welcomed by Swedish refugee authorities on the other side.

The arrangements worked for a time, until a Swedish newspaper in-
discreetly described the operation in a report that fell into German hands.
The Gestapo soon put a guard on the ferry to check the railroad cars, and
this means of escape was quickly put to an end.[4]

Though the Germans had made their most intense effort at rounding
up Jews in the first two days of the *aktion*, they began to intensify their
efforts once again a few days later near Snekkersten. On that day, eight
fishing boats made the crossing to Sweden with loads of refugees. However, the fishermen were greeted on their return by the Gestapo, who quickly
detained twelve of the seamen and sent them off to Horserod, the Danish
detention center.

That same day in Dragor, the Gestapo halted a line of taxis that were
dropping Jews off at the harbor. They fired warning shots at two Jewish
families who were plotting their escape, while the boats waiting to take
them across the sound set sail and made it out into the water. The two
families were arrested, though several other Jews who'd been waiting in
other taxis disappeared into the recesses of the village and were hidden by
accommodating Danes.

One particular Gestapo agent became the most notorious of all the German officers trying to interdict the escape of the Jews. Hans Juhl, who would soon earn the nickname "Gestapo-Juhl," was a former chauffeur for German foreign minister Joachim von Ribbentrop, but as the crackdown on the Jews in Denmark proceeded, he was tapped to serve as the security officer at the port in Helsingor.[5]

Juhl arrived in early October and set up his command post right in the passport control office at the ferry port in Helsingor. He was soon involving himself in activities such as arresting a group of Jews who had been picked up by a Danish vessel that had found them in distress while trying to make the crossing in a rowboat. The Danish ship, a good-sized schooner, was on its way to returning the refugees to Danish authorities on shore when Juhl interceded and took custody of the eight Jews who had been saved. Instead of sending them to a Helsingor jail and into Danish custody, he had them transported to Horserod and eventually to the Theresienstadt concentration camp.

Just a couple of days later, Juhl and a few other Gestapo officers in his command were at Gilleleje, a village nineteen kilometers to the northwest of Helsingor on the very northern tip of Zealand, where there had been several successful evacuations in previous days. One hundred and eighty refugees had been safely transported from Gilleleje to Sweden, according to one account.[6]

Now, a number of refugees were gathered there, looking for a means of escape. A fishing boat was at the dock in the Gilleleje harbor, loaded with Jews, just as the Gestapo came onto the scene. The boat began to leave the harbor, but racing from their cars, the Germans fired warning shots at the cutter to order its halt in the village harbor. When the sailboat failed to stop, Juhl and his men fired twenty to twenty-five more rounds, until finally, the vessel sailed back toward shore, where a truckful of Wehrmacht soldiers rounded up the nineteen Jews on board and hauled them away to Horserod.

The foiled escape failed to deter more attempts from Gilleleje. Refugees continued to flock to the northern tip of Zealand in order to leave Denmark, which became an acute problem for those trying to help the refugees. There was no place to put them all as they awaited transport. Word that other fishing boats would be arriving in port the next day brought more Jews to Gilleleje and increased the difficulties of the townspeople to find hiding places for them. The Jews were directed to farms in the area, ones that were outside the village. The very next day, however, they returned, desperately seeking transport.

To put them up, the village church, built in the sixteenth century, opened its doors, and the refugees were steered toward its attic, a dark, stifling space beneath a red-tiled roof, with no ventilation and buckets for lavatories. Eventually, about eighty Jews—men, women, and children— were crammed into the space there. The church pastor arrived to offer words of comfort to the refugees, but it wasn't long afterward that distinctly German voices were heard outside the door leading to the attic. Gestapo Juhl had arrived with about a dozen of his henchmen.

Juhl would later claim that he had discovered the hiding place strictly by search and chance. He'd come to the church and grown suspicious when gatekeepers had been reluctant to let him in. Another story that was widely circulated was that a young woman, a local, had given up the Jews because she had a boyfriend serving in the German army on the Eastern Front and had thought that somehow she could earn him favors by disclosing the whereabouts of the refugees to the Gestapo.[7]

In either case, the Jews were quickly assembled and marched out of the attic and down to waiting trucks. Like the refugees from earlier in the week, they were taken to Horserod as a way station on their way to incarceration at the Theresienstadt concentration camp, where the Jews already gathered in Copenhagen were being placed, as well. The eighty Jews captured in Gilleleje were the largest group of refugees arrested by the Germans in a single location, beyond the initial sweep in Copenhagen.

Theresienstadt would soon be home to almost all the Jews rounded up in Denmark during the *aktion*.

AS THE TRAFFIC OF ESCAPING REFUGEES INCREASED DURING THE FIRST couple of weeks of October, the threat of Gestapo Juhl and his officers increased, as well. Familiar ports of embarkation could only be used for

German artillery unit posted at the Copenhagen harbor. *Public domain; from the archives of the Museum of Danish Resistance.*

Danish troops readying for the German occupation. *Public domain; from the archives of the Museum of Danish Resistance.*

Danish citizens in southern Jutland greeting the arrival of the occupying force. *Public domain; from the archives of the Museum of Danish Resistance.*

14.

Jorgen Kieler and his sister Elsebet, students at the University of Copenhagen. *Public domain; from the archives of the Museum of Danish Resistance.*

Stjerne Radio, birthplace of Holger Danske in Copenhagen. *Public domain; from the archives of the Museum of Danish Resistance.*

King Christian X, on his daily ride
through the streets of Copenhagen,
accompanied by his devoted citizens,
during the occupation.
*Public domain;
from the archives of the
Museum of Danish Resistance.*

Rabbi Marcus Melchior, Ph.D.,
who would become acting chief rabbi
during the crisis in August 1943.
*Public domain; from the archives of
the Museum of Danish Resistance.*

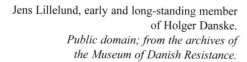

Jens Lillelund, early and long-standing member
of Holger Danske.
*Public domain; from the archives of
the Museum of Danish Resistance.*

Werner Best, Germany's plenipotentiary in Denmark from the Telegram Crisis onward. He controlled civil affairs in the country.
Public domain; from the archives of the Museum of Danish Resistance.

World-famous physicist Niels Bohr and his wife Margrethe escape Denmark in late September 1943.
Public domain; from the archives of the Museum of Danish Resistance.

Three Jewish brothers and their sister on arrival in Sweden in a rowboat on October 6, 1943.
Public domain; from the archives of the Museum of Danish Resistance.

Danish navy scuttles the fleet to prevent Germany from using its ships.
Public domain; from the archives of the Museum of Danish Resistance.

Bent Faurschou Hviid, the Flame,
fierce gunman for HD 2.
*Public domain; from the archives of
the Museum of Danish Resistance.*

Jorgen Staffeldt, leader of HD 2
until his capture
*Public domain; from the archives of
the Museum of Danish Resistance*

Svend Otto Nielsen, a.k.a. John,
vital member of HD 2.
*Public domain; from the archives of
the Museum of Danish Resistance.*

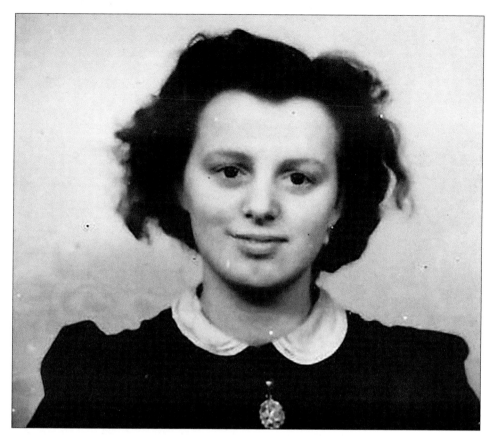

Gestapo photo of
Bente Kieler
after her arrest
in February 1944.
*Public domain;
from the archives
of the Museum of
Danish Resistance.*

Likewise, Gestapo photo
of Flemming Kieler
after his apprehension.
*Public domain;
from the archives
of the Museum of
Danish Resistance.*

The great escape of Danish Jews to Sweden begins in early October.
One of the few photos of an actual rescue.
Public domain; from the archives of the Museum of Danish Resistance.

The famed White Buses bringing Danish and other Scandinavian prisoners home from the camps in 194
Public domain; from the archives of the Museum of Danish Resistance.

brief periods of time before their continued use became dangerous. So it was with Aage Bertelsen's Lyngby group.

Early in the rescue, the group had arranged transport primarily out of Copenhagen and the piers and docks just north of the city, but as time passed and refugees continued to arrive, they decided to arrange a transport out of Humlebaek, a village between Lyngby and Helsingor. By this time, the various transport groups were communicating with one another and sharing who had made arrangements for fishing boats, where they would be located on a given night, and how much room they might have for refugees. Under the circumstances, places on boats were often the subject of bartering and hard choices regarding who ought to have priority in getting a place on a given boat.

On one occasion, Bertelsen found himself arbitrating a dispute that involved a family whose Jewish father was arguing that he needed to bring his wife and child—his wife was not Jewish—along with him on the trip to Sweden. This would have meant taking the space for two other full-blooded Jews. Because at the time non-Jews were not being incarcerated by the Nazis, Bertelsen decided that the Jewish father ought to leave his wife and child behind. They would be safe until they could be reunited with a future journey. Perhaps not surprisingly, the father was adamant that they go with him.

Adding to the complication was the fact that the fisherman who owned the boat was asking 10,000 kroner to take eight passengers on the journey to safety, and he said that he needed an additional 1,500 kroner to pay for the final two passengers.

The money from group funds that had already been raised to pay for these trips was held by Bertelsen. He had the 1,500 kroner in his pocket. So he had the final difficult say in who would stay and who would go. Ultimately, he told the father that he should go to Sweden without his wife and child, and that's what happened.[8]

The very next night, the Lyngby group got word from a contact in Helsingor that as many as eleven fishing boats might be available to take fifteen Jews apiece across the Sound near Humlebaek. The group was able to secure two trucks from volunteers in Humlebaek, and they drove the refugees to a farm outside the village, where more than a score of Jews were already hiding in the hayloft of a barn.

Loading the numbers of refugees hoping to travel to Sweden onto the trucks that night was like loading animals or sacks of grain for market, according to Bertelsen, who aided in the process. Bodies were lifted over the siderails of the truck and stacked on the bed, one on top of another—men, women, children, and babies. Despite the cold-bloodedness of it all, no one complained as they were driven silently up the coast beneath a moon that emerged from beneath the clouds of a chill, rainy October night.

As they arrived at the agreed-upon site of the evacuation, the Jews were left outside in the truck as Bertelsen and another member of the group went into a brewery hall that was serving as the meeting location. Rather than a room full of fishermen ready to sail out into the sound, they found two young men, who quickly explained that they had only one boat at their disposal and it would cost 15,000 kroner for its use. The captain was waiting on the boat, and along with these two, that was the entirety of the rescue crew.

The 15,000 kroner were due prior to embarkation, and at that price it meant that only about ten of the refugees assembled from the trucks and the farm could go. Some haggling brought the cost down to 10,000 kroner, and in total, just fifteen or sixteen of the Jewish family members could be squeezed onto the ship. Once again, Bertelsen had to deliver the news of these limits to the people who had assumed they would all be safe and sound and sailing to Sweden shortly.

After leading the departing group from the brewery, through a garden, and to the narrow path to the boat landing, Bertelsen watched as the vessel set off toward Sweden. "Nobody who has not attended an embarkation of that kind will be able to imagine the feelings that overcome those who are left behind and see the heavily loaded ship sailing off toward safety and freedom. Mingled are rage at human wickedness, sympathy and grief at the misfortunes of the persecuted, the excitement, the uncertainty, and the painful responsibility—above all the responsibility—but also the duty, and an elevating and strengthening feeling of friendship and solidarity of the task. Everything is dissolved into a strange, indescribable feeling of happiness when the work is finished."[9]

While he was walking back from the landing, Bertelsen happened upon one of the young men whom he had been haggling with earlier. The young fisherman, who had facilitated the trip but not sailed with the boat, was wading in from helping load the cutter with refugees, and Bertelsen noticed that he was weeping. The Lyngby teacher put out a hand, and the young man responded by reaching out to Bertelsen. He cursed the Germans. Called them beasts. And told Bertelsen that if he and his friends ever got in trouble with the authorities, they should come back to the landing. "We will get you across, and it won't cost a penny."[10]

OF THE EIGHTY JEWS TRAPPED IN THE CHURCH ATTIC IN GILLELEJE, ONE young man, named Bruno, managed to escape by climbing up a ladder in the loft to the church's bell tower, where he hid out for the night until he was found in a rough way by friends the next morning. A few days afterward, he joined nine others in an attempt to cross over to Sweden in a rowboat. Unfortunately, the dinghy capsized, and though several people on board were either picked up and saved or managed to swim to safety, Bruno was one of three who drowned.[11]

Another young man caught at Gilleleje managed to escape the Gestapo in Copenhagen as he was being transported by the Germans through Denmark on his way from Horserod to Theresienstadt. Nineteen-year-old Gert Lilienfeldt was born and raised in Germany at the height of its growing anti-Semitism, living in Dusseldorf with his family during the rage-filled Kristallnacht. Soon after that fearful night, his parents sent him to Denmark to be part of the Aliyah program, the project that brought young Jewish workers to the agricultural fields of Denmark to learn the skills of Danish farming for eventual use in kibbutzim in a Zionist homeland in the Middle East.

Lilienfeldt had been at a hospital in Copenhagen, being treated for tuberculosis, when the Nazis began their roundup at the start of October.

One of the practitioners treating him, a Dr. Blagvad, arranged his trip to Gilleleje to help him escape.

Once in Gilleleje, Lilienfeldt found himself trapped in the church attic with the seventy-nine other Jews cornered by Gestapo Buhl. Like Bruno, he tried to hide out in the church's bell tower, but Gert was grabbed by the Germans before he could make it there, and they quickly loaded him into a truck bound for Horserod.

As it turned out, Lilienfeldt had a second opportunity for escape when he found himself back in Copenhagen as he was being transported from Horserod to Theresienstadt. The Wehrmacht truck that he was in stopped to allow its load of prisoners to be transferred to a camp truck for the trip into Germany. During the switch, Lilienfeldt saw an opportunity to bolt and did so, right in the center of the city. A nearby taxi driver happened to see the escape and quickly pulled up to Lilienfeldt and offered a ride. The only place that Gert knew in Copenhagen was the hospital where he'd just been treated for tuberculosis, so he asked the driver to take him to Dr. Blagvad back at the hospital. Blagvad, seeing his patient returned, now with a hair-raising tale of escape, took Gert home and hid him for several days, searching for a reliable means to get him over to Sweden.

Dr. Blagvad soon decided to turn to Henny Sinding and the *Gerda III*, which had aided the hospital in transporting refugees a few times earlier. In a matter of a few days, Gert Lilienfeldt found himself at her elbow in the warehouse down by the dock, just opposite where the *Gerda III* was berthed, waiting for the moment when he would have to dash across the open esplanade to the fishing boat.

The German guards were doing their back-and-forth march on the pier while Lilienfeldt waited his turn with his heart in his throat. When he finally got the signal from Henny, he hustled on board the vessel, where one of the crew pointed him into the hold. He piled into the dark, dank space and found himself at the bottom of a pile of refugees with a small child on top of him.

It seemed to take forever for the *Gerda III* to finally shove off. Just before it did, the guards followed their customary routine of coming on board and sitting atop the hold to gulp their morning beers.[12] When the guards finally finished their kibbitz with the crew, they left, the crew started the engine, and the *Gerda III* headed north in the canal and finally out into the harbor, with the refugees on their way to the sound and Sweden.

Barseback was the destination, directly across the sound from Copenhagen. It was about a fourteen-mile trip as the crow flies, and the same one used by the Kielers' group of fishing boats organized by Ulla Lund through the American's help.[13] Because the *Gerda III* was still operating as a lighthouse tender, it had to make a couple of stops en route, which lengthened the journey considerably, especially for the Jews crammed into the vessel's hold. Much later, Gert Lilienfeldt would say that the tension of the trip was relieved only when he set foot on the dock in Sweden and saw a uniformed Swedish police officer there to greet him and the other refugees.[14]

CHAPTER 20

Sweden: A Light in the Northern Sea

WHEN SWEDEN DECIDED TO OPEN ITS DOORS TO DANISH JEWS ON October 2, 1943, it hardly had time to determine just what that might mean to its own people, to say nothing of the Jews that were already beginning to arrive at its shores. The German deportation of the Jews of Denmark and the consequent roundup were reported in Swedish papers as early as October 3. In the papers, there was almost unanimous outrage at the attack and approval of the Swedish government's decision to offer asylum to the Danes seeking refuge. But what was really needed were immediate measures to deal with the influx of refugees.

After three years of official neutrality in the war, marked by Hitler's Germany bullying Swedish foreign ministers and the nation receiving some deep-seated resentment from Allied forces for its stance, it felt satisfying to finally be able to cry "Enough." The occupation of Denmark and Norway in 1940 had not only isolated Sweden from Western Europe and the Allies, but subsequent arrangements with Germany also gave the Reich leeway to send hundreds of thousands of troops through the country in order to subdue Norway, persecute its Jews, and control the airspace and waterways of all of Scandinavia.

The essence of Swedish foreign policy since the beginning of the war had been to keep the nation out of the conflict. As in the case of Denmark and its cooperating foreign policy, the changes in attitude toward Germany that occurred in the fall of 1943 had as much to do with the changing winds of war as they did with an altruistic concern over the fate of the Jews of Denmark. Germany's defeat at the hands of the Allies in North Africa and earlier in the year at Stalingrad in the Soviet Union suggested to both the Danish and Swedish governments that the ultimate winners of the conflagration might well be Western Europe and the United States. To have played footsie with Hitler's Germany might not be a good historic posture for the two governments in the postwar European landscape.

All of this reasoning was sheer speculation in early October 1943, when the Oresund was full of refugees streaming toward villages on the coast of Sweden. What was real were the scores of Jews coming homeless to a land where the vast majority of newcomers had never been, where they generally had little but the clothes on their backs, and where few had the immediate means to support themselves. The pressing questions were: What would they do, and what could the Swedes do to help them?

By the end of the first week in October, the numbers of refugees were increasing exponentially. According to Swedish government reports, that figure stood at about one thousand on the first of October. (The figure included Jews and other refugees who had arrived in Sweden prior to the German *aktion*.) By the end of the year, it would jump to around twelve thousand, of which just under eight thousand were from Denmark.[1] As noted above, they came from dozens of docks, harbors, villages, and landings, up and down the coast of Zealand. At virtually every available place where a boat could be launched, there was a fisherman ready to ferry a frightened Jewish family across the Oresund or a desperate family willing to drag a boat to the water to go it alone.

As it turned out, for each of these sites, there was a corresponding welcoming location on the Swedish side of the sound. In the Malmo district in southern Sweden, the state foreign ministry counted 6,670 newcomers in the span between October 4 and October 16. Ninety-five percent of these refugees were Jewish. By the end of November, the number had increased to 7,600 people.[2] Considering the fact that the entire Jewish population of Denmark was estimated at around 8,000 at the start of the action, it's plain to see that a remarkable story was being written in these early weeks of October.

In Sweden, newspapers and public opinion urged the citizenry to do all that could be done to aid the homeless Jews, and the government heard the sentiments. The Swedish Navy was ordered to keep German boats out of Swedish waters, and fuel was issued to Swedish fishermen so that they could take part in rescue efforts—going out into the sound to look for straggling or floundering boats or guiding others to safe harbors. Soon the Swedish Navy itself would send ships to aid the refugees in the sound.

A Swedish newspaper account of the arrival of the refugees from October 1943 offers a melodramatic projection of the moment a single boat came into a Swedish harbor:

"We are standing on the beach, watching the dark water. Milk white fog was mercifully clouding the surface of the sea, but the moon, green from fear, was shining in the sky. We were waiting for hours . . . , the cold of the night was enveloping our feet. Will anybody cross tonight, some poor refugees . . . will they escape the hunt on the other side?

"The boat draws alongside the quay. A Swedish officer calls out a hearty 'welcome.' The refugees hurry on land with their small bundles. Many fight to keep back their tears, their reactions are overwhelming. A Jew kneels and kisses the soil of Sweden. It is no theatrical gesture. That is what he feels in this very moment. Swedish soil has become holy soil for those who were hunted like animals and had to flee for their lives."[3]

A cosmopolitan non-Jew from Copenhagen, leaving Denmark with his Jewish wife and family, had what appeared to be an uneventful sojourn to Sweden, until it wasn't. Traveling south of the city in a cab to a village on the southeast coast of Zealand, Ulf Ekman soon found himself in the town of Koge. Then he and his wife were ushered farther down the coast to a "god forsaken" (Ekman's description) place called Stroby. Here, the party ran into an acquaintance from Copenhagen, an actor who was dressed in a trench coat à la Humphrey Bogart in *Casablanca*. He was helping old ladies board the boat that all were taking to Sweden.

All in all, Ekman estimated about two hundred people were crammed on board the vessel, which he described as a ketch, or a two-masted sailboat.

When the captain came on board, he announced that there were no reports of German patrols in the area, land or sea, which bode well for the trip, which was being conducted as a nighttime journey in the inky blackness of the northern seas. For the first half of the journey, those promising words of the captain's held true. Then suddenly, one of the ships engines failed, and for more than a quarter hour of tension and fear, the ship sat helplessly adrift in the middle of the sound. The captain had barely gotten the engine started again when out of the darkness a bright light splashed across the vessel and soon revealed itself as coming from a Swedish patrol boat that was approaching out of the black night. Peering into the darkness behind the light, the passengers soon could make out the figure of a man with a megaphone to his lips. The words he was speaking in Swedish, *"Ni skall alla vara hjartlig volkomna I Svertige"* (You are all most heartily welcome to Sweden), were the most comforting Ekman had ever heard in his life.[4]

IT WASN'T ALL KISSING THE GROUND AND BLESSING SWEDISH SOIL, OF course. It was necessary for the charitable organizations, on both the Danish and Swedish sides of the sound, to step into the breech to aid the refugees and find the means to organize and assist this influx. The first camp for Danish refugees was set up at a castle in the county of Skene, which contained the city of Malmo, just across from Copenhagen. The castle grounds were quickly filled, and Swedish authorities made arrangements to house the refugees in a variety of hotels, guest homes, and hostels in the area. In time, most of the Jewish newcomers found their way to reception centers set up in the larger towns in coastal Sweden, including Malmo, Helsingborg, which is directly across from Helsingor in Denmark, and Trelleborg, on the southern coast of the country. [5]

Much of the assistance in the earliest days was provided through individual charity and good works, with people in the towns receiving the refugees and often providing food and shelter in their own homes. Larger acts of beneficence came from the Swedish royal family and the Stockholm Concert Hall, which sponsored a benefit for the refugees featuring a bevy of Swedish artists. Princess Ingeborg, the sister of King Christian X of Denmark, was also a patron and supported further efforts through her husband, Prince Carl, who headed the Swedish Red Cross.

Newcomers arrived in a semi-state of shock and with a profound sense of dislocation, having just experienced, in most cases, the loss of their homes, their belongings, and their homeland, to say nothing of their fears for their lives and the lives of their family. All of this was punctuated by terrifying journeys in the holds of a multitude of fishing boats, only to land in a foreign country.

At the refugee centers, they were given medical exams, supplied with clothing, and assigned a room in one of the centers' dormitories. They were also questioned by both Swedish and Danish police, who were looking for dangerous saboteurs as well as SS officers or German Nazis looking to sneak into Sweden in the chaos of the moment. The beds in the center dorms were made up with paper sheets for hygienic purposes, which left an indelible impression for many refugees who spent their first nights in safety on what felt like crinkly, sterile newspaper.[6]

The only way for the refugees to avoid assignment to a camp was to have a Swedish citizen sign a declaration stating that he took responsibility for the refugee, including economic support. To leave the camps, refugees likewise needed proof of economic support, either by the sponsorship of a Swedish citizen or by reliable employment and a housing contract. A privileged few had the means to bypass the camps upon arrival.

Rabbi Melchior of the Great Synagogue of Copenhagen found work as a state-employed traveling rabbi for Jewish refugees in the camps. He ministered to the thousands who would remain in the camps for lengthy periods of time after their arrival. He went all over Sweden, though he lacked a theological library, service vestments, and any permanent structure in which to offer services. In addition to offering counseling and other ministerial services, he often became a sort of community messenger for Jews who'd arrived and had other friends and family now living in communities apart from one another. He passed along news, greetings, well wishes, and updates from one family to the next.[7]

Another Jewish refugee similarly found himself traveling through the camps after he arrived in Sweden from a harrowing journey from Denmark. Sam Besekow, a theater and film actor and director and a general maven of Danish stage and film production, was sent out as an entertainer after he arrived in Sweden to read an eclectic mix of selections from the works of Hans Christian Andersen and Sholem Aleichem. Besekow, the son of the tailor, who had presented him with the gold cigarette case as a hedge against future troubles way back on the day the Nazis arrived in Denmark three and a half year earlier. He still had the case in the apartment he shared with his wife back in Copenhagen on August 29, 1943, the day he was arrested by police and hauled off to Horserod detention camp.

Aside from being Jewish and performing across the country as an actor through the years of occupation, Besekow had done little to deserve his arrest. He was sympathetic to the cause but not a resister. Of course, given the time, in the wake of the crackdown, not much excuse was really needed to detain a Jewish member of the cultural community.

At the camp, he found himself incarcerated with a number of fellow Jews and intellectuals, who were all in the same position of not knowing what fate awaited them. The barbed wire ringing the encampment was a constant reminder of their imprisonment, and their daily routine of card playing, tutorials, reading, and services was often less than scintillating, but they had each other's conversation, and the response to their incarceration from Danes outside the fences was encouraging. Danish publishing houses sent books, tobacco companies sent their products, even wine merchants and distilleries sent their wares to the camp.[8]

Then on October 1, the beginning of the action against the Jews, Besekow found himself being shepherded from his Horserod barracks and past a group of elderly Jews being loaded into vans by heavily armed guards. He assumed that they were going off to concentration camps in Germany and beyond. Thinking about his own parents and their uncertain fate, for a moment he considered ending his despair by simply joining the group of elderly Jews, climbing aboard the vans, and heading off to Theresienstadt. A friend, however, pulled him out of this fatal instinct and urged him back to the barracks. Remarkably, just a few days later, Werner Best made the determination that Jews married to Aryans would be given their freedom, while Jews with Jewish spouses were to be shipped off to Theresienstadt. Saved at the horrid cost of sending fellow Jews off to their likely doom, Besekow made his way back to his wife in Copenhagen.

Needing to make ends meet, Besekow quickly resumed his old life in Copenhagen, even taking a film job in the days soon after his return. But he and his wife, another Henny, quickly resolved to leave for Sweden. They would never be completely safe in Denmark under German control. They made arrangements to take a boat out of Nyhavn to Malmo. Remarkably, Besekow filmed the final two scenes of his movie on the day he and Henny were scheduled to take the boat to Sweden. He earned 100 dollars for the shoot as well as a promise from the director to put in a good word with the head of Swedish Films Inc. to help him find work on the other side of the sound.

The journey itself sounded as if it might have been with Henny Sinding and the *Gerda III*, though there is no evidence of that. He and his wife were squeezed into herring cases, which were hoisted by the crew into the hold, for the trip to Malmo. They experienced the familiar tramp of German footsteps on the boat's deck, the coughing start of the engine after the guards left, and then the sensation of pulling away from the pier and the achingly slow trip out into the open water of the sound.

When they arrived and settled into Malmo, they had the most pleasant surprise of Sam's life. His parents were still alive and had themselves landed in Malmo, and as with so many others, it was in roundabout fashion. To help pay for their journey, Henny had given Sam's father, Leo, the same gold cigarette case Leo had given Sam three years earlier. When Leo sold it to pay for his passage, he found that it provided enough kroner for he and his wife's passage to Sweden. Unfortunately, after they'd handed the money over to the fisherman who was to take them, the sailor disappeared with the fee and his boat. There would be no voyage from Dragor for Leo and Sam's mother.

They made their way north on the Zealand coast, all the way to Snekkersten, where an old and dear classmate of Sam's, the town doctor, was a ringleader in one of the most highly successful transit units in all of Denmark. Dr. Jorgen Gersfeldt, one of the founders of the Elsinore Sewing Club, was there to take them under his wing. Dr. Gersfelt knew the Besekows well from boyhood visits with his friend Sam at the family home in Copenhagen. He took them into his own home until he was able to secure transit for them to Sweden. The world of Denmark and the resistance was in many ways a small one.[9]

After their arrival in Sweden and their initial reception, refugees were sent to a variety of locations across the country, including hotels, summer vacation homes, hostels, sanatoriums, and by December, camps constructed and overseen by Swedish welfare agencies, which also provided assistance in the form of clothing, household items, and help finding employment. In January, Danish welfare agencies took over the work of the Swedish helpers, providing aid to their fellow Danes. At the same time, the newcomers were required to pay a monthly fee for these services, but only if they had 500 kroner in hand. It remained a free benefit for those who had nothing.[10]

So it was that the majority of the Jews of Denmark settled into a new life as Jews in Sweden. Just how long they would be there and what the future held for them was anybody's guess. They were safe for now, at least, with their feet planted on foreign, but still firm, ground. In a matter of just three weeks in October 1943, almost the entire population of Jews from the nation of Denmark had been transported across the Oresund in a style that would soon prompt many to compare the rescue to the famed boat journey of Allied forces out of Dunkirk to Great Britain.

Thanks to thousands of their fellow Danes, who seemingly had come out of the woodwork to help them and thanks to thousands of Swedes who were now providing similar assistance on the other side, a simple sense of human decency had prevailed.

A final pat on the back was due most importantly to the Jews themselves, who through their own wit, resourcefulness, courage, and on multiple occasions, with their own nest eggs and cold, hard cash had navigated the harrowing escape from the clutches of Nazi Germany.

They had survived the whirlwind of fear prompted by one nation's brutal imposition of its crazed violence on another. Others within the Jewish community of Denmark were not so lucky.

CHAPTER 21

Theresienstadt

THERESIENSTADT WAS A DREARY TOWN LOCATED FORTY MILES NORTH of Prague in occupied Czechoslovakia. Built around a military garrison in the late eighteenth century, the camp originally held thirteen large barracks designed for around two hundred soldiers, but it was reconfigured by Jewish laborers culled from the Prague ghetto after the 1941 uprising. The Nazis intended for the revised camp to serve as a new ghetto for what it considered "prominent Jews," including politicians, cultural figures, scientists, and World War I Jewish war heroes as well as the elderly. To cut costs and manpower, the original plan was for Theresienstadt to be self-governing, with a Jewish administration headed by a council of Jewish elders.[1]

Quickly, however, the camp became used more as a transit center for many more Jews than had been originally planned. In time, they would come from all over Europe, including large numbers from Czechoslovakia as well as prisoners from Austria, Germany, the Netherlands, Hungary, Poland, and also Denmark. For many of these internees, it became an interim stop on the way to extermination camps like Auschwitz. By the time Denmark's Jews began to arrive there in October 1943, there were already forty-five thousand people squeezed into an area about the size of a large cornfield.

The roundup of Danish Jews, as noted, began in Copenhagen on October 1, when just under two hundred Jews, mostly elderly, were arrested by the Gestapo—many from a single nursing home in the city. They were marched onto the German transport ship *Wartheland*, which was parked at the Langelinie dock, along with other Jews who had been picked up by Gestapo Juhl or failed for whatever reason to heed or hear of the pending roundup.

The Germans made other less successful attempts to corral Jews outside of the city at the same time as they began the *aktion* in Copenhagen. At Aalborg in Jutland, Germans had set up transport at the railway station to bring two thousand Jews from the Jutland and Fyn. However, they were only able to find eighty-three victims in their roundup to send to the transport ships in Copenhagen.[2] A number of these detainees were part of the group of young Zionists who'd come to Denmark to study agricultural techniques for use in their ultimate destination, the kibbutzim in the as yet unrealized state of Israel. They had simply not heard word of the roundup prior to its happening.

An eyewitness to the conditions on the transport ship describes them as foul. Old men and women, crying and wailing, made to climb steep stairways to go to a filthy bathroom guarded by German troops. One elderly woman was so infirm that she had to be hoisted onto the ship with a crane.[3]

The *Wartheland* sailed for Germany, to the city of Swinemunde on the Baltic Coast, and landed just a day after it was loaded in Copenhagen. Witnesses of the ship's disembarking in Swinemunde describe a horrific scene of inhuman behavior. Teenage Jewish boys were racing up and down the gangplanks, trying to help the elderly negotiate the difficult descent, while the Gestapo stood by, shouting at and shoving the very people the youngsters were trying to assist. After a time, the elderly Jews grew confused and exhausted by the chaos and began to huddle on the gangplank, which prompted more gibes and kicking from the Gestapo.[4]

From the pier at which they were unloaded, the passengers were steered directly to a row of waiting cattle cars for the trip to Theresienstadt, which was due south of Swinemunde, just over the German/Czech border. Once again, the young Jews helped the elderly into the cars, where they were packed like sardines, fifty or sixty to a car with a single bucket for a toilet.

Among the youngest passengers on the ship was three-year-old Birgit Krasnik, whose family were members of the Great Synagogue of Copenhagen. They had missed the crucial service at which Rabbi Melchior warned of the pending roundup and thus were arrested just a few days later and forced onto the *Wartheland* for the trip to Theresienstadt.

Among the oldest passengers was a woman known as "Cousin Clara," who was in her eighties and toted a hearing trumpet. She was the widow of a Danish naval officer and had arrived in Denmark from the Virgin Islands, where her husband had been stationed many years earlier. The Germans found her name on a list of donors at the offices of the Great Synagogue, and she was soon after arrested, along with two daughters in their sixties. Cousin Clara quickly earned the respect and admiration of her fellow prisoners and was given the additional nickname of "the Admiral" in the camp.[5]

The train trip to Theresienstadt took two and a half days in the packed cars, with only a few moments the entire way for the passengers to get out of the cars to relieve themselves in the open fields. When they arrived, they were funneled through an area called "the Sluice," where they were divested of all their belongings. Men and women were separated at the camp and then steered to filthy and unheated dormitories with the companionship of bedbugs and fleas. Birgit and her mother were shuffled to a special house for pregnant women and women with young children. It wasn't long before the little girl's legs were covered—first in a rash and then in painful, pus-filled blisters, which turned out to be impetigo. She was eventually hospitalized, where she shared a bed with a little boy about her age; Birgit slept with his feet in her face, while hers were in his.[6]

Danish Jews were mixed with Jews from other European countries in the camp, but it wasn't long before a distinction was noticed with the Danish Jews. While other Jews were frequently being moved, placed for "transport" to other camps in the East, the Danish Jews, just under 450 in total, were left at Theresienstadt.

After their arrival at the camp, the Danish Jews were given a "special" reception at which they were served a meal on a white tablecloth, lectured to by a German-Jewish professor of sociology, and given blank sheets of white paper and stamped envelopes, with which they were supposed to write letters home to their friends in Denmark about the pleasantries that could be found in the camp. The evening was topped off when all the newcomers were presented with the first yellow stars of David they ever had to wear.[7]

The routine of camp life was made quickly evident. If a person was physically capable of work, they were sent to do hard, physical labor—men and women. Meals were a sodden soup with the occasion chunk of potato plopped within. Hunger became an ever-present companion to the detainees, joining loneliness, fear, and, in many cases, a despondency that often verged on the suicidal.

What the Danish Jews couldn't know in the early days at the concentration camp is that back in Denmark, the Danish central administration, that part of the government that still existed in Copenhagen, was making frantic efforts to protect the Jews of Denmark who had been rounded up and shipped off to Theresienstadt. What was most surprising about these efforts was that they actually had some effect with the Germans. A month after the roundup, as Danish historian Sophie Lene Bak noted, "One of the most peculiar meetings in the history of the Holocaust was held in Copenhagen." Adolph Eichmann, the man who more than any other was responsible for carrying out Hitler's Final Solution, arrived in the city to sit down with Werner Best.[8]

Despite his role in organizing and advising Berlin on the Danish *aktion* against the Jews, Best maintained a faith in his initial preference of keeping a lid on Danish troubles by treating Danes with a less brutal hand than was being used in other occupied nations. After all, Danish farmers and manufacturers were still providing tons of food supplies and war materials to Germany. And the fact of the matter was that now, with so many Jews living as refugees in Sweden or at Theresienstadt, the Jewish problem was essentially disappearing from Denmark. Most of the Jews of the country were gone or were leaving, without the bother for the Nazis of rounding them up and shipping them to extermination camps. Georg Duckwitz, the German shipping expert who had advised Danish Jews about the coming *aktion* back in September and who remained Best's confidante about

German intentions throughout the crisis, recalled Best telling him at the time of the roundup that he would really like to solve the problem of the Jews of Denmark by building a bridge over the sound.[9] Just let them all make their own way to Sweden. In essence, the fishing boats of Denmark had just served as that bridge. With the thorny exception of the Jews in Theresienstadt.

Having been blindsided by the perfidious actions of the Germans against their fellow Jewish citizens, the remnants of the Danish government, its administrative leaders, tried to use their justified moral outrage to help achieve special consideration for those Jews detained in Theresienstadt. Surprisingly, Best, in conjunction with the Danes, was able to convince Eichmann and Berlin to offer some concessions. First, Jews over the age of sixty would no longer be arrested or deported. Next, deported half-Jews and Jews married to non-Jews were to be sent back to Denmark from Theresienstadt (about twenty-seven people in total, including the two daughters of Sister Clara). All Jews deported from Denmark were to be sent to Theresienstadt, rather than camps that were known, or suspected, to be death camps. Finally, representatives from the Danish administration were to be allowed a scheduled visit to the camp to view how it was being administered sometime in the spring of 1944.[10]

Also discussed and agreed to was the possibility of sending food and clothing parcels to Danish detainees at Theresienstadt. A social service agency in Copenhagen agreed to serve as the conduit overseeing this arrangement, and the first packages arrived at the camp in December 1943. At about the same time, five detainees from the camp who had been mistakenly deported were sent back to Denmark.

The social service agency worked extensively with Professor Richard Ege from the Rockefeller Institute in Copenhagen, who headed the Biochemistry Department at the institute. Ege had been deeply involved in efforts to find money and transport for refugees in rescue operations in October. He had worked extensively with David Sompolinsky and Aage Bertelsen of the Lyngby group, and in the process had compiled a broad knowledge of the Jewish families in Copenhagen and beyond. Ege's academic work included an expertise in nutrition, and when the social service agency charged with providing food and clothing parcels to the detainees contacted him about finding names and addresses of family members, he also volunteered his services helping to provide contents for the food parcels. He was able to convince a number of pharmacists in Copenhagen to donate vitamin pills for the camp detainees, which were hidden inside the parcels in the lining of the packaged clothing.[11]

The parcels were held up by German authorities for several months after the concept was approved by the authorities. As it turned out, it was Ege who found a way to outwit those running Theresienstadt by using the efficiency of the German postal system to subvert the slowdown. The German postal service to Theresienstadt had worked very well from soon after the arrival of the Danish Jews. So instead of using Danish social services to send the packages, as these packages were being slow-walked to their recipients by German authorities, Ege enlisted Danish acquaintances of detainees to send the packages by way of the efficient German mail system, rather than through the camp administration, and suddenly the parcels began arriving for the internees in February.[12]

In an attempt to soften the image of German concentration camps in the eyes of the world, Berlin decided to showcase Theresienstadt as a model for its supposedly humane treatment of Jews in its concentration camps. The visit to the camp by Danish observers, already agreed to by German authorities in early December and scheduled for April, was pushed back a couple of months and now included representatives of the International, German, and Danish Red Cross and a film crew overseen by German authorities. The camp was spruced up for the visit with fresh paint, efforts at fumigation, and most importantly, an effort to make the camp seem less crowded and overbearing. In the world of Nazi Germany, the quickest way to depopulate Theresienstadt was to send more than seven thousand detainees off to camps in the East, probably Auschwitz.[13] Though the Danish camp members were spared this form of execution (a Danish commission, after all, was coming to visit), everyone within Theresienstadt understood what was happening, and dread settled over the camp like a thick blanket.

The Danes who visited along with the Red Cross representatives saw a camp that did not suggest the truth of Theresienstadt. The Jews incarcerated within, who were unable for obvious reasons to counter the impressions being offered to the visitors by the German-led tour, prayed that their fellow Danes would be able to see through the thick layer of propaganda being painted over the camp to understand its oppressions and the miserable existence obscured by the authorities.

"All of Theresienstadt prays that these people, sent by Providence to them, will, in spite of everything, see the vast lie in the whole thing," wrote one member of the camp, speaking of staged scenes presented to the visitors in which the German commandant of the camp was seen playing with detained Jewish children and the beds in the camp hospital were set up with crisp white sheets and down comforters instead of bedbugs and ratty old blankets. Visitors were shown only the first floors of the buildings that housed the internees because no work had been done to clean up the second floors, which were now crammed with Jewish residents who had been moved upstairs to lessen crowding on the ground floors.

Prior to the visit, the camp commander assembled all the Danish Jews in the camp to inform them on how they were to behave: No one was to express any criticism of the camp. If they were asked about the death of a relative or husband or wife, there was to be no mention of malnutrition, typhus, or dysentery. If the visit resulted in a negative report, the extra packages of food that they'd grown accustomed to would be quickly ended, and Danish Jews might soon start to be deported to the camps in the East.

Unfortunately, the Germans on the tour, including Germany's Red Cross representatives, saw nothing but decent accommodations at the camp, and they were encouraged by the reticence of the Jews within the camp to openly express the truths about what they were seeing. Rabbi Max Friediger, the chief rabbi of the Great Synagogue of Copenhagen, who had been detained since the earliest days of the turmoil in Denmark back in late August, had become the spiritual and community leader at Theresienstadt since his arrival there in November. Friediger, hoping to maintain the benefits that the internees were receiving in the form of food packages and somewhat ameliorated living circumstances, decided to hold his tongue about the deceptive gloss that had been applied to the camp.

The representatives of the Danish foreign ministry were likewise satis-fied by the visit and the continued German concessions to the Danish Jews at Theresienstadt. Red Cross packages from Denmark could now contain books as well as foodstuffs, and the few real changes that the Germans had made in sprucing up the camp—creating a playground for the children, for instance—would not be taken away.[14]

PART 3

Resistance

PART 4

Resistance

CHAPTER 22

Holger Danske 2

THE REMARKABLE ESCAPE AND RESCUE OF THE JEWS OF DENMARK, along with the incarceration of those captured by Germans and sent to Theresienstadt, virtually eliminated the Jewish population in the country. It did not, however, end resistance to the German presence in Denmark. In fact, the rescue operations intensified the movement and gave it courage and hope. They also encouraged the SOE to put more resources into the Danish resistance after the destruction of the Exhibition Hall in September and the successes of the Jewish "Little Dunkirk" had given the movement a sense of viability beyond the shores of Denmark.

Because so much of the resistance was active in the rescue, the groups were able to better organize and expand the movement through interconnections formed during these efforts. This was evident in what happened to the group of resisters centered around the Kieler family flat at Raadhusstraede.

As has been told, the original group of friends, family, and students had grown through their work aiding the refugees to now include cousin Svend Kieler and his friend and fellow cadet Erik Koch Michelsen (better known as "Mix") and, after the middle of October when they were fully released from German detention at the Royal Naval base in Copenhagen, about ten other naval cadets from the academy joined the group, as well.

Also included with the coterie was Henny Sinding, who had become paired with Mix in both a working relationship and something more than that. They had become close as they worked together both during the rescue and after. They subsequently met frequently at the Raadhusstraede apartment, where Mix left a lasting and positive impression with both Henny and Jorgen Kieler.

To Jorgen, Mix was reminiscent of his old friend Peer Borup from Horsens, who had been Jorgen's partner in his first attempt at sabotage the summer before. Jorgen noted, "The same big smile, the same lively eyes, the same keenness and impatience to get going. He was also quite confident in his behavior, and I was left with no doubt that he was the leader type. I had great confidence in him right from the start and knew that we would soon become good friends."[1] He referred to Henny as "Mix's girlfriend."

Mix had introduced Henny to the Kieler group during the midst of the rescue, even as both worked largely in separate spheres of the waterfront to evacuate refugees. Mix was already envisioning a broader effort to sabotage the occupiers in Denmark, and he felt Henny out to see if she might be interested in being a part of that effort. She was, and soon she was a regular in the circle of saboteurs centered at Raadhusstraede.

Along with the Kielers and their friends, Henny, Mix, and the ex-sailors, the circle now also included Jens Lillelund, who had become acquainted with the others through their joint work in the rescue. They both had a common connection to the Staffeldt brothers—Mogens and Jorgen—whose bookstore had served as a station for refugees on their way to Sweden. Both the Kielers and Lillelund had steered many Jews to the Staffeldts during the rescue.

To protect his anonymity, Lillelund was now calling himself "Finn." His connections to the old Holger Danske organization were now in the past, and what remnants of the group that existed, including the still-recovering Tom Sondegaard, remained unorganized and inactive in Sweden.

When Lillelund, a.k.a. Finn, hooked up with the Kielers, however, he urged them to help identify the Kieler group's goals and practices by naming themselves Holger Danske 2, a next-generation sabotage organization linked by aspirations to the now-defunct original Holger Danske organization. The reconstituted HD 2 would soon prove to be a central component of a growing sabotage movement in Copenhagen and Denmark as a whole.

It was quickly boosted by the presence of a member of the SOE, whom Finn introduced to Kieler in October. Jens Peter, as the man called himself, was a Dane who had extensive training in sabotage work in England before returning to Denmark to aid the resistance. By the middle of October 1943, the SOE saw opportunity in Denmark for an enhanced resistance effort in the wake of the collapse of the Danish government and the continued plight of the Axis war effort. It seemed like a good time to redouble efforts to supply and aid groups like HD 2, in order to continue to soften the Germans before the coming Allied invasion of Europe.

For their part, the HD 2 resisters wanted nothing more than to aid these same efforts and prove to the rest of Europe and the world that Danes stood strong against the Axis, even if the country's government had accepted compromise agreements at the start of occupation.

Though acts of violence against his fellow Danes were to come, Jorgen Kieler himself said that he and the group never considered themselves at war with other Danes, except those who supplied direct support to the German war machine through equipment and materials. Though they chose to commit acts of sabotage against Danish businesses and institutions, they never thought of themselves at war with Danish society. Instead, they felt they would act as saboteurs "to ensure that Denmark would not end up on the side of Hitler, and also because [their sabotage] avoided air attacks of the population as a whole, reduced the Royal Air Force's losses over Denmark and contributed—to a small extent—to the shortening of the war."[2]

Kieler and Mix welcomed Jens Peter to the Kieler flat in Copenhagen with open arms, and according to Kieler, the SOE agent "didn't beat around the bush." He came into the apartment, set a bag on the table, and like a door-to-door salesman, immediately began to display its contents: detonators, fuses, ignition equipment, and various types of bombs and explosives. They were now armed saboteurs.[3]

A couple of days later, Finn brought another new element into the group at Raadhusstraede. This was "John"—real name, Svend Otto Niel-

sen—a slightly built former teacher of mathematics and physics in a suburban high school outside of Copenhagen. Kieler describes his "lively
eyes" as offering an "ever-changing expression" that suggested his deci-
siveness, sense of humor, and "capacity for friendliness." In photos, a pair
of round-rimmed glasses give John an intellectual countenance, but he
was born and raised in a forested area of Jutland and had hunting and
other outdoor skills, too. He had served in the Danish military prior to
teaching, and because he was more experienced in the world of weaponry
and had slightly more experience in the underground world of sabotage,
he quickly assumed a leadership role with HD 2. He was said to have gone
onto a German airfield once to steal a bombsight directly from one of the
planes hangered there, shooting a guard with a pistol in the process. He
was also fond of costumes, particularly police and medical uniforms. He
had once been hailed to assist some accident victims while dressed in a
doctor's coat. John did the best he could under the circumstances, but he
admitted the victims were no doubt worried about his methods and bed-
side manner. Despite his absence of medical skills, to his colleagues in HD
2, he was cool as a dip in the Oresund.[4]

John soon brought in a younger friend to HD 2—Bent Faurschou Hviid, whose nickname "the Flame" was an inevitable offshoot of his brilliant red hair. The Flame was a twenty-two-year-old man who had been
trained as a hotelier, just like his father, who had operated a spa-resort in
the German state of Thuringia. It was while working there as a youngster
that Bent developed a deep hatred for the Nazi state. He also became an
adept marksman. These two traits would one day merge into purposeful
expressions of his character.[5]

More weapons arrived for the group via the SOE in the form of pistols
and submachine guns. An instructional meeting was held in late October,
at which time the pistols were hauled out and hefted. The lack of experience of the group was evident when a mishandled revolver went off by
accident, putting a deep scar in Jorgen Kieler's desk. There was some fear
that the neighbors might become suspicious about what was happening in
the apartment, and no doubt they were, but nothing more came of it, and
HD 2 continued its training.

Even as the group coalesced, they tried to lead as normal lives as possible. The university students went on with their college studies, the naval cadets went back to their training with the Royal Navy, and Henny continued her work for her father and the Royal Navy. While the sabotage was considered the work of the men in the group, there were exceptions, and the women played crucial roles as lookouts and girlfriends in operations where couples were required for undercover purposes.

Henny later recalled in an interview how she would assist by walking with the boys as half of a lovestruck couple, "not caring about anything in the world except the two of us, while at the same time keeping an eye out for any Germans."[6]

Mix thought it would be a good idea for Henny to learn something about the weaponry that had arrived at the group. He took her to Grib Forest in northern Zealand, and once they were there and tucked deep enough within, he pulled out a submachine gun and showed her how to use it, along with a pistol that he brought, as well.[7]

Elsebet compared the work of her and Bente at the apartment to running a "speakeasy" for the saboteurs, meaning a hideaway for their illicit activities. As the sabotage efforts began and became recurring, Elsebet, Bente, and their friend Nan Moller, who along with her brother, Hans, was one of the original student members of the group, monitored the happenings outside their rooms by listening for explosions out in the night, and then straining to hear footsteps on the stairs up to the apartment as the saboteurs came racing home. "We would sit there in silence evening after evening, counting the minutes until the boys came home and counting the boys when they came in. We were the government, staff HQ, and private soldiers all rolled into one."

They were also just as liable, in the eyes of the authorities, as the guys for the work that they were doing out in the night. If and when the Gestapo came, they would come for one and all. Under the circumstances, they all needed somewhere to meet, "a home where we could live a normal mental life, because the work itself embraced values that could almost knock us off our feet."[8]

CHAPTER 23

First Assignment

AS A GROUP, HD 2 REMAINED LARGELY INDEPENDENT THROUGHOUT its operations, but it was not averse to guidance from SOE, which gave the saboteurs their first suggested target in early November. The American Apparate Company was a radio factory in Copenhagen that made radio and jamming equipment for a Berlin company that supplied the Wehrmacht. After a couple of preliminary reconnaissance ventures at the factory, John and Jorgen returned with several others in the group on a Sunday night, with the intention of placing several bombs within the building when just the company guards would be at the structure.

The sabotage was not particularly well thought out. Jorgen, dressed in the uniform of a Danish auxiliary police officer, went straight up to the factory gate and rang its bell. The plan was for Jorgen to tell the guards at the building that he was there, in his auxiliary police role, to inspect the blackout provisions employed by the company. When they let Jorgen inside for the inspection, John would follow and proceed to keep the other guards busy, while fellow HD 2 members would sneak in with the bombs that were to be placed strategically around the structure.

Things quickly went awry. When Jorgen rang the bell at the gate, instead of opening the gate to allow him inside, the guard opened a window from a floor above the gate and shined a light down in Jorgen's face. He was immediately skeptical of Jorgen's request to come inside to inspect the blackout provisions, and when Jorgen tried to bluff his way in by asking for the address of the factory director, the guard instead ordered Jorgen inside, where he began to dial the police.

John came to Jorgen's rescue, arriving with a pistol in hand. He fired a shot in the direction of the guard as Jorgen raced by on the way out the factory gate. For his part, the guard aimed and tried several times to fire at Jorgen, but the pistol jammed. Everyone and everything made it back to Raadhusstraede unscathed, with the exception of several valuable and much-needed bombs, which were left in a sack behind a hedge at the factory. Luckily, they were still there when Jorgen and Nan Moller returned to reclaim them the next day.[1]

A lesson was learned. They decided to do away with much of the subterfuge in a second attempt at the radio factory and instead employed a tactic that became known among the group as "the direct assault." Four members of HD 2 stood outside the factory, providing cover with guns aimed at the building's windows. A bomb unit ran up beneath those same openings. When the signal was given, the bomb unit smashed open the windows and lobbed incendiary bombs inside the factory, which started several fires. The incendiaries were followed by a ten-kilogram detonation bomb, which sent the guards inside running for safety. By the time the larger bomb went off, the factory was in flames, the guards had left the building, and HD 2 was hightailing it to safety.

Encouraged by their successes in this second go-around, they decided in just a week's time to head out again. They chose to attack a truck repair shop in suburban Lyngby that fixed up vehicles that were being sent to the Eastern Front to supply German troops fighting the Soviet Union in Russia. Unfortunately, they chose to assault the works at just the moment a convoy of trucks were arriving at the shop for repairs.

Jorgen was collared by a Danish police officer whose suspicions were aroused when he saw the saboteurs lurking around the building. The cop followed Jorgen and soon drew his gun, forcing Jorgen to drop his own. Jorgen was marched down the street, and as they walked, the two Danes chatted like two old acquaintances, debating the moral dilemma they found themselves in. Both the Danish cop and Jorgen knew if the officer took Jorgen to the police station and handed him over to the Germans, chances were good that Jorgen would be imprisoned and maybe ultimately executed. The Danish cop explained to Jorgen that he belonged to a non-violent religious group and was not inclined to hand Jorgen over under any circumstances, even if they hadn't been fellow Danes.[2] It was typical of dealings with the Danish police everywhere for HD 2. The cops were deployed by the German authorities and generally followed the lead of the occupiers. At the same time, they were inclined to look the other way at resistance activity if that option presented itself.

The Danish police had been left with the responsibility of maintaining order in Denmark even after the August 29 crackdown, but arrested citizens could be and were frequently interrogated by the Gestapo. Because saboteurs were considered private criminals and not members of a hostile armed force, they were generally remanded to the Danish court system, which was far more lenient to its own citizens than were the German authorities. The natural sympathies of many Danish police officers also leaned in the direction of the Danish resistance, and on a number of occasions, the police actually worked with saboteurs to provide information about potential targets or German police maneuvers.

The Germans were themselves aware of the two-sided nature of the Danish police and the court system, but because of the ongoing state of Germany's compromised relationship with Danish authorities and its own lack of resources, it was unable to fully bring the system to heel. All of which gave Danish resistance groups like HD 2 more leeway than they would otherwise have.

The Danish cop decided in the end to let Jorgen slip away, and that's what he did, escaping arrest at the truck repair shop. Jorgen quickly continued his work with Holger Danske.

A UNIFORM FACTORY ON ALLEGADE STREET IN THE FREDERIKSBERG DIS-trict of Copenhagen soon became the next target for the group. It was a business that had long been making uniforms for the German Weh-rmacht, and it had been a target of unsuccessful resistance sabotage by other cells at least twice before it came in the crosshairs of HD 2.

Using the new direct assault techniques they'd employed at the radio

factory, the group assigned a half-dozen members to the attack, split between a bomb unit and marksmen armed with pistols to provide cover and
knock out searchlights. Once again, the bombers got tight to the factory
so as to break windows and lob in incendiary bombs. These were followed
by more powerful detonating devices. The saboteurs then left the grounds
with the factory in flames soon after the heavier bombs had exploded.

The group was now moving quickly from target to target, getting
council from the SOE, the workers at some potential factories in war-
related industries, and the occasional police officers, whom John had been
cultivating for just this purpose. In one instance, word arrived that a factory in the northern part of Copenhagen was producing sound locators
that the Germans used to pinpoint British aircraft that were flying over
Denmark to drop supplies to the resistance or were on their way to raids
in Germany or Poland. To the British, who would lose over 1,300 airmen
over Denmark through the course of the war, it was no small thing to take
out this manufacturer.

John, Mix, and Jorgen did reconnaissance at the factory, while Finn
sought out details about the business and the structure in which it was
housed. The factory was located at the west end of a large structure that
stretched all the way down to the harbor on the east side. Housed in that
eastern edge of the rambling structure were both the German and Danish
harbor police.

The compound sat on a large lot surrounded by a chain-link fence
that may or may not have carried an electrical charge—no one knew with
certainty. There was a plank fence on the border of the western edge of the
compound, separating a filling station from the factory. The whole area
was lit from dawn to dusk by searchlights.

To the north side of the Industrial Combine, as the compound was
called, sat the Tuborg Brewery. In his information gathering, Finn had
learned that the switch to the searchlights could be found within the brewery, in its machine room. He had also somehow managed to get a set of
keys to the room and thus access to the light switch.

The assault required a large contingent of saboteurs. There needed to
be multiple groups of bombers, multiple numbers of shooters to cover the

work of those planting and throwing bombs, and a contingent to enter the Tuborg factory to turn off the lights and make sure none of the factory workers within interfered with the sabotage.

For the first time in their operations, the armed units would be carrying machine guns, which while presenting more firepower within HD 2 also lifted their activities to a more serious level in the eyes of their enemies, a fact that would have consequences down the line. The Flame and Niels Hjorth, Jorgen's med school classmate who'd been in Varde over the summer, were given the weapons and asked to cover the bombers. Meanwhile, inside the Tuborg factory, John and Jorgen's younger brother, Flemming, covered the lone guard in the attached Tuborg plant.

Members of the bomb squads included Mix, Jorgen, and half a dozen other cadets and recent recruits brought into the group by John and Finn.

The bombs arrived by previous arrangement by taxi at around seven o'clock, which immediately set the clock ticking on the action. John, who'd been given the keys by Finn, led the way into the Tuborg factory, where he and the others soon ran headlong into two Tuborg workers, a boiler attendant and a machine tender, neither of whom knew which of three light switches turned off the searchlights in the yard outside the factory. When the Tuborg workers discovered that the saboteurs were not interested in harming their own factory, they quickly became willing to help solve the mystery of which switch needed flipping. In fact, they called the plant engineer to put the question to him and soon had an answer. In return, the factory workers asked that the saboteurs tie them up to cover any questions that might arise when the authorities came later. Again, the ambiguous feelings of the Danish people toward the work of the resistance was a constant but uncertain factor in the work of HD 2.

The lights went out, and the bomb squad was sent into action. They climbed the plank fence on the western edge of the compound and headed into the open space behind the sound locator factory. The guards, who had been disoriented by the loss of their lighting, suddenly caught the movement of the bomb units in the area between the fence and factory and finally opened fire on the saboteurs. The HD II gun units, led by the Flame, returned fire with their newly-acquired machine guns and raked the western side of the building. A member of one of the bomb units threw an incendiary device into the factory, which soon started a fire. Inside, the guards had to tend to the blaze. That gave the HD 2 bomb units outside time to prepare their larger detonation bombs, which were then heaved inside with the fuses sizzling.

Their role in the action finished, the bomb squads made their exit, through the plank fence this time, as John had loosened some of the boards to make the route easier. He was there counting heads as the bomb units made their way out into the night.

The detonators were on a short fuse, which gave the crew just a few minutes to get away. They were all clear of the factory when the explosions erupted in the night. Three brilliant flashes lit the night sky, signaling that three of four bombs had gone off, enough to do enormous damage to the factory.

Shards of glass rained down on the complex. There were screams in the streets, and passing trolleys came to a halt. The saboteurs disappeared on bicycles and into a pair of taxis waiting outside.[3]

CHAPTER 24

Setbacks

A FEW DAYS AFTER THE SUCCESSFUL SABOTAGE AT THE INDUSTRIAL Combine, John and Finn had arranged to meet at seven-thirty one evening on a Copenhagen street corner in the district of Osterbro. That was just a half hour before the eight o'clock curfew. When their business stretched long, they decided to stay in a nearby flat that they knew to be unoccupied, its tenants now in Sweden, instead of risking a bike ride home post-curfew. When they approached the apartment, however, John had the unsettled feeling that it was being watched by the Gestapo. Finn knew of another place nearby, where a Norwegian seamstress named Hedvig Delbo lived. According to Finn, she had done some work for the first Holger Danske group and was now eager to again assist with the reconstituted organization.

She not only welcomed them into her home but also offered sandwiches, coffee, and a place to spend the night. After dinner, they brought their bicycles into the hallway outside her flat, and then all of them sat down to listen to the BBC before Finn and John were directed to the spare bedroom for the night, across the hall from the main part of the flat. Unbeknownst to the two saboteurs, Mrs. Delbo took the alone time, as they settled into the room, to call the nearby Gestapo headquarters.

As if nothing had changed from their evening friendliness, the next morning, Mrs. Delbo insisted that John and Finn stay for breakfast, which they dutifully ate. After thanks and good-byes, the men hopped on their bicycles and were beginning to pedal away when they noticed two men following them. Further, at the corners on each end of Mrs. Delbo's street, two cars, each carrying three or four more suspicious-looking men, were lurking about. As John and Finn pedaled past, the cars started to shadow the bikes, and the HD 2 members became certain that the occupants were the Gestapo.

Finn saw John stand up on his pedals and reach for his pistol, which was tucked into his trousers. It was a signal to Finn to get out of there as fast as he could, which he did, heading toward a safe house out of the neighborhood.

Unfortunately, John was not so evasive. As he fumbled to get his pistol out and aim, the Gestapo agents got of their car and started shooting. Several shots were fired by the Germans, and at least one of them hit John and knocked him off his bicycle and onto the street.[1]

A witness watching the scene later recounted it for the benefit of the Flame. The passerby, who had loose connections to HD 2, said that he'd recognized John after he fell and that he was running to call an ambulance when the Gestapo approached John, who had managed to turn on his side and finally get his pistol out of his pants. The witness claimed that John shot one of the officers, which prompted the other to level his machine gun at the saboteur, who was finally stopped with a hail of bullets. For good measure, the Gestapo agent clubbed him with the butt of his gun before John was dragged to the back seat of the car and driven away.

Meanwhile, Finn pedaled on and was able to evade the Gestapo and get to a tobacco shop that had become a safe spot for resistance members. There, he contacted both his HD 2 colleagues and his home, where his wife waited anxiously for word of his whereabouts.

CHAPTER 25

The First Death

MORE CHAOS ENSUED FROM THE SHOOT-OUT. NOT ONLY WERE JOHN and the Gestapo man wounded, but another bicyclist, just passing by on his way to work, was hit in the leg by a stray bullet. He was immediately taken by ambulance to Copenhagen University Hospital, along with the Gestapo agent.

The bicyclist was suspected by the Germans to be a colleague of John's, and they were reluctant to have him discharged; instead, the Gestapo corralled a pair of medical students to transfer him to Bispebjerg Hospital. One of these med students was Kieler's old friend and fellow medical student Cato Bakman, who, along with Dr. Koster, had been one of the vital cogs in the Bispebjerg Hospital rescue operation. He had also worked with *Frit Danmark* as a nonviolent member of the Kieler student group and was the student who burst into the assembly at the university to announce Niels Bohr's success in getting Sweden to accept Danish refugees.

The newly married Bakman, whose bride, Andrea, also worked at Bispebjerg as a nurse, set off to find Koster, who had an apartment on the hospital grounds, only to discover that there were six Gestapo agents already outside his door, looking for Koster, as well. Bakman was an athletic young man who, when he spied the agents lurking around Koster's door, assumed they were after him. His first instinct was to run down a hospital corridor to an open third-floor window and leap. Which he did, with the Gestapo on his heels. Leaning out the window, they shot down at him on the grounds below, where the fact that he'd damaged his spine in the fall and couldn't move made him a pretty easy target.

Cato was hit by three bullets and stretchered back into the hospital, where the first person to care for him was the duty nurse, his new wife, Andrea. In addition to his spinal injury, he now had three bullet wounds and other injuries due to the fall. There was little that could be done for him. According to Kieler, he lost consciousness in the night and passed away early the next morning with Andrea and his parents at his side.[1]

Andrea buried her husband, who was never a saboteur but was the first member of HD 2 to be killed for his duty. Andrea herself had helped in the rescues at the hospital and would continue with assistance to the resistance after the death of her husband.

CHAPTER 26

Vengeance: First Attempt

I N THE WAKE OF JOHN'S ARREST, THE FLAME VISITED A POLICE CONTACT at the local headquarters to sniff out any information he could about John's fate. He learned that despite being shot eight times, his friend was still alive and had been taken to Vestre Faengsel, Copenhagen's main prison. His current status and his future in the hands of the Germans remained uncertain.[1]

Holger Danske 2 had not yet had to deal with such an overt act of betrayal, and it quickly mobilized for a response. Finn could think of no other way that he and John had been betrayed, other than by Hedvig Delbo, but the group decided to put the supposition to a test. First, they sent a lovebird couple, in this case Mix and Henny, to stroll by and linger around Mrs. Delbo's apartment and see if their presence might prompt any reaction. It did; HD 2 observers soon spotted two Gestapo cars parked at either end of the street. There was also a suspicious-looking handcart parked outside her building, with Christmas trees for sale. The cart, the group subsequently learned, was concealing a machine gun.

Deciding the time was not good for an action, Finn then called Mrs. Delbo directly to tell her what had happened earlier to him and John and to tell her that his cover was blown, that he would have to go to Sweden. Could he come by, debrief her, and say good-bye? She begged off and instead tried to coax more information out of Finn about his plans and the plans of Holger Danske 2. How would he get to Sweden? Would the group be assisting? She might have to leave Copenhagen herself. Probably go back to Norway.

To Finn and the others, when he informed them of the conversation, it was another clear indication of her guilt. What was more, it seemed to the group that she was dangerous, not simply to Finn but also to HD 2 as a whole. Something needed to be done about Mrs. Delbo. Something soon and drastic.

The group had never planned a liquidation before, and the morality of the decision was far from easy. After all, these were good Danes, many of them clean-cut students who couldn't have dreamed of shooting another human just a few months earlier, young people who had just spent the past few weeks helping to save the lives of desperate people on their way to Sweden.

Finn volunteered to do the shooting; in fact, he wanted to do it as a debt to John. But since the notion of a liquidation was a collective decision, the others wanted to have some part in it, too, to take responsibility, as well. The plan, as it evolved, was for Henny, carrying a sample bit of fabric, to ring Mrs. Delbo's doorbell and ask if the seamstress might be available to make her a dress from the material. Henny would go in and discern if any Gestapo were lurking about in the apartment. If not, she would go to the flat's front door and open it for Finn, who would have followed her into the building. The plan was straightforward after that: Finn would shoot the *stikker* (Danish for snitch) and would, indeed, head off to Sweden with his family.

It didn't work out quite as planned. Henny was able to get inside Mrs. Delbo's apartment and found no Germans there, but there was one other customer, who was taking forever getting sized. Henny's patience was severely strained, as was Finn's as he waited, pacing in the hallway. Henny tried to get Finn to come inside to do his business regardless of the other woman's presence, but he insisted that it just be Mrs. Delbo within.

Meanwhile, out in the street, two other HD 2 members who were watching over the action, including Mix, attracted the attention of the police and were ultimately dragged down to the station for questioning. Henny, left to her own devices, soon quit the apartment, as did Finn.[2]

He came back by that night with a pistol, silencer attached. The Flame served as his only companion. There would be no more elaborate ruses. Finn rang the bell to her apartment and waited. When Mrs. Delbo opened the door and saw who it was, she let out a scream. Finn raised his pistol and fired. The seamstress fell, and the assassins, assuming their mission was complete, turned and hightailed it out of there.

In fact, Mrs. Delbo was not dead.

A visit by the Flame the very next day to his contact at the local police station revealed that not only had Mrs. Delbo received only a superficial wound the evening before, but she also was even then in the police station being quizzed by the Gestapo about what had happened. She had identified her shooter as Finn, and according to the cop informing the Flame, they were already printing up copies of his photo to be passed around to the police all over the city. Finn's days in Copenhagen were essentially over.

And so were Mrs. Delbo's. The Gestapo helped facilitate her escape to Norway, where the Norwegian resistance would make two more failed attempts on her life in the next several months before she decided to come back to Copenhagen. There, she took an assumed name and once again hooked up with the Gestapo. It wasn't an association that could last. On March 9, 1944, an unknown resistance fighter—not from HD 2—assassinated her in her new apartment. It was said that the police found 35,000 kroner in her flat, presumably from her work as a snitch for the Germans.[3]

CHAPTER 27

New Territory

WITHOUT FINN AND WITHOUT JOHN, HOLGER DANSKE 2 WAS SOME-what rudderless. The Flame and Jorgen Kieler were both presumptive leaders, but both lacked experience in sabotage and neither had the connections to other underground groups that were needed to find directions and weapons for continued acts of sabotage. Finn had been familiar with the SOE and BOPA, the Communist-led resistance fighters who had been pioneers in the resistance movement and had continued to carry out actions through the fall, particularly in the brutal form of executions at a pair of cafes in Copenhagen that were popular with German officers and their Danish girlfriends. To carry out their attacks at these establishments, BOPA had placed bombs beneath tables occupied by the Gestapo and their friends, killing multiple people and causing turmoil within the ranks of various resistance groups.

Finn had also been connected to the Freedom Council, which was a group founded in September by both establishment and resistance figures, including Frode Jacobsen, the humanitarian writer and student of philosophy from Jutland, who was now one of the principal leaders of the council. He was the student of Kierkegaard and German literature who, along with his German-born wife, had vowed to quit speaking the language altogether when Germany began its occupation of Denmark in 1940. Now, he was a leading figure among the various groups trying to foment resistance in the country. It was the Freedom Council's goal to organize the various groups, including BOPA, the SOE, Holger Danske 2, and a growing group of expatriates in Sweden who wanted to continue the fight from the other side of the sound into a semblance of a unified front that might be able to unite with the Allies when the time came to help battle to the Germans on Danish soil.

As it turned out, the bookseller, Jorgen Staffeldt, was tabbed by the Freedom Council for the position as the new leader of HD 2; it also turned out that he and the group had to become readjusted to their new situation quickly. The SOE wanted an act of sabotage performed quickly, and it was not to be performed on the group's familiar home turf in Copenhagen but rather on the other side of the country, in the city of Varde, near the west coast of Jutland.

PART OF THE REASON THAT HD 2 WAS TAPPED FOR THE ASSIGNMENT WAS that it had already made a connection to Varde: that was where Kieler's medical school and resistance friend, Niels Hjorth, had served an internship at a local hospital over the past summer. Along with hooking up with the local resistance while there, Hjorth also made the acquaintance of a pair of friendly police officers in town, one of whom introduced Hjorth to an SOE member who had been parachuted into the area during the summer.

There was a steelworks factory in the city that the Allies wanted destroyed as quickly as possible. So quickly, in fact, that they let the Danes know that if it wasn't destroyed by sabotage on the ground, the RAF would be forced to bomb it from the air, despite the fact that the factory was located in the center of Varde and a bombing raid would wreak havoc in the town, endangering the civilian population and the Danish workers at the site.

So it was that just days after losing Cato Bakman at Bispebjerg, as well as John and Finn to the Gestapo and exile in Sweden, respectively, that a group of ten saboteurs made the cross-country trip from Copenhagen to Jutland intent on destroying the Varde steelworks. Among the coterie were Jorgen, the Flame, and a mix of students and navy cadets. They took the train across Zealand and Fyn to the Great Belt, where they had to take a ferry over the waterway separating the two islands.

There was no train service across the central part of Jutland, so the resistance fighters split into groups and were forced to squeeze into a pair of taxis, a fact that drew eyeballs from at least one German vehicle driving along the same roadway. It was a moment in the occupation when Danes could be certain that almost any vehicle on the road, with the exception of taxis, was likely to be Germans or Danish police. Despite any suspicions about the overloaded vehicle, the Germans didn't pull the taxi over.

The saboteurs ended up at the home of the police constable in Varde, the same connection Niels had made as an intern at the Varde hospital in the summer, and who had subsequently hooked him up with the SOE in the fall. There the group sat around the kitchen table plotting the particulars of the attack, using excellent drawings done by the local resistance group to acquaint themselves with the lay of the land. Local resistance members also supplied the saboteurs with the knowledge that four or five security guards would be on duty and that they were in regular contact with the local police, calling in every half hour to the station.

When the plan was agreed to, the HD 2 group wasted little time before heading off to the steelworks in pairs, cutting their way inside the chain-link fence. Once inside the grounds, they quickly found the guardroom, kicked in the door, and took the guards completely by surprise. The guards volunteered the keys to the factory and then allowed themselves to be locked in the air-raid shelter.

It took another hour to place and wire the bombs inside the structure. Because of SOE's direct involvement in the activity, a supply of good munitions was readily at hand; eight bombs were distributed using plastic explosives linked by Cordtex detonating cords. Partway through rigging the bombs, the Flame took one of the guards to a telephone to have him call in the regularly scheduled all clear to allay any suspicions at the police station. In a matter of minutes afterward, HD 2 had vacated the premises.

The resulting explosions were so successful that the plant shut down for six months afterward. The British were extremely pleased, and the story of the sabotage was picked up all the way across the Atlantic by the *New York Times,* whose December 13 headline read DANES BLOW UP PLANT MAKING GERMAN ARMS.

The story suggested that forty to fifty saboteurs had taken part in the raid, about five times the number of HD 2 members who had actually been involved.[1]

The reputation of HD 2 was greatly enhanced by the attack. It soon became the go-to resistance organization for what were called flying sabotage operations, and getting supplies for further actions from the SOE was no longer a problem.

THEY WENT TO HORSENS OVER CHRISTMAS, VISITING THE KIELER FAMILY's old stomping grounds and using the occasion to hook up with Jorgen's old friend and fellow saboteur Peer Borup. Peer had lined up several small jobs for the group to take care of, including blowing up an engineering firm and a company that manufactured condensed milk for German use.

After the holidays, HD 2 headed back to Copenhagen, where Niels Hjorth found their next target. He had made a connection with a foreman at a large and well-known shipping firm called Burmeister & Wain (B & W), which made repairs for German Navy ships at a wharf-side plant in Christianshavn. The foreman let Niels know that no work was done at the company on Saturday evenings, when only a skeletal crew guarded the business. In December, BOPA had targeted the company and caused significant damage to some drilling equipment, but quick repairs at the business had sent it back into production just a month later. Now, with the words of Niels and his contact for reassurance, HD 2 decided to hit B & W after getting the go-ahead from Jorgen Staffeldt.

Mix took the lead on the project, which in retrospect seemed to have a lot of moving parts for a still-inexperienced group of saboteurs. The first essential was to get a buy-in from the Copenhagen harbor police, who would be asked for the use of one of their motorboats, which was to be used to tow another boat, a dinghy, that they planned to hijack from the harbor and take to a designated berth. There, ten members of HD 2 would be waiting to climb aboard the craft with weapons and bombs. The police

motorboat would then tow the dinghy to a canal near the company compound. Once there, the crew of HD 2 members would storm the company, place their bombs, hop back on the dinghy, and be towed to a nearby
bridge, where their escape from the harbor was to be covered by the Flame
and another group of Holger Danske 2 saboteurs.

The various components of the plan aside, the one thing that everyone
seemed to agree on going into the attack was that HD 2 was well-armed
for the venture. According to Mix, everyone had a pistol and there were
twelve submachine guns available, plus, he said, "masses of hand grenades.
We were determined to carry out the operation against all odds. We did
not want to allow ourselves to be stopped by any accidental occurrence
while we were on the job, but were prepared to shoot it out with whoever
stood in our way."[2]

In addition, the cadre carried seven bombs with a total of 412 pounds
of TNT. These were explosives the group had bought themselves with
money, Mix writes, that was left over from the collections used to pay passage for Jews traveling to Sweden. The bombs were packaged at the apartment in Raadhustraede and carried in rucksacks on "wobbly" tricycles to
a departure wharf in Christianshavn.

They quickly ran into problems. The dinghy that they'd chosen to pil-
fer was blocked in by another motorboat on the dock whose pair of owners
were not interested in moving quickly, and, by the way, one of them was
an owner of the dinghy. In the confused set of circumstances pervading
at the time in Denmark—where both the police and the general populace
were often sympathetic, if not downright supportive, of the efforts of the
resistance—the two turned out not to be entirely dissuaded by the fact
that their boat was being stolen when they realized that they were inter-
fering with the work of saboteurs. They ultimately let the HD 2 contingent,
which included Jorgen Kieler, who was designated to serve at the helm,
and Klaus Ronholt, who'd helped Elsebet raise money for the rescue in the
fall, steal the vessel as long as they promised to bring it back.

That brought about the next problem: the Danish police motorboat
that was supposed to tow the dinghy to the canal beside the factory not
only failed to show up, but what arrived in its place was the German har-

bor police, who were not only armed with their own submachine guns but also had numerous questions about what was going on with the dinghy. The saboteurs quickly dumped their pistols overboard, but they were then towed into custody and placed under arrest at Langelinie Pier by the Germans.

While Jorgen Kieler and the trio of cadets, who had been with him on the dinghy, waited at Langelinie to be interrogated by the Gestapo, Mix and the ten or twelve other saboteurs continued in the action. They were finally able to locate the harbor police motorboat that they'd expected earlier in the evening. It turned out that one of the two officers involved in the subterfuge got cold feet, and he took a good deal of convincing to continue on with the action.

Now the bombing of the plant was back in the hands of Mix and his retinue of saboteurs. They quickly decided to stick to the plans of the sabotage, minus the dinghy. With the help of yet another naval cadet, whose knowledge of the harbor was crucial to the exercise, they navigated to the plant and landed at the canal within the compound, where they were greeted by two guards with pistols and two with submachine guns. According to Mix, they caused no trouble.[3]

Flemming Kieler might not have agreed with this assessment. Along with carrying a machine gun, Flemming was literally strapped with one of the bombs that was soon to be used on the plant as he trudged toward his assignment with the HD 2 bomb squad. The bomb was so large that it stuck out over the top of Flemming's head as he carried it toward its destination. Suddenly, a guard stepped in front of him, pointed a pistol at his chest, and ordered Flemming to raise his hands. Cool as a cucumber, Kieler indicated in a direct manner that what he was carrying in the rucksack on his back was a bomb, and if he was shot, chances were good that it would go off and kill them both. The guard was not interested in risking his own life and finally surrendered his weapon to Flemming, who proceeded to the bomb's designated location.[4]

Mix occupied a spot somewhere near the middle of the large compound. He used whistles to signal to the disparate teams locating the bombs to advise them if dangers had arisen and when they should get back to the boats. When all was ready, they ordered their captured guards into the plant's air-raid shelters and placed the bombs. Mix gave the signal to get back to the boats and then counted as the men returned. They waited a quarter of an hour, started to sail back to their starting berths, and then listened as the first explosion sounded over the waterfront. It was quickly followed by five more.

The fuse had failed on a sixth bomb, but the explosions of the first five were electric and filled the night sky over the Copenhagen harbor with the echoes of destruction. Henny Sinding was tracking what was happening from a room in Christianshavn that her father had recently rented for her and her sister. She not only knew the intimate details of the sabotage but also was soon to be involved in its aftermath. The plan was for Mix and the HD 2 members to return to the Sinding sisters' apartment to stow leftover gear from the attack.

As the saboteurs sailed back to their original point of departure, with thanks for the borrowed police boat, Henny had gone out into the streets of Christianshavn after the first explosion and was there when the subsequent blasts lit the sky purple, and "aglow with flames and rising embers."[5] She knew by these indicators that Mix and the others had done their work, but she had no idea if all or some would be returning from their mission.

The boys were supposed to return to her place by car, but as Henny waited, and waited some more, they failed to show up. Then she saw them, on foot, lugging heavy suitcases, just down the street from her apartment. They'd all pulled up the collars of their jackets to better disguise their identities (though certainly their heavy suitcases distinguished them on the street).

Once inside Henny's building, they lugged the suitcases up to the apartment, shoved all the furniture within to block the front door, and then spent the night guarding the gear, which turned out to be pistols, machine guns, and grenades.

THROUGH ALL THIS HIGH EXCITEMENT, JORGEN KIELER AND HIS THREE companions were at Langelinie, housed in a cabin aboard a German vessel guarded by sentries. As they waited for the Gestapo to arrive to interview them, the students frantically tried to get their stories straight. This was a first for them, being quizzed by the vaunted German security forces, and they had little time to perfect and sync their tales. Not surprisingly, the Gestapo were quick to punch holes in their accounts of what they were doing on a dinghy that was not theirs when they interviewed the four separately.

The major concern for the quartet was that they not be linked to the attack on B & W, which had just occurred and was obviously the most pressing concern of the Germans. All four admitted to the Gestapo that they were students at the university. Under the theory that it was better to confess a partial crime than being found out as fellow saboteurs in the B & W bombing, they told their interlocutors that they'd pilfered the dinghy with the idea of sailing it to Sweden. They said that they were fearful of a *razzia* (a police raid) at the university, which had prompted their decision to escape across the Oresund.

The discrepancies in their stories were pointed out to Jorgen when the officer interviewing him returned after a break with three sheets of paper containing transcripts of his colleagues' interrogations. They didn't match his story. This prompted a trip to a small room where a pair of Danish guards were assigned to put the screws to the HD 2 quartet. The torture turned out to be a seemingly endless series of deep-knee bends that lasted for an hour or two, until the guards grew as tired of watching the students as the students were exhausted by the exercise. The guards ended up simply taking Jorgen and the others back to the interrogation room.

By this time, the Germans had gotten their hands on an unexploded bomb that had been picked up by a German disposal squad at the site of the B & W attack. The officer interviewing Jorgen brought it into the interrogating room as a visual display of what he suspected Jorgen and the others had been involved in when they were apprehended. During this round of questioning, he made Jorgen entirely ill at ease by holding the bomb and swinging it around by its fuse and then setting it down with a bang on the table between them.[6]

As luck would have it, however, it was the fact that Kieler and the others were being held at Langelinie by the Gestapo when the bombs at the plant went off that cleared them from suspicion in the most serious transgression that the Germans were considering them liable for. They were still charged with the theft of the dinghy but sent to the Danish judicial system, which was obviously preferrable to German imprisonment but still meant they would continue to be held in custody, now in the Copenhagen Vestre Faengsel jail.

While he was in prison, Jorgen would subsequently learn that his sisters, Elsebet and Bente, had received a visit from the Gestapo at the apartment at Raadhusstraede. They were visited by a section of the Gestapo separate from the one investigating the sabotage; this contingent was interested in the underground press and was looking for evidence of Jorgen's involvement with *Frit Danmark*. Fortunately for Jorgen, the fact that he was at the same time being held by another branch of the Gestapo was never connected by the Germans, and he proceeded through the Danish justice system with a consequently more lenient punishment. Jorgen and Klaus were sentenced to eighty days of incarceration and a fine of 200 kroner for the theft of the dinghy, which had already been returned. They were given credit for eight days of time served and Klaus's parents paid the fine. For reasons that Jorgen never completely understood, except as a measure of the confusion and leniency of the Danish judicial system at the time, they were then released, still owing seventy-two days of jail time to the state that would never be served. They didn't need to be told twice that they were free to go.[7]

CHAPTER 28

Menace of the Peter Group

B Y MIDWINTER 1943–1944, THE SHAPE OF THE GLOBAL WAR WAS BE-
coming more apparent. It was inevitable that the Allies would soon
be invading Western Europe. Then, with the Allies coming from the west
and the forces of the Soviet Union continuing to advance from the east,
Germany would soon be squeezed in a vice by these great powers. More
desperate hours, days, and years were to come, but it was evident that the
time had arrived to prepare for the final struggle. In Denmark, the resistance movement continued to grow, in part to make sure the Allies understood that despite the Danish government's cooperative strategy through
much of the occupation, the people of Denmark stood in support of Allied
efforts.

After the reorganization of Holger Danske and the creation of HD 2 in
October, other resistance groups decided to follow suit and even took the
Holger Danske moniker. Holger Danske groups 3, 4, and 5 were formed
between December 1943 and May 1944. HD 3 and HD 4 disbanded quickly, but HD 5, which included the Flame and a newcomer to the organization, Jorgen Haagen Schmith, nicknamed Citroen, would become notorious saboteurs and resistance fighters.

In Sweden, refugees, both Jewish and—in ever-increasing numbers
now that the evacuation was essentially over—political and resistance figures, organized a military unit called the Danish Brigade with the idea
of eventually joining Allied forces in a final battle for Denmark, if and

when that moment came. Sweden provided a 25 million kroner credit to the Danish legation to help fund, train, and organize this brigade, which would eventually include familiar figures like Herbert Pundik and several exiled Holger Danske members.

As the intensity of the resistance movement increased through the course of the war, the numbers of political refugees in Sweden swelled. The routes of escape had already been well-established during the Jewish exodus. Now they were being used by downed Allied pilots, government officials, former military personnel (including comrades of Volmer Gyth, the members of the Danish intelligence service who'd assisted in the escape of Niels Bohr), and the increasing numbers of resistance fighters who were being forced from Denmark by pressure from the Germans. In the reverse, these same routes were being used to bring arms and ammunition from Sweden to Denmark as well as to return resistance fighters like Jens Lillelund (a.k.a. the Finn), who was back in Denmark by May 1944 after his brief self-imposed exile following the attempted assassination of Mrs. Delbo in December.

After its rescue efforts with Jewish refugees slowed to a trickle in October, the Elsinore Sewing Club started to shift gears and use boats that its members had collectively purchased to continue to run missions to Sweden and back. One of its members, the bookbinder Erling Kiaer, had taken the lead in the changing nature of the mission of the club. He was piloting one of the group's new boats in early 1944 when it was attacked by the Gestapo as it was pulling away from a beach just north of Elsinore. Its passengers included several Jews who had lingered in Denmark, working with the resistance. Among those injured in the shooting was one of the original members of the Elsinore club, police detective Thormond Larsen. Kiaer and the group were convinced that their plans had been given away by an informer. It prompted the sewing club to suspend its activities and caused Kiaer to send his own family to Sweden. He stayed behind and eventually continued making the illegal trips across the sound.[1]

The *Gerda III* as well continued in its service to the resistance, even as Henny focused on her work with HD 2. Perhaps surprisingly, her father, Paul Sinding, the straightlaced commander of the Lighthouse and Buoy

Service in the Copenhagen harbor, took over many of the resistance duties pioneered by his daughter. As with other boats employed in the Jewish rescue efforts, the number of refugees on board declined steeply after the middle of October, but under Paul Sinding's guidance and say-so, the *Gerda III* became focused on supplying Danish fighters with military equipment and radio transmitters smuggled from Sweden to Copenhagen. [2]

The change in Paul Sinding from a parent accepting his daughter's dangerous passions to joining her in active participation in the same might signify the growing strength and resolve of the general Danish population in its opposition to the Germans and, by extension, the government's co-operation policy. The sabotage attacks against Danish businesses carried out by resistance groups like HD 2 were growing more accepted within Denmark as a whole as a necessary response to the continued German occupation.

These sentiments were bolstered by the Freedom Council, which grew more powerful within both resistance circles and the general public by offering an economic and political framework for the use of sabotage against Danish businesses. The council published a pamphlet in December 1943 titled "Are You a Nazi?" which argued that Danish patriots should applaud the use of sabotage to damage and subvert German efforts that continued the war. "If you want a shorter war, a faster end to the occupation and the defeat of Nazism, then you must support—not oppose the freedom movement in word and deed. These words are not for those who *have* understood the meaning of the freedom struggle, but for those who unwittingly support the cause of Nazis."[3]

This had been the logic of resistance fighters like Jorgen Kieler for many months now, and it had led him and other unlikely saboteurs toward the extreme measures they were now employing to fight the occupation. Even those who had applauded government measures to preserve the country from the devastation of an all-out blitz when Germany occupied the country in April 1940 were now coming to see the necessity of overt acts of violence against those businesses and individuals who continued to support the German war effort.

The change in the political temperature in Denmark did not go unnoticed in Berlin. While its response to the exodus of the Jews of Denmark had been somewhat ambiguous—it might have been a bit embarrassing to lose so many refugees to Sweden, but it did take care of the problem of the Jews in Denmark and it satisfied the Danes, didn't it?—the Third Reich could not tolerate the sort of open rebellion that seemed to be brewing in Copenhagen and Jutland in early 1944. Especially given the coming Allied invasion of Western Europe and the possibilities of a rear guard force joining the Brits and Americans against the Germans.

In response to the increase in sabotage and resistance actions, German authorities decided it was necessary to step up their own police authority in Denmark. In February 1944, Germany formed a counterterrorism group composed of and initially led by SS officers who worked under the motto "Terror against terror." The Peter Group, as the division came to be known, were a specially trained unit of German soldiers who were soon joined by Danish volunteers, most of whom had been a part of the Schalburg Corps, a unit of Danish soldiers who had served on the Eastern Front for the German Army under Christian von Schalburg, a Danish Nazi.[4]

The violence and ferocity of the Peter Group shocked and terrified the Danish community. Leaders in the group tended to choose victims whose deaths would have the greatest intimidating impact on a wide swath of Danish society. One of its first victims was the well-known and revered playwright and Lutheran pastor Kaj Munk (who had corresponded with Elsebet Kieler when she was sorting through issues of whether or not she could participate in violent resistance efforts). His was the first of what came to be called "clearing murders"—usually very public murders of well-known community figures. Munk had been arrested by the Gestapo in January 1944 for defying a ban on preaching at the National Cathedral for an Advent service. His body was found in a ditch in central Jutland about a month later, near the town where he had served for many years as a pastor.

The work of the Peter Group would continue and grow even more vicious through the coming year. The fact that a number of Danes were actively involved in the group would add to the growing hate and bitterness between those fighting the German occupation and those aligned with it. The Peter Group would ultimately be involved in about ninety clearing murders before the war was through. In addition, by August 1944, it was placing bombs in carefully chosen targets, such as a pair of passenger trains in Jutland, private residences whose owners refused to work for the Germans, and to further intimidate and terrorize the populace, a number of popular entertainment venues, including the famed Tivoli Gardens in Copenhagen.[5]

The repression was widespread and fearful. A month before Munk was arrested, Gestapo agents had apprehended a pair of SOE parachutists who had been working with the Hvidsten group in Jutland for many months, bringing in supplies to resistance fighters throughout Denmark by means of air drops. After being tortured by the Germans, the pair gave up the names of the owner of the Hvidsten Inn and his family members, who had been vital components of the smuggling operation and subsequent distribution of arms and munitions: Anton Marius Fiil; his son, Niels; his two daughters, Gerda and Kirstine; Kirstine's husband, Peter; and several friends and acquaintances who had worked with the parachutists from the SOE to hide and distribute supplies and people were arrested in March 1944 and taken to the Gestapo headquarters at the university at Aarhus.[6] In all, twelve members of the group were arrested, and by June, eight members of the group had been sentenced to death, including Anton Marius Fiil, son Niels, daughter Kirstine, and Kirstine's husband, Peter. With the exception of Kirstine, who was spared the firing squad at the last minute and instead sent to a penitentiary in Germany, all the prisoners were executed on June 29. The day before her husband, her son, and her son-in-law were shot, Gudrun Fiil, the wife of Anton Marius and mother of Niels and Kirstine, was allowed a visit with her family for a few hours. Cold comfort. At midnight that evening, the men were called into a room and told they would be shot at four the next morning. The Germans were as good as their word.[7]

CHAPTER 29

The Demise of Holger Danske 2

O N THE HEELS OF THE ULTIMATELY SUCCESSFUL B & W OPERATION and his first stay in a Danish prison, Jorgen Kieler decided to take a short break from resistance activity and head back to Horsens for a little rest. Unfortunately, a Gestapo raid of local resistance figures there sent Kieler quickly back to Copenhagen, along with his old friend Peer Borup, who was one of the people wanted by the Gestapo in Horsens.[1]

Just a day after they were back in the city, Niels Hjorth got a message from his police contact in Varde. A local resistance group in the nearby city of Aabenraa needed help in carrying out acts of sabotage against a pair of local factories that were supplying parts for German U-Boats and planes. There were no experienced saboteurs in Aabenraa, and the Varde resistance group, with whom HD 2 had worked on the steelworks assault in December, was short fighters, so the SOE agent in the area, along with Niels's police contact, thought of the Copenhagen group and made the call.

Niels and Jorgen made a preliminary trip to Varde in early February. They scoped out the area and recognized several immediate difficulties: Aabenraa was a very small town in the southern end of Jutland, full of ethnic Germans, many with deep ties to and sympathies with Germany, hardly a reliable base of operations for a resistance group looking for like-minded compatriots. In addition, the town itself was physically so small that it offered little in the way of hiding places should something go wrong in the operation. And it was far from their familiar stomping grounds in Copenhagen.

Despite these reservations, Jorgen and Niels were swayed by the fact that they trusted the Varde resistance group, which would take the lead in the operation, as well as by the presence of the SOE agent and his support of the operation. Holger Danske 2 wanted to show its support for the coming Allied invasion in any way it could, and if the British were suggesting that the attacks on these two manufacturers were important, the Copenhagen group would assist.

Kieler summoned his HD 2 saboteurs to Aabenraa, and fourteen arrived by the Jutland Express on February 4 to a snow-covered landscape in south Jutland. They were joined there by a handful of Varde fighters, and all met up at the home of an auto mechanic in town named Koch, whose place would serve as the headquarters of the operation.

Holger Danske 2 had used up much of its munitions on the B & W attack, and a number of its pistols were lost. The group was able to recoup some TNT in Copenhagen, but they had to rely on the Varde group for the bulk of the explosives to be used. This ultimately amounted to twenty bombs with Cordtex fuses to be attached. One of the Varde resistance men had floor plans for both factories—called Hamag and Callesen—but the Koch home turned out to be a mile and a half from each of the businesses. The group decided to gather at a local landmark, the Aabenraa Castle, close to the side-by-side factories, and use it as the staging area for the attack.

At midnight on February 6, at the castle, they divided into two groups, each designated to attack a particular plant, and set off for their destinations. In all there were about twenty attackers. Just six were assigned to the smaller facility, Hamag, because it was known to have no anti-sabotage guards at the facility. That group was armed with pistols and one submachine gun. They carried five two-kilogram bombs, which were quickly placed at strategic locations within, focused on wrecking the metal works machinery. With no guards to deal with and unlocked doors, their work was done quickly and without incident. They set timers on the bombs at half an hour and soon exited.

The larger portion of the squad, which included Jorgen, brother Flemming, Niels Hjorth, and Klaus Ronholt, headed for the Callesen site, which quickly proved more problematic. The entrance to this plant was through a heavily barricaded gate guarded by a pair of security guards. There was no way to get in without being spotted by the guards and alerting everyone within, so HD 2 decided to send a unit armed with pistols and machine guns to go behind the compound and enter through a neighboring property with the hope of surprising the guards from behind. The problem was that at the bottom of the fence circling the back of the factory was a large pile of scrap metal. In the process of scaling the fence and landing on the other side, they couldn't help but make a clatter.

Even worse for Jorgen and the others was that in the midst of the attack, as the plan shifted from going in the front entrance of Callesen to the back entrance, one of their local guides, who was helping steer them through this unfamiliar terrain, disappeared from the action. Once inside the compound, they were without their eyes and principal navigator, and they became momentarily lost. They had brought the sketches of the plant done earlier, but in the hurried situation, the sketches didn't help in situating them and the clock kept ticking. They finally found and followed a set of trolley tracks in the yard that led them toward the back entrance.

More hiccups followed. The gate in back was padlocked shut, and once they arrived there, they could hear the voice of one of the guards inside, obviously on a phone call to the local police, saying, "I'm speaking from Callesen's. Persons unknown have entered the compound."[2]

It was a moment that called for decisive action, and Jorgen took it. He used his submachine gun to shoot off the lock and then kicked open the gate. Inside, two guards lay prone on the floor. The receiver to the telephone that they'd just been using was still off the hook on a table beside them, meaning that whatever police department was on the other end of the line had certainly heard Jorgen's submachine gun blasting the lock from the gate.

The HD 2 bomb unit had rushed into the factory behind the gun unit, once the gate was opened, and was now in the process of setting up twenty-two bombs, again focused on the plant's metalworking machinery.

Just as the bomb group was attaching the Cordtex fuses to the explosives, word came to Jorgen and the unit behind the factory that the Danish police had arrived at the front gate. The saboteurs were able to subdue them, but in interrogating the police the resistance fighters learned from them that fifty German soldiers were in the area, and they now had presumably been warned of the attack.

As if on cue during the Callesen drama, the five bombs at the Hamag plant went off as planned. To Jorgen and the others, it was a sign to get out of the plant, posthaste. The order was given to light the fuses. and both the bomb squad and the armed HD 2 group exited the site just as a second police car pulled in. The Germans were there in ten minutes more.

It was near two-thirty in the morning of a dark Danish night in a south Jutland territory that none of the Copenhagen saboteurs knew well. Peer, Klaus, Niels, and Jorgen, along with two of the Verde operatives, headed off to the home of Koch, the local auto mechanic, where they were hoping to safely spend the night.

The twenty-two bombs in the Callesen factory had not yet exploded, nor would they ever.

THE REST OF THE NONLOCAL SABOTEURS WENT OFF TO HOMES IN THE area where arrangements had been made for their stays. The plan was simply for the resistance fighters to head for unguarded railway stations and find their own ways back to their hometowns once things had cooled down, mainly to Copenhagen and Varde.

The next morning, when the saboteurs had hoped to begin their trips back to their homes, they found the Aabenraa region was thick with Germans. The group staying with Jorgen at Koch's house discussed the failure of the operation at Callesen. Despite all the troubles they'd faced and despite the presence of German forces, they decided to make another attempt at the plant, but only if they were able to replenish their explosives. One of the Verde group, Jens Jorgensen, set off on the morning train to a small town near Varde with an empty suitcase and the hope that he could fill it with TNT supplied by the local resistance. No such luck. He was quickly collared at the railway station by the Gestapo and was being driven to the police headquarters when he was shot in the chest during an attempted escape.

Meanwhile, the remaining contingent of Copenhagen HD 2 saboteurs at Koch's home gathered in Koch's workshop, located in a separate shed. The group consisted of Peer, Niels, Klaus, Jorgen, and Viggo, the last of the Varde resistance fighters still left in Aabenraa. Klaus suddenly came running to the others with word that two German cars were driving up to the house. He shouted that the Germans had shot Koch's landlady. Then, in the process of looking out from the workshop to see what was happening, the resistance team was spotted, and a shot fired at them by the Germans hit Klaus in the leg.

Everyone scrambled to escape the workshop as the Germans searched Koch's house and headed in the direction of the saboteurs, peppering the shed with bullets as they came near. With his good leg, Klaus was able to kick out a window in the shed, but in the process of climbing out, he badly cut his good leg and was now bleeding profusely from both limbs as he started to run with Jorgen through the surrounding snow-covered farm fields.

The German military police, who had been staying at a nearby inn, heard the shooting and commotion and joined the Gestapo in pursuit of the saboteurs. Meanwhile, back at the shed, the Germans found the mortally wounded Peer Borup with a bullet wound to the back of his head. Though the Gestapo wound up taking him and the landlady by ambulance to the hospital in Aabenraa, there was nothing to be done for Jorgen's old Horsens friend. He was dead on arrival.

Klaus and Jorgen continued to make their way across the fields, with Niels and Viggo in an adjacent field. Klaus's legs were bleeding profusely, and he called out to Jorgen to say that his legs were wooden and he didn't think he could go on. Jorgen put Klaus on his back for about 150 yards until they reached a nearby farm. There, they met a very nervous elderly couple, and Jorgen worried for a moment that they might be ethnic Germans, primed to turn them in, but then they pointed to four bicycles in a shed by their house and indicated that the escaping saboteurs could take them if they wanted.

Niels and Viggo had arrived by then, and they grabbed a pair of the bicycles as Jorgen tried to bandage Klaus's legs. They were able to proceed through a woods and out onto a road, where they soon heard a car coming. Niels and Viggo continued on after the car passed, but Jorgen and Klaus stayed in a roadside ditch and Jorgen took the time to more adequately tend to his companion's wounds. He ripped his own shirt into strips to help stanch the bleeding and dress the wound. He detected no breaks in either leg, despite the apparent bullet wound, but Klaus's blood loss was severe. While working on Klaus, Jorgen discovered that he, too, had been hit by a stray bullet in the hand. Between the two of them, they were leaving a brilliant red trail in the snow for anyone bothering to look.

Jorgen was able to help Klaus up on his bicycle, and they continued on for a while until they came to the top of a hill from which they could see in the distance a railway line that might have been their salvation. They could also see, in the same view, a German vehicle traveling along the road. They went back to the ditch to hide once more, but the moment they did, a second car pulled up from the opposite direction and bullets started to fly toward them.

Jorgen had a hand grenade in his pocket but no pistol. Without the Germans being clumped together so it could take out the bulk of the enemy, the grenade would be an ineffectual weapon. Jorgen peeked his head up and counted six Germans surrounding them. He knew that he and Klaus had two bad options: They could either surrender or lob the grenade and be shot for the effort after the explosion. They decided to take option one, and they emptied their pockets of the grenade, identification, and train tickets, which they hid in a pile of leaves in the ditch. Then they came out with their hands up.

The two were searched, and an interrogation began with questions focused on the two (Niels and Viggo) who got away. When Jorgen was less than helpful in answering, he got hit in the head with a rifle butt. The Germans then propped Klaus on one of the bicycles that were in the ditch where Jorgen and Klaus had left them, and the two were forced to retrace their steps back toward Aabenraa, including traveling past the farm where they'd been given the bikes.

During the hike, Jorgen felt a sharp pain in his neck. And when he was allowed to take off his jacket to cover Klaus, who was shivering, he discovered another bullet wound near his collar bone. He'd apparently been hit by a stray bullet while hiding in the ditch.

A pro-German crowd gathered in the streets and began yelling at the saboteurs of the factory as they were marched through Aabenraa. Someone hollered at Jorgen and Klaus that they ought to be strung up. Another told Jorgen that he would be best served by telling the truth to the Germans.

They were taken into the custody of the local arm of the German military police in town, and while Jorgen was locked up, Klaus was taken by ambulance to a German-run hospital in a nearby community.

So ended the last sabotage of Holger Danske 2.

MEANWHILE, NIELS AND VIGGO WERE ABLE TO MAKE THEIR WAY TO SAFE-ty after a trip that included help from a vicar and a doctor in a small Jutland town north of Aabenraa. They got aid as well from a priest in another community, but a taxi driver who was said to have been "a good Dane" almost gave them up by dropping them off in the lap of a German barracks. Niels ultimately got to Odense and then Copenhagen the following day, while Viggo made it all the way back to Varde, where he filled in the remaining members of the group on what had transpired.[3]

Back in Aabenraa, Flemming and Georg Jansen, one of the HD 2 navy cadets, had both been involved in the successful Hamag plant sabotage and had stayed in a separate safehouse in the area. In an effort to hook up with Jorgen and the others, they made the mistake of heading back to the Koch house in the wake the German attack against the Callesen saboteurs. Flemming and Jansen arrived in the aftermath of that raid, saw the house swarming with Germans, and quickly understood that they needed to get away. To avoid their own capture, they started to head down a side road but were spotted by a local pub owner who was friends with the

Gestapo. She immediately reported the sighting, and the German police were quickly on their tail. The two were arrested and taken back to Koch's house, where, along with the homeowner, they were kicked and punched and forced to walk naked around the room by a Gestapo agent, who would cuff them every time they passed by. Another Gestapo agent broke Jansen's jaw with a cruel pistol whip to his head.

The German's found Flemming's identification card and photograph in a bag that he was carrying, and they were able to link him to the resistance, a fact that prompted more beating and abuse. Finally, some of their clothing was returned to them, and they were hauled out to a waiting truck and driven to the same German military police lockup in Aabenraa that was now housing Jorgen.

Jorgen was taken from inside the jail and placed in the back of the same truck. Needless to say, it was not the sort of reunion that the brothers had envisioned when they set out on their separate tasks a day and a half earlier. Though the brothers were ordered not to talk in the back of the truck, in whispers they were able to communicate the information that Peer had been shot, but Klaus was in custody in a German hospital. They were then driven to the Gestapo headquarters in the town of Kolding, and from there, they were soon transported back to Vestre Faengsel in Copenhagen.

NEWS OF THE FAILURE OF THE SABOTAGE EFFORT AT AABENRAA, THE SUB-sequent apprehensions of the Kieler brothers and Klaus, and the death of Peer Borup soon reached the headquarters of HD 2 in Copenhagen through Niels. Alarm bells rang throughout the resistance community. The sense of peril was felt not only because of what had happened in Jutland but also because of what might happen when the Gestapo put the screws to those who had just been captured. Jorgen Staffeldt quickly ordered that all members of HD 2 should immediately go into hiding in preparation for escapes to Sweden. The understanding was that evacuation was the best option—both for the safety of individual members and also for those facing interrogation by the Germans.

Also causing alarms were Gestapo raids in Varde and Horsens, where

Peer Borup's funeral was turning into something of a statement event. The whole town had put out Danish flags to salute the young resistance fighter and thumb their noses at the Germans, which prompted the Gestapo to come around and order them all down. The fact that the Kielers and Nan Moller and her brother were all from Horsens, along with Peer, put a bull's-eye on the town in German eyes.

When the Gestapo came, they even marked Dr. Ernst Kieler, father of the four HD 2 members—Jorgen, Flemming, Bente, and Elsebet—for arrest. When the German police knocked on the Kieler front door, the last and youngest of the siblings, teenage Lida, answered the door and called for her mother, Margrethe, who, in a voice loud enough to alert her husband, let the Germans in. The doctor snuck into the family coal cellar when the Gestapo entered. Lida and her mother feigned an ignorance of the German language to obfuscate the questioning, which was largely and frighteningly focused on Bente and Elsebet. Eventually, Dr. Kieler grew concerned about his wife and youngest daughter and came up out of cellar, where he was nabbed by the German police, who arrested him and took him to a Gestapo holding place in Aarhus to face a lengthy interrogation.[4]

Back in Copenhagen, Henny was staying in an apartment that Mix had arranged for her in Nyboder. She was able to say tearful good-byes to her parents at their home on nearby Christianshavn Kanal. In the process, and to explain the need for her evacuation, she had to confess to them just how deeply involved she was in the resistance. Neither her father nor mother offered words of reproach, for which she was deeply grateful.[5]

Mix had arranged for the journey to Sweden through some of his fellow naval cadets. February 16 was set as the day Henny and Mix would be evacuated to Sweden, and the two met on a street in the city before heading to the Staffeldt brothers' bookstore. While they were there talking in a back room of the store about all that had transpired in the last few days, an employee of the Staffeldts came in and said there was a gentleman in front wanting to see the brothers. Suspicious of what was happening, Henny and Mix exited from the back of the store, while the brothers, Jorgen and Mogens, went up front, where they were promptly arrested by the Gestapo.[6] Among other matters in their interrogation, the brothers were shown photographs of Lillelund, John, and the Flame and asked to identify all three.[7]

Obviously, the police were closing in on everyone. In fact, on that same day, Elsebet and Bente were arrested at their apartment in Copenhagen. They had begun the day, like Henny, planning their escape to Sweden. Elsebet decided to change her hairstyle and put on full makeup for a photo for a false passport. She and Bente had just sat down for dinner at home with a friend when a couple of Gestapo agents rang the bell and told the sisters that they were being arrested. They were given time to finish their dinner, but afterward, when Elsebet asked if she could use the bathroom to take off her makeup, she was shocked when one of the agents followed her inside and watched as she removed the red nail polish that she'd just put on that morning. She said later that she didn't want to see the polish wearing off day after day as she sat in Vestre Faengsel.

Henny had to wait a few more days before she was able to make her escape, by which time Mix had already gone. On February 20, through his arrangements, Henny was taken to a villa in Lyngby, where three other HD 2 members were waiting. The wind was howling that night on the sound, and they couldn't travel, so it took them one more sleepless night before they were picked up by a Danish Coast Guard boat and finally set out across the Oresund.

There was one last scare as they were making the crossing: a German patrol boat spotted them as they were motoring out in the sound. It fired shots at the Danish Coast Guard craft and actually hit the boat that Henny was escaping on, but there was not enough damage to prevent it from continuing the journey to Sweden, which is where it arrived on the morning of February 22.

Henny and Mix were soon together again. He joined the Danish Brigade, the fighting unit of Danes training and preparing to do battle when the time came in the final push to rid Denmark of the German occupiers. Henny joined as well and was assigned secretarial work that eventually evolved into work at a firing range.[8]

As welcome and safe as they felt in Sweden, both kept their eyes to the west, across the Oresund, always watching what was happening in Denmark.

CHAPTER 30

Refugees in Sweden

T HE NUMBER OF DANISH REFUGEES IN SWEDEN CONTINUED TO SWELL,
even as the number of Jews arriving had dropped to near zero. Along
with a growing number of resistance figures, like Henny and Mix, who
had escaped the Gestapo, some fishermen who had participated in the
rescue also chose to leave Denmark, along with some teachers and intellectuals who had freely expressed their anti-German opinions and feared
repercussions.

With these, there were a number of Danes who had left Denmark for
opposite reasons: they were feeling the stigma of being ostracized by their
fellow Danes. These included women with boyfriends in the German military, Danish Nazis who had lost their livelihoods through their allegiances
to Germany, and stikkers and collaborators who feared for their lives from
resistance assassins. As can be imagined under the circumstances, there
were occasions of conflict between these refugees and others over political
differences in Sweden, including instances where women with German
boyfriends, so-called *tyskertos*, had their hair cropped tight to the scalp.[1]

The trauma of the circumstances for the Jewish refugees remained
paramount. Torn from their homes to settle in a foreign land, they took
some comfort in the community of their co-religionists, who were likewise ripped from what had been familiar, but it wasn't enough. Many of
these and the several thousand Jews who were already in Sweden suffered from what would, in the modern era, come to be recognized as

post-traumatic stress disorder. The condition was recognized at the time by the Swedish Refugee Administration, though they labeled it "camp psychosis" and attributed the symptoms of the conditions they saw—nervousness, irritability, apathy, and depression, among other disorders—to the idleness and communal life enforced upon them by their conditions.[2]

In a number of cases, Jewish families were physically separated by the escape. Some children of Jews stayed hidden in Denmark after their parents were forced to flee the country.[3] The age range of these youngsters was from infanthood, just a few weeks old in some cases, to late teens. For the most part, they either stayed with relatives, at children's homes, or with private families who took them in as foster children. The families trapped in these circumstances often faced the long-term consequences of these disruptions. Parents felt enormous guilt and shame, while children suffered from feelings of neglect and betrayal. Young children who stayed with foster parents and in children's homes often became attached to their new surroundings and felt betrayed for a second time when they were reunited with their biological parents and forced to return to a home life that had been violently stripped from them many months earlier.

Because of the ongoing German occupation and continued fears of Jews, including Jewish children, being rounded up and sent to the camps, the hidden children and those caring for them had to be diligent about keeping their identities under cover. According to historian Sophie Lene Bak, "All over Europe hidden children were presented with two ultimate demands: silence and rejection of their Jewish identity."[4] The rejections usually came in the form of baptisms into the Christian faith. These were done both by the foster families and, in a number of cases, by Jewish families themselves, hoping to protect their children, just prior to their escape from Denmark. The lingering effects of these disassociations would have impacts for decades to come.

The uncertainty of the circumstances for the Danes in Sweden remained oppressive, but there were positive experiences, as well. As the war progressed through the spring and summer of 1944, news of the largely successful invasion of the Allies spread through the camps and buoyed their attitudes, but no one could tell how long these Danes would have to gaze across the Oresund to their home country. Some, like the Jewish actor Sam Besekow, settled into a life very much like the one he'd left behind: performing readings and plays in and near Stockholm, including acting in the first Kaj Munk drama to be staged after the playwright's murder; giving readings of resistance poetry; and staging a vaudeville-style revue for a receptive audience at a theater in Stockholm.[5]

Similarly, Aage Bertelsen, the Lyngby schoolteacher who was so deeply involved in the rescue, left Denmark as the heat on rescue efforts got turned up in late October. He wound up as headmaster at one of the many schools in Sweden that opened their doors to Danish refugees beginning in late fall 1943. A number of other exiled Danish teachers likewise found employment teaching in the camps. Almost all of the young Jewish students, including Anita Melchior, daughter of Rabbi Melchior, remembered positive experiences from their days in Swedish schools, and many, if not most, picked up Swedish as a second language.[6]

Some university students were able to continue their studies, as well. They did it through the Danish schools from which they were removed, in some cases smuggling exams from Sweden to Denmark in order to have their papers received and graded by their own professors. In other cases, they switched their studies to receptive Swedish schools, continuing their work with little or no disruption.[7]

The illegal routes that were established during the rescue continued to serve as a pipeline for the resistance movement as it continued through the spring and summer of 1944. Not only did the resistance members keep on bringing to Sweden a steady stream of downed pilots, resistance fighters like Mix and Henny, and others who found themselves on the wrong side of German law enforcement, but they also were able to return large amounts of arms for the resistance, including machine guns and munitions.

These routes were also used to provide a steady flow of information between the countries, in the form of mail, illegal newspapers, scientific material, radio equipment, and propaganda materials. In return, news from anti-German voices in Denmark was quickly delivered to the BBC and American radio services based in Sweden, which were ready to broadcast to the world what was happening in Copenhagen and beyond.

After its initial reluctance to be involved with the troubles of Denmark at the start of the occupation, and despite its still somewhat compromised position with Germany, Sweden had become a solid assistant to the Danes as the struggles went on. Ebbe Munck, the longtime resistance figure stationed in Stockholm, was a central figure in organizing and encouraging the collaborative efforts between Swedes and Danes, beginning during the rescue and extending on into the many months that followed. He saw that the illegal lines of connection established between the two countries could be used as models for continuing communication. Establishing coast-to-coast intelligence lines would prove vital to both the refugee aid associations in Sweden and the resistance groups in Denmark.

The connections between cities close to one another, on each side of the sound, were already well-established, like those between Copenhagen and Malmo as well as Helsingor and Helsingborg, but in time, more distant cities and routes were connected, too, like the link between Jutland and Gothenburg, in the northern reaches of Sweden. In time, the relationships became symbiotic, so that Danish fishing boats sailing from Jutland and carrying refugees might meet Swedish boats with a load of fish midway between the coasts. They would then swap cargos, so that the Danes could be seen as bringing back a haul of cod to avoid any suspicions with authorities overseeing their work.[8]

Gradually, the spontaneity and chaos of the original efforts to get refugees across the Oresund to Sweden was replaced by a more systematic effort that eventually included the Swedish government in the form of the Danish-Swedish Refugee Service, which established a route and organization on both coasts that included telegram services, a signal system, passenger assembly information, and financing services. Liaison officers in both Sweden and Denmark coordinated efforts and linked the Danish underground world of resistance to Swedish aid workers.

Jewish community members in Sweden, principally in the coastal towns of Malmo, Helsingborg, Gothenburg, and Stockholm, combined their gifts with donations from international Jewish aid foundations to help fund all the services required for the Jewish refugees. More funds came from the Danish ambassador to the United States, Henrik Kauffmann, who offered Danish funds from the moneys that had been frozen in accounts by the U.S. government at the time of occupation and an additional 50,000 dollars raised in donations from Jewish American organizations.[9] A number of the newcomers had business or family connections to people in Sweden, and these folks were generally quickest to find apartments and work and move out of the camps and into something approximating a normal life. It was the poorer people who stayed the longest in the camps and whose needs were most difficult to meet. According to one survey, the number of refugees in the camps, Jews and non-Jews combined, was pegged at 2,750 on January 1, 1944; that number had dropped to 825 by the middle of September.[10]

By the end of the war, the total number of Jewish refugees to Sweden numbered around eight thousand, while other refugees came to around nine thousand. The non-Jews were largely young, often working class, and typically involved in the resistance in one form or another. Most had left their families in Denmark and tended to populate the camps, which ran all the way to the north in Sweden, to regions that existed in harder circumstances of wilderness and cold. They provided physical work in pioneer settings, including logging in the forests, building roads, and clearing land for agricultural purposes.

The sociological and cultural differences between the refugees at times led to occasional conflicts. There were times when non-Jewish refugees, who might have taken severe risks in helping Jews escape on fishing boats, would find themselves in the camps, losing out in prime camp appointments to the very people they had helped escape.[11] The sensibility of the non-Jews was exacerbated by the fact that, at least initially, the number of Jews signing up for the Danish Brigade was less proportionally than non-Jews. Among the latter group, this was considered a sign of a lack of appreciation for the efforts of the secular Danish population in aiding

Jews during the rescue and beyond. In fact, by the end of the war, these numbers would even out and Jews would compose about 15 percent of the total members of the brigade.[12]

All of this was transpiring as the war in Europe began reaching its climactic stages. In June 1944, Allied forces had assaulted the beaches of Normandy and soon made inroads into the French countryside, while to the east, the Soviet Union had made advances against the Wehrmacht, inching inexorably toward Germany.

CHAPTER 31

Resistance Continues

A CROSS THE ORESUND, DESPITE THE ABSENCE OF HOLGER DANSKE 2 IN the Danish resistance movement, the fight against the occupation continued. Encouraged by what was happening on the Western Front, resistance fighters from the BOPA group hit the Globus factory just outside of Copenhagen. The attack came on June 6, D-Day, and was designed to thwart the Globus company's work in constructing parts for the German V-2 rocket systems, which would soon become the heart of Germany's efforts at raining cross-channel destruction on England.

Just two weeks later, BOPA destroyed another Copenhagen factory, the Danish Rifle Syndicate, which had been manufacturing small arms, anti-tank weaponry, and artillery for the Germans. A fire subsequent to the attack in downtown Copenhagen burned the factory to the ground as thousands of Copenhagen residents watched.

Elsewhere, the Flame, that vitally active HD 2 saboteur, had teamed of late with another Holger Danske freedom fighter named Jorgen Haagen Schmith, nicknamed "the Lemon," to form a deadly duo of resistance assassins, dedicated to the liquidation of a number of stikkers in various parts of Denmark. No one was more wanted by the Gestapo than this pair of killers.

For these continued acts of rebellion, the people of Denmark anticipated reprisals, and they were quick to come. The Royal Danish Porcelain factory, a landmark business in the capital, was blown up by the Germans.

Also, the student union at the University of Copenhagen, the beating heart of the campus, whose students, including the Kielers, were linked by the Germans to many aspects of the resistance, was ransacked by Danish troops serving in the German Army's Schalburg Corps.[1] The Schalburg Corps likewise laid waste to the Tivoli Gardens, the famed amusement park in the heart of the city, which had provided respite to the people of the city throughout the occupation.

In an effort to cool the temperature in the city, Werner Best declared a state of emergency and instituted a curfew in Copenhagen. The measure backfired: on June 26, more than a thousand workers at the B & W shipyard, the same factory that HD 2 had sabotaged in December, walked off the job. The workers sent a letter to Best, explaining that the curfew that he'd set, from eight in the evening to five in the morning, allowed them no time to work in their vegetable gardens. To maintain their work at home, the letter said (with winking asides to its Danish readers), the workers would have to leave their work each day at noon.

Support for the workers was general throughout the city. Not only did the citizens applaud the walkout, they also took up the same demands. Everyone was now clamoring for eight hours a day before curfew to be able to work in their gardens. Other factory workers picked up the call, as did small business owners, postal workers, streetcar workers, and telephone operators. Everyone was walking off the job. Business in the city ground to a halt. Public transportation, both within the city and out to the suburbs, was no longer running. Everyone seemed to be congregating in the streets to light bonfires and encourage one another. Not only was the resistance alive and well in Copenhagen, it also seemed triumphant.[2]

Best responded by closing the highways as well, cutting off food supplies into Copenhagen. He also cut off gas, water, and electricity and ordered military police from all over Zealand to come to the city to maintain order. In the midst of these measures, it was learned that the Germans had executed six members of the Fiil family and friends, the Hvidsten group that had been arrested months earlier.

Again the streets erupted in protest. Cars were overturned, bricks were pulled from the cobblestone streets and heaved at the police, barricades were erected, and sniping small arms fire broke out between the two sides, resulting in a large number of casualties among the population. In all, twenty-three Danes were killed and over two hundred wounded.[3] German artillery was even brought into the bustling Vesterbro neighborhood in downtown Copenhagen as a final warning that things could escalate even further.

Finally, the two warring sides reached out to find a solution to the chaos. Georg Duckwitz, with his experience in the shipping industry, including with both B & W management and the striking workers, helped get the two sides to the table for negotiations. Best agreed to pull the much-despised Schalburg Corps from the front lines of the conflict and promised that Wehrmacht patrols would no longer fire on citizens. He also said that he would end the state of emergency if the strike was resolved. With these assurances, the Freedom Council, who were more and more becoming the voice and institutional arm of the resistance movement, called for strikers to return to work, which they soon did.

As the temperature cooled in Denmark for Germany, it was rising on other fronts in dramatic fashion. As the Allies continued to make inroads in France, toward Paris and beyond, the troubles of maintaining order in Denmark seemed incidental to the existential problems the Third Reich would soon be facing. Yet even in the wake of the general strike, it was obvious that troubles with the Danes would continue to exist unless some drastic measures to clamp down against the resistance were undertaken.

CHAPTER 32

Vestre Faengsel

JORGEN KIELER WAS SENT BACK TO VESTRE FAENGSEL PRISON IN COPEN-hagen a few days after his arrest with Klaus Ronholt outside Aabenraa on February 10. Klaus accompanied him on the journey from Jutland to the prison, and the two occupied the same cell for a few days, until Jorgen was moved into a separate block with another prisoner who claimed to have been part of a sabotage cell in Aarhus.

Henry C., his new cellmate, had a stunning bit of news for Jorgen. He said that he had been in touch with Jorgen's old colleague from HD 2, John, who much to Jorgen's surprise, had actually survived the rain of Gestapo bullets that had riddled him in the wake of his and Finn's attempt to liquidate Mrs. Delbo back in December. According to Henry, John was now housed at a nearby cell in Vestre Faengsel.

Jorgen was savvy enough about the ways and means of the Gestapo to be suspicious of his new cellmate. Vestre Faengsel was rife with inform-ers, and Jorgen's connections to Holger Danske were well-known, as were John's. Just a day after his introduction to his new cellmate, Jorgen was interrogated by two Gestapo agents for the first time, and they assumed the classic good cop/bad cop guises with him. The one called Falkenberg was fluent in Danish and, Jorgen would later learn, was raised in south Jut-land to ethnic German parents; the second Gestapo agent was Neuhaus, the "friendly" cop of the pair, a native of Hamburg. In the course of the interview, Jorgen learned something of what the German police knew of his past operations with HD 2, including the B & W sabotage. The agents confirmed that they had connected him and his brief previous stay at Vestre Faengsel to that widely known bombing. They also questioned him about the Aabenraa sabotage, but he gave up no information about the group beyond what they already knew.

The day after this first interview was the day the Gestapo rounded up Elsebet, Bente, and the Staffeldt brothers. Jorgen would find out later that Elsebet and Bente were interviewed by Neuhaus upon their arrival at Vestre Faengsel. He would also come to find out that Neuhaus was interviewing Flemming, as well.

Jorgen was seen by a German doctor about a week after his arrival and was told that he likely had a fracture of the spinal column that ought to be x-rayed. The doctor advised laying down on his cell mattress as much as possible, to which Jorgen sardonically replied that he would pass that word on to his guards and the Gestapo.

The very next day, Jorgen got to meet John, who was jailed in a cell by himself. His head had just been shaved, and tufts of hair still surrounded him on the cell floor. He looked wan and tormented, according to Jorgen, a far cry from the confident leader he'd been when first introduced to the HD 2 group the previous fall. Their conversation was constrained by their shared understanding that anything they said together would be used against them. John admitted to knowing Jorgen, but he said it was because both had dined at times at Cannibal's Kitchen, the student cafeteria at the University of Copenhagen.

Jorgen and Elsebet exchanged glances in passing within the prison a few days later. She was made to stand with her face to the wall as a group of prisoners, including Jorgen, passed her and a group of women prisoners in the hall, but they were able to catch each other's eyes.

The family's concern for each other was acute, and to Jorgen, the knowledge that his father, Ernst, had been taken into custody was particularly hard because it extended his worry about how his mother, Margrethe, and his youngest sister, teenage Lida, would take care of themselves without his father's income. He didn't have long to learn how they were faring. In the first week of March, both came to visit him at the prison.

It turned out that they had quickly made arrangements to stay in Copenhagen at the place of a friend who had no involvement with the resistance, where they would presumably be safe from the Gestapo. But as Jorgen put it much later, anyone who entertained the idea that his mother would sit idly by in a Copenhagen flat while most of her family was incarcerated "didn't know the temperament of Margrethe Kieler." She soon marched to Vestre Faengsel to ask the authorities when she might visit her four children.[1]

The boldness of her request apparently had its effect. Soon, she and Lida were greeting Jorgen in his cell and, because a German guard was present, trying their best to constrain the depth of feelings surging between them.

Like a proud mother, she talked about the attention paid to the arrests throughout the country and the fact that she had received numerous bunches of flowers from friends and sympathizers. His father, Jorgen learned, was being transferred from custody in Aarhus to the Horserod camp in northern Zealand. The Gestapo had apparently lost interest in him.

Jorgen and his mother hugged as the meeting came to an end, and Lida and Margrethe soon moved to a town near Horserod, where they were able to visit Ernst later in March. They also traveled one more time to visit Jorgen in Vestre Faengsel, this time in Elsebet's cell with Bente present. Once again, one of their Gestapo watchdogs (Neuhaus) was present, so they could not speak freely. But at least each knew the others were alive and well, all things considered.

In March, Jorgen was taken to a hospital and x-rayed, which revealed that he had received a skull fracture back in Aabenraa as well as a fracture of his neck vertebrae. He was also driven back to Aabenraa by the Gestapo as part of the investigation into his crimes there. Much to Jorgen's displeasure, the Germans spent a lengthy amount of time searching in the ditch where he and Klaus had hid out from their pursuers, until they finally came upon the grenade that the two saboteurs had left behind. The weapon was carefully bagged and taken by the police back to Copenhagen.

In quick succession when he got back to Vestre Faengsel, Jorgen got to see Flemming, who looked to his worried brother to be severely jaundiced. Of course, their meeting was once again monitored by Neuhaus, so there could be no expressions of concern and no catching up on family news. In fact, the two had been allowed to meet only as part of the continuing investigation into the Aabenraa action. Afterward, Jorgen felt compelled to confess to his involvement in both the B & W and the Aabenraa sabotages in order to limit mention of any other sabotage that he was part of. He also knew that the Gestapo already had enough evidence of his involvement in these two affairs to make any professions of his innocence pointless. Better to admit partial guilt to some of his activities than beg deeper questions about the broad range of sabotage conducted by HD 2 over the last several months.

As part of the continuing investigation, Jorgen was soon taken by Neuhaus to see John in the hopes that placing the two Holger Danske colleagues together would loosen the tongues of both. And the first thing John whispered to Jorgen, as he lay on his cell cot with a blanket over his lower torso, was "Speak softly. I'm sure they're listening."

John asked about who had and who had not been arrested, specifically mentioning Finn, and Jorgen told him that he had made it to Sweden. John told Jurgen how disappointing it was for him to see Jorgen locked up now in Vestre. He'd hoped, of course, that the resistance work would have continued. Jorgen whispered to John that his two Gestapo tagalongs seemed particularly interested in the whereabouts of the Flame, but that he had provided nothing to them on the matter.

The Gestapo's interest in their conversation was not acute enough to prevent John from relating details of the story of what happened to him after the attempted assassination of Mrs. Delbo. With seven bullet wounds puncturing his body, including one that had shattered a femur, he was tossed in a Gestapo car and hauled to the Dagmarhus jailhouse in Copenhagen. There he was dumped unceremoniously on a cold hard floor and examined by a German doctor, who said he had at best a couple of hours to live.

John was then given over to Falkenburg and Neuhaus, the same Gestapo agents who were taking the lead on the entirety of the HD 2 sabotage cases. The two officers reminded John of the doctor's recent prognosis and advised him to unburden himself of all the ill deeds that he and his colleagues had been perpetrating. To further encourage him, they kicked his broken leg at the thigh and then twisted the lower part of John's leg outward at a right angle from its normal position. John kept denying everything, and they continued to ask him questions. When he finally passed out from pain, they threw a bucket of water in his face and started grilling him all over again. When he passed out a second time, he woke up in a German hospital to find that his wounds had been bandaged, but they did nothing to his leg. He was finally brought to Vestre Faengsel and placed in a one-man cell. He could not put weight on or move on his leg, but no one was given permission to come and take him to the toilet. He tried to minimize his bowel movements by not eating and instead used the soup that he was given to wash with. His mattress and blanket became grossly soiled, and the stench in the cell was beyond foul, yet no one was allowed to open a window. Even the German doctors refused to visit him.[2]

That day, in his cell with Jorgen, John illustrated the story by pulling back the blanket covering his wounded leg. The lower part of his leg was pulled up toward his thigh bone, as it had been in the original torture. The white bone now poked through the jagged flesh. When he asked why they couldn't have at least set his broken leg, he was told that there was really no point, he would soon be shot, anyway.

Things had improved marginally in John's incarceration. He was now washed and carried to the toilet once a day. Jorgen, too, had seen some relief in his circumstances; he'd been put to work in the kitchen, which involved washing the stairs and corridors as well as delivering meals to the cells. He later learned that he was being watched closely in the new assignment, and again, there was a particular interest and hope between Neuhaus and Falkenberg that Jorgen would somehow reveal something about the Flame as he did his work around the prison.

In the wake of John's betrayal and capture in December, the Flame had focused his resistance work on the liquidation of Gestapo agents and

Danish informers. In the process, he had killed a growing number of each and became the prime target of Gestapo efforts at rooting out the scourge of these assassinations. These were tasks Jorgen had no knowledge of.

For Jorgen, his work around the prison was a means to speak to friends and keep in touch with other members of the resistance. John was glad to have this visit from Jorgen and hoped for more, as well. He also would have dearly liked to get outside for some fresh air, and Jorgen promised that he would see if he could get someone to sanction a breath of something beyond the rank air of the cell. Jorgen put the question to an orderly in the prison, who seemed friendly. A week and a half later, April by this time, Jorgen helped carry John out into Vestre's exercise yard for forty-five minutes of sunshine and blue Danish sky.

The respites were allowed to continue over the next few days. In their visits to the prison yard, Jorgen and John got to know one another in ways that they'd never had the opportunity to learn, even when they were serving together in HD 2. For instance, through all their closeness in working together as saboteurs, Jorgen had never learned John's real name—Svend Otto Nielsen—or details of his upbringing. He'd grown up in the countryside, one of two brothers whose father worked as a land steward in Rold Skov, a large forest in Jutland, north of Aarhus. The two sons had learned to hunt from an early age and often went out with their father, bringing home small game for the dinner table. As a young man, John had wanted to serve as an officer in the merchant marines but wound up getting a degree in mathematics instead, with which he became a secondary schoolteacher. He had served in the Danish military in the early 1930s, was married to Grethe, and had a three-year-old daughter who had been taken by her mother to Sweden after John's arrest. Their absence, and the fact that they were in no position to aid him, of course weighed heavily on his state of mind, leaving him with a deep sense of abandonment.

John was buoyed by Jorgen's visits and the trips out into the prison yard. They would talk at times about a future where they would gather at a cabin in the Norwegian mountains, and he, walking on two good legs, would head out into the woods to hunt as he once had. They talked about the rumors of the coming Allied invasion and what would happen in Denmark once the Germans were defeated. His spirits would ebb and flow, but always there was a deep-seated acknowledgement that his time was running short. And Jorgen's, too.

On April 20, Hitler's birthday, they heard through the prison grapevine that the resistance had liquidated two collaborators. Two days afterward, there was an attack against German soldiers in Copenhagen, and unrest followed. A group of resistance fighters was brought into Vestre Faengsel from a German prison, and word spread that there would soon be reprisals—executions—to compensate for the attacks. Jorgen was certain that John would be among those killed.

They had a last visit together in the prison yard, and Jorgen helped John back to his cell. Waiting for them there was Falkenberg, the second of the two Gestapo officers who had been on his case and Jorgen's from the beginning. "It was him," John whispered to Jorgen. "It was Falkenberg, who tortured me."[3]

Jorgen shook John's hand for a final time, and then he was forced to leave the cell. Outside his own cell the next morning, Jorgen heard the opening of the heavy door at the main entrance to the prison, followed by the tramp of boots in the echoing hallways of the prison. German soldiers had arrived; it sounded to him like a whole regiment. An impressive number for one crippled Dane who couldn't even walk to his own execution. Jorgen heard the prison commandant coming toward John's cell and then heard as they carried him down the hallway and out of the prison.

Walking past John's empty cell later that morning, Jorgen got a peek inside and saw a plate of sandwiches on a table there. Beside them was an unsmoked cigar.

The next day, he passed his sister Elsebet on the way to the exercise yard and whispered the news to her. "Greetings from John," he said. "He was shot yesterday."[4]

IT WAS ON HITLER'S BIRTHDAY THAT ELSEBET AND BENTE WERE PLACED together in Elsebet's cell, where the two would stay until Bente's release. The cases against them were not nearly as serious as those against their brothers, and the rumor was that they would probably soon be transferred to Horserod.

Meanwhile, Jorgen was being interrogated daily, which required a trip outside of the prison to the Gestapo headquarters at a building called Dagmarhus, near Copenhagen's City Hall Square. The focus of the interrogations continued to center on the Flame, and interestingly enough, among the questions from Neuhaus was one in which Jorgen was asked if he had recognized his former HD 2 colleague within the prison on his lunch duties, delivering meals. Which suggested to Jorgen that the Gestapo had no clear idea of what the Flame looked like and couldn't even be certain if they had or had not already apprehended the notorious assassin. He continued to provide no useful information to his interrogators.

Jorgen managed to smuggle out a letter to his father in which he tried to emphasize the good news from prison. It looked like neither Elsebet nor Bente would be brought before a court and both might soon be on the way to Horserod. Flemming's liver was less inflamed, and Bente's bladder infection was better. His own wounds were giving him less pain, though sciatica had set in his back and was causing much discomfort. And by the way, Jorgen added, he and Flemming would be sentenced soon and probably condemned to death.[5]

On a trip to Dagmarhus in the second week of May, Jorgen happened to see in passing Ebba Lund and her boyfriend on Raadhuspladsen street. They did not see him in the Gestapo car and, of course, he could not shout out a greeting, but it served to emphasize the strangeness of his circumstances—passing his old life in the streets of Copenhagen, normal and unaware, on this May day as he was being driven to the harsh realities of his new life as an about-to-be-interrogated prisoner of the German Gestapo.

Just a week later, Jorgen got to meet with Bente, Elsebet, and Flemming in Vestre. He was later able to sneak a letter out to his father with Bente, telling him news of the gathering. Bente was going to be released. She would soon be free and would hopefully be able to deliver the letter he was writing:

"Elsebet and Flemming are keeping a stiff upper lip," he wrote. "But the many executions do put a certain strain on the atmosphere in here. . . .

We live in a little world, surrounded by bars and grilles. But life is large in here too. You just have to live your life as a human being, shut everything else out. You see your friends as a shining example, a light that will suddenly be extinguished by ten bullets. But then a miracle happens. The light fades, but a glow remains in our eyes. On the other side, a total collapse can also be seen. You get to know people in here. If I escape with my life, this will be an experience I would not have wished to have been without for anything. . . . I promise you that whatever the future may hold, I will accept it with my head held high. Our cause can never die."[6]

CHAPTER 33

Strike

IN LATE JUNE, JORGEN GOT PERMISSION TO CELEBRATE FLEMMING'S birthday with Elsebet, his mother, and Lida at the new Gestapo headquarters, a newly constructed building called Shellhus, near Dagmarhus in downtown Copenhagen. Margrethe and Lida had been brought down to Copenhagen for a final visit with Jorgen and Flemming and were staying in a flat in Osterbro.

In conjunction with the family visit at the headquarters, Jorgen took the time to talk with his prosecutor, who expressed regret that he would be asking for the death penalty for the two brothers but said there was no way to escape this fate. Perhaps his heart had been somewhat softened by seeing the family together. But his sympathies aside, he wasn't able to do anything about the pending punishment. No one in the city seemed in the mood to forgive and forget.

These were unsettled times in Copenhagen. Saboteurs blew up a building the same day that his mother and daughter arrived in the city, and the very next day, the Germans executed eight resisters from the town of Aars in retaliation for the bombing. The executions of the Jutland fighters didn't satisfy the bloodlust of the Schalburg Corps. The next day featured attacks on the Royal Porcelain Factory, the student union at the University of Copenhagen, and Tivoli Gardens.

Events in the city soon cascaded toward chaos. Jorgen was no longer working in the kitchen, which meant he wasn't able to wander around the prison delivering meals and couldn't keep up on what was happening nearly as much as he could before. But he did learn about the fate of the Hvidsten Group—Marius Fiil and his family and associates, who had been arrested months earlier—eight were executed on June 29. Five others, including his daughters Tulle and Gerda, were spared the firing squad but given long prison sentences instead.

The general strike in Copenhagen began quickly afterward, with the walkout at the B & W factory triggering the wider "Go Home Early" strikes across the city. These were followed by the countermeasures instituted by Best, including the shutoff of gas, electricity, and water. The same strictures came to Vestre Faengsel and the apartment that Margrethe and Lida were staying in (now joined by the suddenly free Bente).

The fact that the water was turned off at the prison allowed the inmates to empty the lines and use the hollow pipes to communicate from floor to floor by tapping out messages via Morse code.

Flemming and Jorgen's case was scheduled to be heard at the end of June, but the day came and went and the brothers remained in their cells. Word came through the various grapevines at Vestre that seven inmates had been deported to Germany rather than be executed. Was it a positive sign?

The strike came to an end in the first week of July, and the water and power soon returned to the prison. So, too, did permission to use the exercise yard. Elsebet was heading out to the yard soon after when the woman in line ahead of her turned and whispered, "They've shot my husband, my father, and my brother." Elsebet was stunned by the words until she realized a few moments later that the woman who was talking to her was Tulle Fiil. Later, Elsebet passed Tulle's cell door to express her deepest sympathies.[1] In the next couple of days, Tulle asked that Elsebet be allowed to come and join her in the cell that she and her younger sister shared.

In the two days following the end of the strike, no one came to Jorgen's cell to collect him for trial. All he and Flemming could do was continue to wait for their final sandwiches and cigars. Finally, Neuhaus arrived with the blunt news: they had been saved by the strike and would not be sentenced. In addition, Elsebet would be going to Horserod in a few weeks' time.

Jorgen surmised that in the wake of the invasion at Normandy and the rebellion in Copenhagen, the Germans in Denmark were afraid of creating an open revolt. There was also an attempt on Hitler's life on July 20, which no doubt shocked all the German forces in the Reich.

As was reported in subsequent documents,[2] the real explanation for why the Kielers were spared execution had as much to do with the shooting of the Hvidsten group as the strike in Copenhagen. Best had set up the Gestapo tribunal in the city in order to expedite the cases of the saboteurs and resistance leaders languishing in Vestre Faengsel, but it turned out that setting up a tribunal in a Copenhagen was not what Hitler had in mind when he had ordered Best to combat sabotage in Denmark with terror. He simply wanted terror and not deliberation. In fact, deliberation—letting the Hvidsten group stay in prison for weeks in the city prior to their execution—was precisely what was causing the unrest, in Berlin's estimation.

CHAPTER 34

Froslev

SO THE GESTAPO TRIBUNAL WAS SENT BACK TO BERLIN, AND THE SENtencing of Danish prisoners was postponed. In August, Jorgen and Flemming were sent to the Froslev camp in southern Jutland, where they joined their father and Elsebet, who had recently been transferred from Horserod.

The camp was run by German authorities, but compared with others in the system, particularly the concentration camps in Germany, Froslev and Horserod were considered "holiday camps."[1] The guards were German, but the camp was in Denmark, and food was provided by Danish sources and was decent.

The fact that the camp was near to the German border presented a cautionary note to those housed at Froslev—the camp's proximity to Germany made for a more expeditious transport to those concentration camps across the border. However, for the time being the Kielers were as satisfied as they could be in captivity, sharing accommodations in a hut with their father, who had become a sort of friendly camp doctor, both during his stay here in Froslev and before, while he was in Horserod. Both Jorgen and Flemming got to join him in his rounds, where Ernst served as both doctor and news information service. Somehow, he'd acquired the use of a radio, with which he listened to news of the advancing invasion, and he spread word of the Western front around the camp.

When the radio was discovered, Dr. Kieler was carted off for interrogation to a German town just across the border. His sons, daughter Elsebet, and many others in the camp feared for what might happen to him, but he came back just a couple of days later.

As it turned out, they ought to have feared more for their own fate. By mid-September, preparations were being made at Froslev to transport about two hundred prisoners to a concentration camp in Germany.

Spared were Elsebet and Dr. Kieler. Among those packed up and prodded toward a string of trucks waiting to take them across the border were Jorgen, Flemming, Klaus Ronholt, Georg Jansen, and Jorgen Staffeldt from HD 2. Also being moved were Koch, the auto mechanic from Aabenraa; his landlady, Hilda Lund, who had helped hide the HD 2 members on her property after the attack in Aabenraa; and a number of saboteurs from Varde who had helped with the last attempted bombing.

CHAPTER 35

The Police Are Arrested

THE GERMAN RELATIONSHIP WITH THE DANISH POLICE FORCE HAD been fraught with distrust and lack of cooperation on both sides from soon after the occupation began. During the escape of the Jews, when in many cases, Danish law enforcement openly aided refugees and those assisting them, the divergence of interests became acute. Likewise during the general strike in July of 1944, when Danish police refrained from acting against strikers. It was growing more and more apparent to Werner Best and the German ministers in Denmark that law enforcement in the country not only couldn't be trusted, but because they also were armed and uniformed, they represented a potential threat to German force. Late in the summer of 1944, Best decided to do away with the problem.

On September 19, air-raid sirens rang out through all of Denmark, bringing out Danish police officers from Copenhagen to Odense to Aarhus and many major towns in between. As the city constables gathered at stations to assume their air-raid duties, they found themselves greeted by Gestapo and German troops, who disarmed and arrested the officers and began the process of shipping thousands off to concentration camps in Germany. In all, there were about ten thousand Danish police officers, of whom just under two thousand were detained and deported. These included coast guard officers. Many officers serving in small Danish towns were simply disarmed and asked to swear that they would do nothing to interfere with the work of the occupying power. Also treated with more leniency were officers over the age fifty-five. Best also allowed the guards outside King Christian's residence at Amalienborg to remain on duty for ceremonial purposes. They were the only uniformed police left in the country.[1]

The disbanding of the Danish police force left the nation of Denmark in a state of lawlessness that prompted heightened criminality. Black marketeers brazenly set up shop around the country, openly selling coupons, cigarettes, and other contraband and rationed items. Danish saboteurs were able to receive munitions and arms at such heightened levels that German trains traveling from Norway began to bypass northern Jutland, where the railroad tracks were being blown up at such a persistent rate that it made travel not only perilous but also uneconomic.[2]

Quite a few officers managed to escape in the process, and most of these quickly joined the underground. The police officers who were not so fleet or lucky were sent in two deportations to concentration camps at Neuengamme and Buchenwald.

CHAPTER 36

The Flame

ON OCTOBER 18, 1944, BENT FAURSCHOU HVIID (A.K.A. THE FLAME) was having dinner at his flat with his landlady and some friends when there was an insistent knock on the door. A German voice demanded to be let in, and the Flame, who was caught unarmed, ran upstairs to see if there might a way to escape over the rooftops there in Gentofte, just north of Copenhagen. He looked out the window and saw the neighborhood crawling with Gestapo. They had finally caught up with the most wanted man in Denmark, and the Flame had good idea of what was in store for him when he was captured.

Which is why he had long kept a cyanide tablet in his coat pocket and why he swallowed it just before the Germans burst into the upstairs room in which he was breathing his last.

His friends down below said later that the Gestapo cheered as he lay there in his death throes, and when they dragged him down the stairs and out of the house, they did so with a slow deliberation, letting his head bounce on every step as he descended feet first.

CHAPTER 37

Aarhus

THE GERMAN RESPONSE TO THE INCREASED RESISTANCE IN JUTLAND was an anticipated increase in counterterrorism. The Gestapo hit back with ferocity, arresting resistance figures in central and north Jutland in such numbers that the underground members of the resistance there were fearful that it would be decimated. They soon reported this to London.

By October, the SOE, now working in conjunction with the American Office of Strategic Services (OSS), was anticipating the ultimate defeat of Nazi Germany. One of the missions that they pressed upon the Danish resistance was to ensure that Gestapo archives be preserved, not only to save an accurate record of who was who among the German security agents but also for future reference in terms of postwar accountability: they wanted to know both among the Germans and their Danish stikkers, who did what.

Gestapo archives in Jutland were housed in two buildings at Aarhus University in central Jutland. When the SOE-OSS sent word to the Danish resistance that they wanted the Gestapo records saved, the news arrived in Denmark at the most precarious moment in the all-out assault of the Gestapo against the local resistance. Needless to say, the locals, at that moment, were less concerned about postwar matters of justice and retribution than they were about simply surviving. The same archives that Allied intelligence operations wanted preserved were currently providing information that was leading to the capture, torture, and deaths of numerous freedom fighters in northern Jutland at present.

That was the sum of the message sent by the leader of the central Jutland resistance, a man named Fritz Tillisch, to SOE-OSS headquarters in London when they learned of the request to save the archives:

"Underground in Jutland about to be torn up by Gestapo," Tillisch telegrammed. "It is more important to destroy archives and save our people than to save archives and have our people destroyed."[1]

That succinct and powerful message had its effect. The Allies soon began to make planes available for a bombing of the Gestapo headquarters in Aarhus, which took place on October 31.

The planes took off from Scotland and came into Aarhus that day, flying low beneath the clouds. They completely surprised the Germans, dropping their bombs right on the target. There were two resistance workers being interrogated at the headquarters at the time. Both survived the blast. The number of Germans killed was in the range of 150 to 165, according to Tillisch. An additional twenty or thirty Danes were dead. "Most of them informers. All card indexes burned. We are very thankful to you," Tillisch said in a subsequent telegram.[2]

The success of the raid was so complete that the idea of a low-level bombing raid on Shellhus, the new Gestapo headquarters in Copenhagen, began to be bandied about in London as well as in Denmark. There were numerous reasons why Shellhus presented a much more difficult target than Aarhus for such an attack, beginning with the fact that the Gestapo had begun to house resistance leaders within the confines of the building, in essence holding them hostage against precisely the sort of bombing that the Allies were planning.

The outline of the attack was drawn up, but implementation was delayed. Copenhagen had far more antiaircraft batteries than north Jutland, and the low-level Mosquito planes used for the Aarhus mission were being used by the score to help the Allied fight throughout Western Europe. As the war ticked on, Allied bombing priorities had to be decided upon. Was the Shellhus bombing a high or a low priority? Time would tell.

CHAPTER 38

Porta Westfalica

IN ALL, JORGEN AND FLEMMING KIELER AND NEARLY TWO HUNDRED other detainees left Froslev in mid-September on their way to their first experience in a German concentration camp at Neuengamme, which was a small town just east of Hamburg in Germany. After a tortuously slow train ride that included an overnight stop in Hamburg, a bombing raid, only one toilet stop, only one opportunity to get some water at a station, and no food, they pulled into Neuengamme on the second morning of their journey.

They spent just a few days in the camp, where the prisoners were stripped naked and had their heads, armpits, and genital areas shaved in an attempt to lessen the prevalence of lice on their bodies. They were given a small bar of soap, which was supposed to last a couple of months, and then were allowed to shower and given a set of clothes, which included a shirt, trousers, and a jacket, which according to Jorgen looked like they'd been assembled by "the rag-and-bone man."[1] There was no regard for size, and no belts were provided to ameliorate fit. Detainees were also given a pair of slippers and happenstance hats, which made for a comical assemblage of headwear among the new campers, including some wearing women's hats and another in a Catholic priest's biretta. Not that that the functionality of the head coverings mattered much. According to Kieler, they would soon learn that their chief purpose was to doff them in proper respect to the guards.

They spent the next two days learning the ropes of the German camp system. There were various categories of prisoner, each assigned a signifying color: political prisoners wore a red triangle on their chests; criminals a green one; homosexuals a pink one; Jews, yellow; asocial elements, black; and religious prisoners, purple.

In the presence of SS guards, prisoners were expected to snap to attention and take their headgear off. If they weren't quick about it, prisoners would be immediately whipped. Each morning and evening, prisoners were marched to a square for roll call, which featured two sets of gallows. There were two hanged Russians in their nooses on the morning of the Kielers' arrival. Incongruously, the roll call also featured a camp orchestra composed of prisoners, who played a variety of symphonies and popular music during the morning and evening calls.[2]

Food, which would grow continually scarcer through the fall and winter until it reached starvation diet levels, began at Neuengamme with turnip and cabbage soup. As a Sunday treat, they received goulash with a few nibbles of stringy meat. All of the food was served in dirty bowls and eaten with fingers. The food smelled rank and rotten enough to take away all appetite—until the serious hunger set in.

In addition to the SS guards, prisoners were subject to the abuses of the Kapos, camp guards who were usually Germans and often had criminal histories themselves. These guards lived in fear of their SS superiors and tended to curry favor with their bosses by meting out brutal punishment to the rest of the prison population.

Neuengamme was one of a series of work and concentration camps in eastern Germany, and it served as a sort of transit camp, where inmates were often quickly assigned to other camps in the system, which served various needs and functions for the Reich. So it was with Jorgen and Flemming, who were glad to soon be assigned to a different camp; it was hard for them to imagine worse circumstances than those in their original posting. The fact that the new camp, Porta Westfalica, was said to be based at a large hotel added to their sense of hopefulness. The accommodations had to be better than Neuengamme.

The transport selection process seemed to focus on whether or not prisoners had any skills at operating machinery, which was a much-needed competence in Germany. People without it were assigned to more menial and dangerous work, like tidying up bomb-damaged districts of German towns.

The Kieler brothers were being sent to Porta Westfalica to supply cheap labor for the construction of massive underground plants that were intended for use in building airplanes for the German Luftwaffe. The RAF and American air forces had been devastating the Luftwaffe for months with air raids. Heinrich Himmler, the head of the concentration camp system, offered to provide the labor for these gargantuan projects in the form of prison labor. One of the first camps chosen to provide these workers was Porta Westfalica.

About two hundred prisoners at Neuengamme, of whom close to one hundred were Danes, were chosen to go to Porta Westfalica. Most of the Danes were members of the resistance and designated as political prisoners. Before the trip began, air-raid sirens sent inmates and guards alike to a shelter, into which SS guards and the Kapos hurried the prisoners with curses and blows from their clubs. They seemed to Jorgen to be equally fearful for their own lives as for the possibility of inmates escaping.[3]

Afterward and just before departure, the prisoners were given new clothing: a striped prison uniform with trousers, coat, and cap. Each of the Danish prisoners' uniforms had a patch with a red *D* for "Danish" on the jacket. They were also given a sweater and boots to replace the scant footwear they had been initially issued. The boots were not distributed with regard to size and consisted of wooden soles and leather sides sewn together roughly. No laces were supplied to tie the sides of boots together.

The train ride to Porta Westfalica took almost two full days and was carried out through railroad cattle cars crammed with fifty prisoners each. The inmates were ordered to sit in rows in the car with their legs spread wide open, so that each layer of prisoners would sit between the legs of the row behind them. They could not talk or move and were watched over by a pair of SS guards, who occupied a central space between two sections of prisoners stacked on either side of the car.

According to Kieler, the pain caused by this posture over the long hours was excruciating, but even the slightest movement was threatened by a whipping or the prominent display of the submachine guns in the laps of the SS tenders.[4] About halfway through the trip, the train arrived at Hamburg, and its passengers were told to sleep in the same position in which they had been so painfully traveling. The car doors were closed and locked. Anyone who even dared to stretch his legs was kicked by a guard.

When they finally arrived at Porta Westfalica and had their first chance to actually stretch their legs and take a first glance at the hotel that would be their barracks, they were actually encouraged. It was a two-storied structure with a high and steeply-sloped tiled roof with dormers, turrets, and timbered framing accenting its sides. It did, indeed, look like a nice vacation spot nestled in a north-central German river valley for a German burgher and his family. Until Jorgen and Flemming saw an ominous handwritten sign in the yard behind the main structure that read, in Latin,

HIC MORTUI VIVUNT (HERE THE DEAD LIVE)

Behind the hotel, through the yard, ran a long path that led to another large, nondescript structure. Here was a large hall, called the theater, that was almost the length and width of a football field. On one side of the interior of this hall was a thicket of bunks arranged vertically in blocks of four. Prisoners were not given assigned bunks because there were not enough bunks for all the inmates, nor were there adequate blankets, which meant that each evening there was a mad, sometimes violent, scramble for blankets and bunks.

At one end of the hall, the Kapos bunked in a walled-off area. In another corner was the camp infirmary, which held a few dozen bunks for the desperately ill. In the middle of the hall, at the foot of the inmate bunks, were tables lined by a collection of stools. This was the camp mess hall, where again, a limited supply of dirty metal bowls meant for an eternal squabble between prisoners trying desperately to get food.

The meals were looked forward to for no aesthetic reason. Only hunger drove the inmates to clamor for the chunks of rye bread, turnip soup, black pudding, pickles, fish guts, and remnants of beef culled from bombed cattle that were served in the hall. The latrines were foul beyond description and placed right next to the kitchen, which only added to the disgusting ambience.

The constant string of roll calls added to the misery. There were morning work shifts and evening work shifts, and each required a roll call for the whole camp. Inmates were made to line up to be counted, and any small bit of insubordination, usually made up, would prompt the Kapos to whip the internees or beat them with a cane or rubber truncheon, and then start the process all over again.

Any attempt at escape was met with swift and brutal punishment. Prisoners were either shot on the spot or hanged a short time after being caught. The hangings took place in the theater at roll call, and the corpse would be left hanging for all to see.

Work details opened with a three-mile hike from the hotel to a mine set near the Wesel River in north-central Germany. Jorgen and Flemming, who were able to share a bunk in the hall—a straw mattress and pair of threadbare and filthy blankets—were also linked in work details, along with a column of about seventy other inmates, mostly Russians but with a few Danes thrown in the mix.

The work shift began at four-thirty in the morning and ended at six in the evening. Work consisted of hacking out and shoveling rocks and rubble from a large mine gallery into dumping wagons to create space for the underground airplane manufacturing centers that Himmler imagined would save the newly minted Luftwaffe planes from Allied bombing raids before they were even finished being constructed. At first, the Kieler brothers, both with flaccid muscles from having been shut in prisons for months, were eager to stretch their bodies. They began their first few work shifts by applying themselves with vigor to the job at hand, but they were quickly advised by the Russians, who were more experienced in work-camp life, to save their energies. "Work slowly. Do you want to work for the Germans?"[5]

Prisoners at Porta Westfalica came from seventeen different nations, according to Kieler, and there were about fifteen hundred housed there when he and the contingent of just under one hundred Danes arrived there in the fall of 1944. The majority were from the Soviet Union, but there were groups of Polish, French, Dutch, Belgian, Spanish, Italian, Czech, Bulgarian, and Greek prisoners, as well.

They were a mix of prisoners of war and red-starred resistance fighters, along with some German criminals and antisocial elements. The camp chef wore a purple star on his jacket, indicating he was a Jehovah's Witness.[6]

The Danes in the camp had all been part of the resistance and, along with the French and Soviet inmates, were the most homogenous of the groups at Porta Westfalica. The Danes and the French arrived at the camp at approximately the same time and formed a bond over mutual efforts to maintain some sense of civility under their awful circumstances.

Because of their fellow Aryan connections to the Germans, the Danes received some small benefits through the camp administration, in Jorgen's words, "whether we wanted them or not."[7] This included being able to write and receive letters from their parents, which is how Jorgen and Flemming were able to receive the news that their father and Elsebet had been freed from Froslev on October 1. The mail was sporadic, and letters had to be written in German so the guards could read and censor them—which, of course, limited the number of Danes who could take advantage of the privilege.

Packages could also be received, though they rarely made it through the Kapos, and if they did, they were often opened and picked over. Late in the year, the Danish Red Cross saw to it that parcels arrived with regularity, and the food and clothing that was sent from home was deeply appreciated and welcome. The packages did cause levels of animosity with other prisoners, who were unable to receive similar largess. Unguarded bunks and no space for storage prompted theft. Also, when hunger and starvation began to set in, the rich food that arrived from home prompted serious bouts of diarrhea, which was a particularly wretched condition given the crowded bunks and vile lavatories.

Danes were also frequently chosen for positions of some trust within the camp. After a couple of months, Jorgen was picked to work as a medical orderly in the camp infirmary, which gave him an escape from the hard labor in the mine. One of the patients he tended to was his fellow HD 2 leader, Jorgen Staffeldt, who had contracted tuberculosis and was very ill. The two Jorgens, who had not really known each other very well back in Copenhagen since Staffeldt only became a part of the group late in its activities, now bonded through their joint incarceration at Vestre, at Froslev, and now here in Germany.

Staffeldt, along with his brother, Mogens, had operated the Nordic Bookstore, the well-known center for resistance and rescue operations in Copenhagen. Both had been arrested the same day as Elsebet and Bente, way back in February, and each had trekked through the Danish prison system from Horserod to Vestre to Froslev. The divergence had come in October, when Mogens had been freed from Froslev and ultimately made his way to Sweden, while Jorgen was sent on to Germany and was now in the misery of the infirmary at Porta.

Jorgen could do very little for his fellow prisoners. There were few disinfectants and bandages. Mine work by its very nature was hazardous, and broken arms and legs "were not infrequent," according to Jorgen.[8] Without anesthetics and with deficient medical expertise, it was impossible to perform most operations. Appendicitis, for example, generally resulted in peritonitis and death. Usually, the best that the staff at the infirmary could do was assign patients to "light duty," which often meant peeling potatoes and avoiding the hard mine labor for a few days. In his first few weeks at the infirmary, in early December, Jorgen had already seen two Danish resistance fighters die in the ward, and a fellow HD 2 member, one of the naval cadets named Jorgen Salling, had to be evacuated back to Neuengamme with a severe illness.

Meanwhile, resentment and animus toward the Danish privileges slowly escalated among the other nationalities through the early winter, until matters reached a boiling point around Christmas, when Danish prisoners began to receive extra food and a bounty of clothing through the Danish Red Cross. They got new jackets, underwear, scarves, gloves, and pairs of clogs.[9] All of which were looked upon with envy by the rest of the camp.

On the day that the Kapos doled out the packages to the Danes in the camp yard, the guards stood back as an assembly of Russian prisoners began to gather menacingly in an area opposite the Danes. Slowly but inexorably, other nationalities joined the Russians, and their numbers swelled until they were many times more than the Danish prisoners and they inched closer. The Kapos stood by, watching sadistically and expectantly for mayhem to follow.

At the last instant, a Danish farmer from Jutland named Nikolaj Nikolajsen, who had been arrested for storing secondhand weapons for the resistance in a shed on his little farm in the province of Schleswig, stepped forward. He was a large, strong man and was highly regarded by all in the camp for his helpfulness and egalitarianism, whether it was heaving particularly heavy rocks while working in the mine or carrying one of the Russians, who had gotten ill while working, all the way back to the camp on his back so that he wouldn't miss roll call. As the Russians and their cohorts oozed forward toward the wealthy Danes, it was Nikolaj who stepped out of the crowd between the would-be combatants and raised his arms. Remarkably, he was able to stanch the bloodbath. He turned to his fellow Danes and said, "And now we are going to share everything."[10]

The divided packages served as the basis for a Christmas celebration in the camp. The internees were given a day off from work, but even this blessing was compromised by the fact that it meant both day and night shifts had to fight for the use of the bunks at the same time because there were not even enough beds for more than one group to use at a time.

The camp authorities did put up a Christmas tree with electric lights, but Jorgen had to spend much of that day with the patients in the infirmary, about fifteen or twenty, which included Jorgen Staffeldt, who was still desperately ill with tuberculosis.

Dinner was a porridge made of oats and supplemented by the contents of the Danish packages shared by all. There was a somewhat feeble attempt to sing Christmas carols in a handful of different languages—Danish, French, and Polish.

At the end of the evening, Jorgen was able to get outside in the yard with his brother Flemming to look up into a cloudless sky. They thought of home and family and searched for familiar constellations in the crisp winter night. They were able to find the North Star, but not much else before the cold drove them back inside.

Jorgen Staffeldt died the next morning, information that Jorgen Kieler soon passed on to Flemming. He was the thirteenth Danish resistance fighter to die at the camp, and more were to succumb over the next months as food supplies continued to be cut from the starvation diet that already pertained in the camp.[11]

THE WAR OUTSIDE THE CAMP KEPT GETTING WORSE FOR THE GERMANS. The repercussions of that fact within the camp were to heighten efforts to finish the work in the mines. Camp inmates were whipped into digging at an even faster pace. Jorgen's work in the infirmary came to an abrupt end, and he was sent back to the rocks, this time in a new mining gallery blasted out of the river valley hills. A new group of experienced miners from Germany's Saar region were now overseeing the work. Their attitudes about their new circumstances varied by personality, but the prevalent tone seemed to accept the notion that the work that was being done here in these mines for the Reich could perhaps save all of Germany from Allied destruction. If they recognized the fact that the laborers they were pushing to extremes were starving and simply could not do the work that was demanded of them, they ignored the fact and pushed them harder. "The civilian miners," in Kieler's words, "appeared to think that they could shovel their way to a German victory."[12]

Jorgen was paired with a man who was a baker in civilian life. In camp life, he was nearing what was called the *Muselmann* stage—the condition where extreme emaciation and starvation combine to make victims virtual walking skeletons who are fast succumbing to listlessness and apathy.

At the close of their last day working together, Kieler and his partner fell behind while trying to fill a dump wagon with rocks and stones that had been blasted from the mine wall by explosives. This debris was then shoveled on top of them by a civilian ganger, who despite the prisoners being overwhelmed, kept raining the debris over them, even as Kieler and the baker tried to defend themselves with shovels and hands. They were soon buried from their shins upward to their faces in rocks and rubble. Blood ran from every pore of exposed flesh, and still the debris kept coming until the baker finally collapsed before the whistle blew ending the workday.

The final indignity was that Kieler had to finish shoveling these rocks into the wagon lest they miss the roll call and hike back to Porta, where they faced punishment. Meanwhile, their tormenter walked away.

Somehow, Kieler was able to both get the rocks in the wagon and lug his partner to roll call. From there, the baker was sent on to the infirmary, where he died in a matter of hours.

Rumors of the stoning spread around the camp, but of course, nothing was done about it. An SS doctor who was inspecting the infirmary asked Kieler how he and the baker had sustained their injuries. It was a rare moment of sympathy from a German authority, and Kieler took advantage to try to tell him about the stoning and that he'd been shot while working in the resistance, which was adding to the intense pain he felt in his back. He also told the doctor that he was a medical student and that his own father was a doctor, trying to connect at a personal level with the German doctor.

It worked to a degree. The SS doctor asked Jorgen about his father's practice: What kind of medicine was it? Where did he work? At the end of the talk, Jorgen found himself grateful when the doctor gave him eight days off from digging in the mines.[13]

CHAPTER 39

Henny and Mix

AT THE CLOSE OF 1944, HENNY AND MIX WERE STILL IN SWEDEN, STILL working and training with the Danish Brigade. Their romance had deepened and Mix was eager to get married, while Henny was just as determined not to wed until after the war. Mix was also eager to get back to Denmark to continue the fight against the Germans before there was no longer a war to take part in.

On New Year's Eve, 1945, at a gathering of their brigade colleagues, he asked her to marry him, and once again, she said not until their exile was over. They separated in melancholy, and two days later, she received a note from someone at his brigade camp. He had left, she was told, taking his weapon and ammunition, headed for the Oresund. There, he swiped a rowboat and muscled his way across the sound, landing in Denmark beneath the looming batteries of the Kronborg castle.

It wasn't the last good-bye. The illegal but active courier service between Denmark and Sweden soon brought news of Mix from Denmark. His mood was good, he said, though he missed her and his friends at the brigade in Sweden. He was attached to a sabotage group in Denmark that was plotting "a very good job," one that would make "world news." The plan involved cutting off coal shipments for Germany by blowing up a large shipment at the entrance to the port of Copenhagen.[1]

It didn't go as planned. The plot was revealed to the Gestapo by a Danish stikker, and on February 27, 1945, the Germans arrived at his apartment in Copenhagen and knocked on the door. Mix answered with a pistol in his hand. He shot and killed one of the agents and wounded a second one, but Mix himself was shot in the leg in the process. He was ultimately captured and arrested by the German police, who took him to Vestre. He was being taken by guards to face a firing squad there when he was hit by a volley of bullets during an escape attempt. Erik Koch Michelsen (a.k.a. Mix) was just shy of his twenty-second birthday when he passed away.[2]

CHAPTER 40

Negotiations

FROM VERY EARLY IN THE WAR, WHEN RESISTANCE FIGHTERS HAD FIRST been arrested in Norway and then when the first Communists in Denmark were arrested and sent to German camps, an informal connection between Germany and a diverse group of Scandinavian individuals had developed with the expressed interest of trying to negotiate for the care and condition of those Nordic people who had been incarcerated by the Germans. From Norway, a journalist named Odd Medboe had used long-standing ties with academic figures in Germany to broach the subject of the possible release of Scandinavian prisoners on humanitarian grounds. Medboe also traveled to Copenhagen for talks with Admiral Carl Hammerich, the Danish minister of social welfare, who quickly understood the necessity of organizing some means of safe and caring evacuation for Scandinavian prisoners, if and when they might be released. Danish authorities began to negotiate directly with the Germans, looking for a way to release some of these prisoners. Hammerich organized a fleet of trucks, buses, ambulances, and private cars, to be ready when the time came to pick up prisoners from their desperate circumstances in the camps.

The arrest of the Danish police force provided the impetus for the first rescue. On December 1, 1944, German camp authorities notified Denmark that two hundred of its police officers who had been placed at Buchenwald after their arrest could be picked up and transported back to Denmark.

Hammerich's squad of miscellaneous vehicles, which he'd dubbed the Jutland Corps, was ready to go. On December 5, four buses and four ambulances, along with doctors, nurses, medicines, food, and a healthy sum of schnapps to bribe recalcitrant German border guards, set off from Copenhagen for Buchenwald. They returned in a matter of days with 198 Danish police officers and headed for Froslev. One Danish officer had died en route. Hammerich, meanwhile, heard of the successful mission while in a cell at Shellhus, the Gestapo headquarters in Copenhagen, where he'd recently been incarcerated for resistance activities and was awaiting further interrogations.[1]

Negotiations between Danish Red Cross officials and German authorities continued that winter, and a few small convoys from the Jutland Corps were able to bring home handfuls of internees from Germany to Denmark in a similar fashion to the first load of police. But it wasn't until a Swedish diplomat named Count Folke Bernadotte became involved and broadened the issue to include prisoners from Norway and other Western European nations that a plan for a large-scale liberation began to be worked out.

At this point in the war, the forces of the Soviet Union were already in East Prussia and moving rapidly to the west. The crucial Battle of the Bulge had been waged on Germany's Western Front and won by the Allies, who were now on the brink of reaching the Rhine. The Third Reich was not quite in its death throes, but the bells would soon be tolling. All of this formed an incentive for the Germans to consider how their treatment of concentration camp internees would be viewed in a postwar Europe.

Count Folke Bernadotte seized the moment to offer his services on behalf of the Scandinavian prisoners incarcerated in German concentration camps. Bernadotte was a grandson of the king of Sweden (his father was the second son of the king, not in the line of succession), a high-ranking member of the Swedish Army, and a vice-chairman of the Swedish Red Cross. He was also well-connected in the ranks of Allied high command, where he had worked on behalf of American and British pilots who'd been interned by the Germans after forced landings in Sweden.

In early February 1945, Bernadotte was invited by General Dwight

Eisenhower to meet in Paris to discuss the overall state of the war, what might evolve in Europe after the fighting, and what role neutral nations like Sweden might play in the coming postwar landscape. While there, Bernadotte also met with the Swedish consul general, and the two discussed the possibility of doing something for all those prisoners currently languishing in German concentration camps.

Back in Stockholm, Bernadotte had a meeting with the Norwegian foreign minister, who implored the count to use whatever influence he might have in the matter to release the Scandinavian prisoners currently being held in German camps, which would include both Danes and Norwegians.

To even broach such a sensitive subject with Germany, Bernadotte knew that it would be necessary to speak with the highest authority he could find to make sure the talks would have their desired effects. This was not a matter that should get lost in the thickets of diplomatic bureaucracy; better to approach the top immediately. In the middle of February, he made a trip to Berlin to meet with Heinrich Himmler, the architect of the German camp system. Rather than saying that he was there to discuss the possible release of the camp internees, Bernadotte said that he wanted to discuss deteriorating Swedish-German relations and how Sweden's currently hostile feelings toward Germany might be ameliorated.[2]

Not surprisingly, Himmler, at the beginning of the talks, would not even consider that Germany had done anything to earn Sweden's hostility, but as they continued to negotiate their differences, he asked Bernadotte if there were any concrete proposals that he might have that would improve the current situation between the two countries. Bernadotte decided to lay his cards on the table: Would Germany be willing to release its Scandinavian prisoners in concentration camps to be transported and then imprisoned in Sweden?

Himmler's quick answer was "No." If he were to do that, Western media would call him a war criminal who was only interested in trying to save his own neck at this last minute. But he did have a counterproposal: What if, in exchange for a German concession, Bernadotte and Sweden ensured that sabotage in Norway and Sweden would come to an end?[3]

Bernadotte said bluntly that the German request to end sabotage in the region was impossible. Neither he nor the Swedish government had any means to bring a halt to the politically organic sabotage in their neighboring Scandinavian countries. It seemed the negotiations were at an end, but then Himmler surprised the Swedish diplomat. He offered to gather all of the Norwegian and Danish inmates and place them in a single camp where the Swedish Red Cross could look after them. He also agreed to release the sick and aged and to allow women prisoners with children to return to Denmark and Norway once they had been settled in the camp. The Swedish Red Cross and the Swedish Army would be given the task of gathering all the eligible Scandinavian prisoners in Germany and transporting them to the chosen camp, where they would be readied for evacuation back to Sweden.

The Germans kept their word, and the transfer of prisoners soon began. The single camp chosen to hold the Scandinavian prisoners was Neuengamme, the same transit camp that had briefly held the Kieler brothers before they were shipped to Porta Westfalica. The Swedish Red Cross, in conjunction with the Swedish Army, oversaw the initial transportation requirements (soon to be supplemented by help from the Danish Assistance Corps). Thirty-six buses were requisitioned for the move, to be driven and operated by Swedish Army personnel.

The logistical problems of the rescue were many. The eligible Scandinavian prisoners, who included, aside from the elderly, desperately ill prisoners, women, children, POWs, political prisoners, and those Danish policemen who had been arrested the previous fall, were housed in a variety of camps throughout Germany. To gather them all would take a matter of weeks, traveling over dangerous German highways.

CHAPTER 41

Shellhus in Copenhagen

ON MARCH 21, 1945, A SQUADRON OF RAF MOSQUITOES ATTACKED AND bombed Shellhus, in the heart of Copenhagen, at the ongoing request of the Danish resistance, who had been eager for such a raid since one in Aarhus the previous October. The conditions were similar: the Gestapo had used the new building, Shellhus, as its city headquarters since it had been finished the year before, storing archives, interview notes, and even prisoners within the facility, thus accumulating and keeping vast amounts of information on the ways and means of the Danish resistance in the country. The Germans were using this warehouse to collect the means necessary to gather and arrest scores of Danish fighters across the land. The resistance wanted that storehouse destroyed and had pressed the RAF for that to happen sooner rather than later.

The resistance knew that the prisoners were being kept on the top floors of the building and advised the Royal Air Force of that fact in the hope that the bombers could somehow spare the twenty-six members of the resistance who were inside.

As at Aarhus, several waves of bombers flew at the structure that morning, keeping low to the ground, just before nine in the morning, heading south to north up the Zealand coast. Most of the bombs of the first wave hit their targets, but one of the planes was flying so low that it actually hit a lamp post and crashed near a French school.

The pilots of either one or two planes in the second wave of bombers were confused by the smoke rising from the crash near the schoolhouse and dropped their bombs there, rather than on the Shellhus building, killing 123 teachers and children in the process. It was the worst single casualty toll in all of the war in Denmark.

Shellhus was gutted by the explosions and fire, and much of the Gestapo archives were destroyed. Fifty Gestapo workers were killed in the bombing, along with fifty Danish employees. Nine RAF fliers were lost. Flames and smoke filled the skies over Copenhagen. On the streets could be heard the wail of sirens and the cries of victims perishing in what had been a quiet March morning in the city.

Of the twenty-six resistance fighters detained at Shellhus at the time of the bombing, eighteen managed to survive the devastation. One who didn't make it was Admiral Carl Hammerich.[1]

CHAPTER 42

The White Buses

With the Luftwaffe having been decimated by this stage in the war, Allied planes owned the skies over Germany, and they were targeting moving transports on the highways and railroads below them. American and British air commanders could not guarantee safe passage for the vehicles in the prisoner release operation. To help alleviate the danger, all of the thirty-six buses were painted white, with the Red Cross insignia on both sides, in an effort to distinguish them from military vehicles. The mission was quickly dubbed the White Bus Rescue.

The buses were readied and transported by ship from Sweden to Odense in Denmark on March 11, where a number of Danish support vehicles, including trucks, a field kitchen, and food and gasoline supplies, joined the convoy. They crossed the Danish-German border and split into two groups, with one heading east to pick up prisoners in the eastern part of Germany and one headed south to gather prisoners from central and southern German concentration camps. They were then going to transport the internees back to the camp in Neuengamme.

By mid-March, the White Buses were transporting Scandinavian prisoners from a number of camps in Germany to Neuengamme. By the first of April, 2,000 had arrived at the camp from Sachsenhausen, 600 from Dachau, and 1,600 Danish policemen came from Buchenwald.[1] With these additions, Neuengamme was soon overflowing with prisoners, and the camp commander determined that the excess non-Scandinavian internees would have to be placed elsewhere. This meant that all the Polish, Czech, French, Ukrainian, Dutch, and Russian prisoners had to be moved. And since the German camps no longer had the means to transport their internees, the Red Cross buses were drafted to do the job for them.

The non-Scandinavian prisoners, who had not had the benefit of Red Cross packages over the last several months, were in far worse shape than those Danes and Norwegians who had at least had some extra food and supplies. Many of them were so sick and starved that they had neither the strength nor the energy to make it from the camp to the buses. The White Bus personnel had initially not been allowed to enter the camps for fear of what they would see and report about the conditions within. That changed when these human skeletons were forced to make their way from the camp interiors outside to the waiting buses and simply couldn't do it.

Resentment was directed at some of the Danish prisoners for their relative good health as well as the fact that they were now being evacuated while prisoners of other nationalities were simply being shifted to other concentration camps. A Danish policeman leaving Buchenwald was seen stuffing a bag full of clothing, blankets, and bread while leaving behind, with no apparent concern, starving, half-naked prisoners of other nationalities.[2] Even some of their fellow Danes were looked upon with scant regard. One Danish Communist had been imprisoned at Neuengamme when the policemen arrived recalled being recruited by a couple of high-ranking Danish police officers, who had just arrived at the transit camp from Buchenwald, to haul their luggage into the barracks from the buses. The notion that anyone would even have luggage in the camp environment that he had been living in seemed amazing to him.[3]

Even with the special treatment of Scandinavian prisoners and the Danish police, they were still not being released from Neuengamme by the end of March, which prompted another visit to Germany by Count Bernadotte. As opposed to his February meetings with Himmler, Bernadotte now found the Reichsfuhrer to be nervous and worried by the coming end of the war. No doubt considering what was coming after the end of the Reich, Bernadotte told Himmler that conditions in Neuengamme were "vile" and urged the immediate release of all prisoners.[4]

Himmler agreed in principle to the idea of releasing all of the prisoners but hoped it could be done in staggered intervals. Bernadotte agreed to the proposal, and once again, the Danish police were put at the top of the list of inmates to be evacuated. They were to be followed by Scandinavian invalids from the camps, who would be taken to Sweden for medical treatment; a group of Norwegian students who'd been imprisoned for political reasons early in the war; then women and children; followed by Scandinavian civilians who had been imprisoned for a variety of nonviolent offenses.

Two convoys left Neuengamme on April 3 and April 5, both carrying Danish police. The first transport carrying the ill left on April 8. By the middle of April, the floodgates were opening, and the White Buses were making daily trips from Germany to Denmark and then on to Sweden. There was still no mention of the Danish Jews interned at Theresienstadt.

CHAPTER 43

Porta Westfalica for a Last Time

JORGEN AND FLEMMING KIELER, ALONG WITH SEVENTY-NINE OTHER Danish prisoners at Porta Westfalica, received orders to bathe and get ready to leave for Neuengamme on March 18. The 81 Danes were what was left of a total of 225 Danish prisoners who had arrived at the camp the previous fall. The rest of the Danes had either died in this camp or had been sent on to a similar fate at another of the death camps. On March 19, the Danish prisoners watched as their fellow campmates marched off to their daily work in the mines. They were kept back and, instead of going to work, were handed the last of their Red Cross packages and then marched off to the railroad line, where they were loaded into cars and reversed the horrible trip they'd made the previous fall back to Neuengamme. This time, they could stretch out, could eat what foodstuffs were in their Red Cross packages, and were given straw to rest on.[1]

At Neuengamme, the new Danish arrivals from Porta Westfalica became reacquainted with the Danes who had remained in Neuengamme. These included several acquaintances of the Kielers from Horsens, who had apparently been rounded up after the resistance had swelled in the city in the wake of Peer Borup's death and burial the year before. A subsequent Gestapo crackdown in the area had bolstered the number of Jutland fighters now incarcerated in German prisons.

It was in this moment of reacquaintance that Jorgen learned several of the Varde resistance fighters were still in the camp, but unfortunately,

Koch, the man who had housed them on the assignment, had not survived.

Neither had his old HD 2 stalwart friend, Klaus Ronholt, the comrade who had gone out with Elsebet to the manors of Zealand to raise money for the rescue, the one who had first been nicked with Jorgen on the B & W assault in Copenhagen and then interrogated for a first time by the Gestapo at Langelinie, the one who had occupied a ditch with him after the last failed sabotage attempt at Aabenraa in south Jutland, and the one who'd been with him in Vestre and Froslev and, finally, Porta Westfalica. Now, Klaus was gone, too, like so many other of the resistance fighters. There was no time to mourn him or all the others. No time to mourn anyone.

At Neuengamme, Jorgen was sent back to work in the camp infirmary, where once again, he encountered many cases of tuberculosis. He was also beginning to feel the first signs of pleurisy in his own condition—chest pain, coughing, a high temperature—and he guessed these might be signs that he had himself contracted tuberculosis. Again, there was too much to do in the infirmary at the moment to treat his own symptoms.

The work in the infirmary was frenetic and made more so by all the activity surrounding Neuengamme as Scandinavians from a variety of different camps from across Germany were being brought in on the White Buses to soon be transported back to Sweden on the same buses for processing.

In early April, Count Folke Bernadotte himself showed up at the camp and visited the Neuengamme infirmary to inspect matters to make sure things were progressing as they were supposed to. It was from Bernadotte himself that the Kielers and other Danes at the facility first learned what was happening—that they would finally be going home.

Even with the presence of this Swedish count saying it was true, even given the remarkable change of circumstances in their lives over the past few days, even after being shifted from Porta Westfalica to Neuengamme and being handed their Red Cross packages, even having taken a relatively leisurely train ride to the camp, and even with the pretty certain knowledge that the war was coming to an end, that Germany was going to be defeated, and that there was a distinct possibility they would survive this horror, even with all of this, it was still hard to credit that they would soon be going home.

And then it happened. The wheels of negotiation kept turning, and prisoners at Neuengamme kept being transported out of the camp. The White Buses kept rolling in with prisoners from elsewhere and rolling out with ex-prisoners on the road to freedom in Sweden. Until finally, on April 20, the infirmary at Neuengamme was emptied and Jorgen and Flemming Kieler found themselves being loaded on those same buses and heading back to Denmark. The brothers did not share the same bus ride, but they were in the convoy together as it traveled over the border from Germany and back home to Denmark. [2]

Through mile after mile of German countryside, Jorgen looked out the bus window with the thought that he would never care to see this land again, but his mood buoyed as he entered the border town of Padborg in Denmark, not far from the Froslev prison camp that he'd stayed at only a few months earlier.

Outside the bus window, he could see crowds of people standing at the roadside, waving greetings to the prisoners who were finally coming home. As the bus slowed to a stop, he could see a familiar face, his own mother in the crowd, scanning the windows of the buses as they fanned by, looking anxiously, expectantly, for her sons inside, but uncertain if they were or were not on these buses, indeed, uncertain if they were alive or dead. She had made the trip down from Horsens to the border with a prayer on her lips but no definite knowledge of their whereabouts.

As the bus finally eased to a stop, Jorgen rushed off and hurried through the crowd toward her. He had remembered on the ride home that today was her fifty-fifth birthday, and as they hugged, he greeted her with that simple message, "Happy birthday, Mother."[3]

CHAPTER 44

Theresienstadt Once Again

WORD OF THE PENDING RELEASE OF THE DANISH JEWS OF THERE-sienstadt arrived at the camp office of Rabbi Friediger on Friday, April 13, 1945. A Danish vehicle pulled up outside his door, and a young Czech woman burst inside to inform Rabbi Friediger, who had a hard time believing her. "I thought she was making fun of me. You see, I had told her several times that I had dreamt of our return home and that they would come to fetch us by plane or with thirty or forty buses from Copenhagen."[1]

The Danish car soon disappeared, but the hope continued to augur well. That afternoon, Friediger was called to camp headquarters. There, he met a Danish doctor, Johannes Holm, who had just been negotiating the evacuation of the Danish Jews from Theresienstadt with some recalcitrant Gestapo officers who remained reluctant to the last gasp of the Final Solution to release Jews from their clutches. Holm had organized a convoy of Danish vehicles to rescue the Danish Jews when negotiations between Bernadotte and the Germans broke down over whether or not to let the Jews go. According to historian Leni Yahil, Holm interceded and was finally able to convince the Germans to sanction the transfer—with the help of cases of Danish food and schnapps for the officers.[2]

The Danes were soon told to pack their belongings, and word of the pending release spread quickly through the camp. Joy and disbelief mixed in a cauldron of confusion and uncertainty. Could it really be happening? Could they really be going home? Rabbi Friediger walked through the prison to assure the internees that it was true, they were leaving Theresien-stadt. He found one family in tears, seated in the midst of their packing, simply unable to continue with this last chore, unable to believe that they were going home.

But then the White Buses arrived, and the next morning, on Sunday, April 15, the Jews walked down the streets of the camp, which were now lined with other internees of different nationalities who were being left behind in the camp. They cried and waved to the Danes. There was even a band playing as the Jews approached the gates of Theresienstadt, which remarkably stayed open as they approached and walked through to the waiting buses.

There were 35 buses filled with the Jews of Theresienstadt, 423 people in total. Though the transportation came from Denmark, Bernadotte had insisted that the drivers be Swedish, and so it was that Swedish drivers took the wheels for the drive through bombed-out Germany. The journey included a trip through Potsdam, which was still smoldering from a recent air raid, and through decimated Dresden, whose destruction was a shock-ingly awesome sight even to the most camp-battered passengers.[3]

It took two days to make the drive to Denmark, with the buses spend-ing overnights parked on the sides of the open roads, staying away from the bombing raids being conducted in cities all over Germany and hoping their white color and red crosses would protect them to from the incessant bombing. When they passed the frontier into Denmark, they were greet-ed with waving flags, school children lining the streets, flowers, candies, singing, and cigarettes tossed their way. It was hard for the stunned in-ternees to realize that all of this joy was expressed for them.[4]

The Germans still controlled Denmark, however, and not only were they not partaking in the celebration, they also waved the refugees quickly through Jutland, then east across the outer belt, as if they had no business coming home. In Fyn, the Germans sounded the air-raid sirens to keep lo-cal citizens off the streets. There would be no celebrations there, no shouts of joy to greet the refugees as they had at the border.

The buses drove on to Odense, where the refugees paused to spend the night. Then it was into Zealand the next day, and finally to Copenhagen, where a loud welcome from thousands of Danes filled the streets. So many came out to greet the refugees that again the Germans were annoyed by the display of joy. Through loudspeakers, they warned the citizens that the refugees might be sent back to Theresienstadt if the demonstrations continued.[5]

Ferries awaited the White Buses at the port in Copenhagen. The Jews were driven straight onto transports for the quick passage to Sweden. The fact that they had to continue on to Malmo was heartbreaking for some, who had waited so long for this return, but once again, the long-suffering group endured.

The Jews of Denmark were home but not yet home. The former inmates were placed in quarantine in Swedish refugee camp barracks and awaited the next link in the chain of events that would ultimately lead them back home.

That came on May 5 with the announcement that Germany had capitulated to the Allies. Denmark was free.

Among the first group of Jews who were allowed back into their native country after the liberation were those Danes in Sweden who had volunteered for the Danish Brigade. That included young Herbert Pundik, the refugee teenager who, at age eighteen, had just barely made the minimum age requirement to enlist in the brigade a few weeks earlier. He was sent with his unit to a frontier post in southern Jutland, right at the border, not far from the Froslev prison. He was stationed there as a steady stream of defeated German soldiers arrived, heading for home on their own two feet. As they shuffled over the last few yards to cross the border, the brigade members thought they'd have a little fun with the weary, defeated Germans who were on their way home. They gave them two choices: they could run back to Germany or goose-step across the border.

Writing of this moment many years later, a grown-up Pundik wrote, "Since then I have often thought of this victorious attitude in shame. For it was not we who had won the war. It had been won by the allied soldiers and the European resistance movements. We merely came to sweep up afterwards."[6]

This was a moral and generous perspective. But he and the rest of the survivors of the German occupation did more than just sweep up afterward: they lived to tell their stories so the world could know what happened there and could say that, at least in Denmark, almost all the Jews survived.

ACKNOWLEDGMENTS

ALL MEMBERS OF THE KIELER FAMILY SURVIVED THE WAR AND WENT on to live long and fruitful lives. Scars from the struggle remained, however. After their return to Denmark and the end of the war, both Jorgen and Flemming, along with others of their Porta Westfalica fellow prisoners, continued to suffer from the ill effects of their starvation diets and the tuberculosis contracted while in the camps. As Jorgen continued his medical studies in the years following his release, he also began a study of the health of concentration camp victims that would eventually lead to his involvement in a newly founded postwar organization called the Freedom Foundation, which Jorgen joined and would become chairman of, serving in that position for more than a dozen years. It was an organization that, among other duties, dealt with issues of compensation for those who had suffered during the war.

Jorgen took his medical degree from Copenhagen University in 1948 and married another doctor, Eva Fausball, in 1947. His principal medical work over the years was conducted as a research scientist, working in the field of cancer studies, a field in which he became internationally known for his research on the causes of the disease. Among other honors, he served as head of the Danish Cancer Research Society.

Flemming Kieler also got his medical degree, in 1951. He married Maria Mikkelsen, and they settled in Horsens, where Flemming became a general practitioner of medicine. Along with his sisters, Elsebet and Bente, he converted to Catholicism in the years after the war. Elsebet became a student and scholar of the faith and published a number of books on various aspects of the religion; Flemming, too, published works on ethics, morality, and theological issues.

Jorgen Kieler avoided writing on the subject of the war, the resistance, and his incarceration until the 1980s, when he was encouraged by his friend, the Nobel Prize–winning writer and fellow concentration camp survivor, Elie Wiesel, to write of his experiences. Kieler subsequently became a historian and memoirist of the camps and the resistance. He interviewed and collected stories from a number of his colleagues from the resistance and published several histories, including *Hvorfor Gjorde I Det?* (Why Did You Fight?), and an English version of his memoir, *Resistance Fighter*.

In an era when many Danish historians have written sympathetically of the Danish government's cooperation policy during the war, suggesting that it allowed Denmark to not only save its Jewish population but also to bring the nation relatively unscathed through the conflagration, Kieler remained an adamant critic of the government's occupation policies, arguing that by appeasing Germany in the conflict, the Danish government helped prolong the consequent suffering of many other countries. In the words of journalist Bent Blunikow, "For Kieler [the war] was not just a narrow national struggle, but an effort against Nazism in all its forms" ("Jorgen Kieler dead at 97 years old," *Berlingske*, Feb. 19, 2017).

This book owes a great debt to Jorgen Kieler and the whole Kieler family for their story, heroism, and moral courage. My gratitude and admiration for them is deep.

I also owe thanks to the many narratives of the war and the plight of the Jews that I have used to write this book, including Aage Bertelsen's *Oktober 43*; *The Rescue of the Danish Jews*, with its reminiscences by Sam Besekow, Rabbi Bent Melchior, Jorgen Kieler, and Herbert Pundik, as well as by the book's editor, Leo Goldberger; Herbert Pundik's *In Denmark It Could Not Happen*; and *Boats in the Night: Knud Dyby's Story of Resistance and Rescue* as told by Martha Loeffler.

Of great value as well were the oral histories recorded at the United States Holocaust Memorial Museum in Washington, DC, which, primarily in the 1990s, collected a number of filmed interviews of Danish participants in the rescue of Denmark's Jews. There, I was able to see and get a sense of the character and personality of several of the figures who would be central to this story, including Henny Sinding Sundo, Frode Jacobsen,

Jorgen Kieler, Ebba Lund, Bent Melchior, Herbert Pundik, and many others whose stories are not here included. The archives at the museum also provided a wealth of photos and documents pertaining to the escape and rescue that were essential to the research for this book.

Likewise, the Museum of Danish Resistance has been of enormous value to this book, not only in a visit to its collections in Copenhagen but also in providing its photographs and for daily online visits to its documentary archives. There can be found a comprehensive collection of information on the history and details of the lives of the thousands of Danes involved in the resistance, along with guidance on how to find out more about their actions and deeds.

I also need to thank the University of Aarhus and its Department of Culture and Society for the website they have created, danmarkshistorien.dk, which features hundreds of articles on Danish history written primarily by the scholars of Aarhus. These articles provided a wealth of background information for this book, and the site, as with the archives at the Museum of Danish Resistance, was a frequent online stop for me.

Other books and scholars have contributed to my understanding of Denmark, the resistance, and the plight of the Danish Jews during the war. *Nothing to Speak Of* (The Danish Jewish Museum, 2011), by Sofie Lene Bak, is a comprehensive study of the wartime lives of Danish Jews in Denmark and Sweden. Bo Lidegaard's book *Countrymen* (Alfred A. Knopf, 2013) is a compelling account of the rescue of the Danish Jews written by one of Denmark's best journalists. *Henny and Her Boat*, by Howard S. Veisz, offered a thorough and well-written account of the exploits of Henny Sinding and the *Gerda III*. And scholar Leni Yahil wrote the first and in many ways still the most thorough history of the Jews of Denmark during the occupation, *The Rescue of Danish Jewry* (1969, Jewish Publication Society of America).

Thank you to Wendy McCurdy, Ann Pryor, and Stephen Smith at Kensington Publishing and my agent, Farley Chase.

I'd also like to thank my wife, Susan; my son, Sam; Evan West; my daughter, Hannah; and Sean Bruton. Thanks as well to guide Agnethe P. for her assistance and expertise with my research in Copenhagen, Dragor, and Helsingor.

NOTES

CHAPTER 1

1 William Shirer, *The Rise and Fall of the Third Reich* (New York, Simon & Schuster, 1960), 699.

2 Niels Wium Olesen, "The Occupation on 9 April 1940," danmarkshistorien.dk.

3 J. Brøndsted and K. Gedde, eds., *The Five Long Years,* vol. 1 (Aarhus, Denmark: Aarhus University, 1946), 108.

CHAPTER 2

1 Jorgen Kieler, *Resistance Fighter,* trans. Eric Dickens (Jerusalem and New York: Gefen Publishing House, 2007), 12.

2 Niels Wium Olesen, "The Occupation on 9 April 1940," danmarkshistorien.dk.

3 Kieler, *Resistance Fighter,* 20.

4 Frode Jacobsen, report from 1975 about occupation of April 9, 1940, danmarkshistorien.dk.

5 John Oram Thomas, *The Giant-Killers* (New York: Taplinger Publishing Company, 1976), 192.

6 Thomas, *Giant-Killers,* 194.

7 *Kristeligt Dagblad,* September 4, 2015.

8 Aage Bertelsen, *Oktober 43* (New York: G. P. Putnam's Sons, 1954), 24–25.

9 Howard S. Veisz, *Henny and Her Boat* (North Charleston, SC: CreateSpace Independent Publishing Platform, 2017), i–iv.

10 *Dansk Biografisk Leksikon.* Essay by Jorgen Haestrup.

11 Leo Goldberger, ed., *The Rescue of the Danish Jews* (New York: New York University Press, 1987), 121.

CHAPTER 3

1 Dr. Marcus Melchior, *A Rabbi Remembers* (New York: Lyle Stuart, 1968), 163–64.

2 Melchior, *Rabbi Remembers,* 163–64.

3 Goldberger, *Rescue of the Danish Jews,* 158.

4 Bent Melchior interview, 1996, United States Holocaust Memorial Museum digitized collections.

CHAPTER 4

1 "Kongens Fødselsdag," Danmark på Film, danmarkpaafilm.dk/film/kongens-foedselsdag. Film footage of the day.

2 The king did, however.

3 Kieler, *Resistance Fighter,* 27.

4 "Kongens Fødselsdag," Danmark på Film.

5 "Alsang, 1940–1943," danmarkshistorien.dk.

6 Harold Flender, *Rescue in Denmark* (Princeton, NJ: Princeton University Press, 1963; reprint, Holocaust Library), 31.

7 Flender, *Rescue in Denmark*, 31.

8 Kieler, *Resistance Fighter*, 26.

9 Kieler, *Resistance Fighter*, 28.

10 Christian Wenende, "In the Name of the King or Traitor to the Crown?" *Copenhagen Post*, March 5, 2018.

11 Kieler, *Resistance Fighter*, 30.

12 Kieler, *Resistance Fighter*, 35.

13 Ellen Levine, *Darkness over Denmark* (New York: Holiday House, 2000), 32.

CHAPTER 5

1 Kronborg was built prior to Shakespeare writing his timeless play about the melancholy Dane, but he was nonetheless aware of the existence of the new castle and its placement in Helsingor on the Oresund.

2 Knud Jesperson, *A History of Denmark*, trans. Ivan Hill and Christopher Wade (Red Globe Press, 2004), 32–33.

3 Thomas, *Giant-Killers*, 262.

4 Thomas, *Giant-Killers*, 266.

5 Thomas, *Giant-Killers*, 83.

6 Keiler, *Resistance Fighter*, 40.

7 Thomas, *Giant-Killers*, 83.

8 Goldberger, *Rescue of the Danish Jews*, 79.

9 Hans Kirchoff, "The Telegram Crisis," https://lex.dk/Telegramkrisen.

10 Levine, *Darkness over Denmark*, 39.

11 Kieler, *Resistance Fighter*, 41.

12 Kieler, *Resistance Fighter*, 42.

CHAPTER 6

1 Leni Yahil, *The Rescue of Danish Jewry* (Philadelphia, Jewish Publication Society of America, 1969), 118.

2 Kieler, *Resistance Fighter*, 45–46.

3 Kieler, *Resistance Fighter*, 46.

4 Maria Holm, "'Star Radio' a Symbol of Resistance," *From One Heart to Another* (blog), March 24, 2016, mariaholm.blog/2016/03/24/star-radio-a-symbol-of-resistance.

5 Thomas, *Giant-Killers*, 193.

6 Aage Trommer and Tage Kaarsted, "Beginning Resistance," from Gyldendal and Politiken's Danish history, lex.dk.

7 David Lampe, *Hitler's Savage Canary*, (London and New York: Arcade Books, 1957; reprint, 2010), 36.

8 Niels-Birger Danielsen, "Hvidstengruppen," https://lex.dk/Hvidstengruppen.

9 "Kirstine 'Tulle' Fiil, 1918–1983," danmarkshistorien.dk.

CHAPTER 7

1 Thomas, *Giant-Killers*, 32.

2 Richard Rhodes, *The Making of the Atomic Bomb* (New York: Simon & Schuster, 1986), 55.

3 Thomas, *Giant-Killers*, 35.
4 Thomas, *Giant-Killers*, 35.

CHAPTER 8

1 "Augustprøret 29. August 1943," danmarkshistorien.dk.
2 "Leksikon," *Danmark under Besættlsen og Befrielsen,* https://web.archive.org/web/20080308113437/http://www.besaettelse-befrielse.dk/leksikon_n.html#9._april_1940.

CHAPTER 9

1 Thomas, *Giant-Killers*, 193.
2 Thomas, *Giant-Killers*, 193.
3 Lampe, *Savage Canary*, 34.
4 Thomas, *Giant-Killers*, 192–96.
5 Lampe, *Savage Canary*, 35.
6 "Leksikon," *Danmark under Besættlsen og Befrielsen,* https://web.archive.org/web/20080308113437/http://www.besaettelse-befrielse.dk/leksikon_n.html#9._april_1940.
7 Flender, *Rescue in Denmark*, 39.

CHAPTER 10

1 Kieler, *Resistance Fighter*, 52.
2 Goldberger, *Rescue of the Danish Jews*, 143. From a reminiscence by Jorgen Kieler.
3 Kieler, *Resistance Fighter*, 58.
4 Kieler, *Resistance Fighter*, 60.
5 Kieler, *Resistance Fighter*, 62–64.

CHAPTER 11

1 Flender, *Rescue in Denmark*, 42.
2 Goldberger, *Rescue of the Danish Jews*, 43. Essay by Jorgen Haestrup.
3 Goldberger, *Rescue of the Danish Jews*, 43–44.
4 Goldberger, *Rescue of the Danish Jews*, 42.
5 Flender, *Rescue in Denmark*, 46–47. Describes Duckwitz's initial effort to intervene about the telegram. More recent scholarship casts some doubt on this account.

CHAPTER 12

1 Flender, *Rescue in Denmark*, 47.
2 Flender, *Rescue in Denmark*, 48.
3 Rhodes, *Making of the Atomic Bomb*, 482.
4 Rhodes, *Making of the Atomic Bomb*, 482.
5 Rhodes, *Making of the Atomic Bomb*, 483.
6 The escape of Bohr is told in *Giant-Killers, Making of the Atomic Bomb,* and *Hitler's Savage Canary,* with slight variations in each. The most dramatic version, in *Savage Canary,* describes gunfire and shooting as the fishing boat made its way out of Danish waters.
7 Yahil, *Rescue of Danish Jewry*, 148–49.
8 Bertelsen, *Oktober 43,* from the introduction by Hedtoft, 17.
9 Bertelsen, *Oktober 43,* 18–19.

CHAPTER 13

1 Levine, *Darkness over Denmark*, 70.
2 Herbert Pundik, *In Denmark It Could Not Happen* (Jerusalem and New York: Gefen Publishing House, 1998), 11–12.
3 Pundik, *In Denmark It Could Not Happen*, 11–12.
4 Lampe, *Savage Canary*, 81.
5 Bo Lidegaard, *Countrymen*, trans. Robert Maas (New York, Alfred A. Knopf, 2013), 98.
6 Pundik, *In Denmark It Could Not Happen*, 14.

CHAPTER 14

1 Yahil, *Rescue of Danish Jewry*, 185–86.
2 Yahil, *Rescue of Danish Jewry*, 185–86.
3 Richard Petrow, *The Bitter Years* (New York: William Morrow and Company, 1974), 222–23.
4 Flender, *Rescue in Denmark*, 97.
5 Kieler, *Resistance Fighter*, 97.
6 Pundik, *In Denmark It Could Not Happen*, 106.
7 Kieler, *Resistance Fighter*, 99.

CHAPTER 15

1 Flender, *Rescue in Denmark*, 96.
2 Bertelsen, *Oktober 43*, 31.
3 Pundik, *In Denmark It Could Not Happen*, 30.
4 Bertelsen, *Oktober 43*, 33–34.
5 Flender, *Rescue in Denmark*, 73.
6 Kieler, *Resistance Fighter*, 100.
7 Flender, *Rescue in Denmark*, 106.
8 Kieler, *Resistance Fighter*, 99.
9 Veisz, *Henny and Her Boat*, 60–61. Veisz's book is by far the best source available for the comings and goings of the *Gerda III* and all those associated with it.

CHAPTER 16

1 Dan Kaznelson, "Northern Light in White Coats," *Dansk Medicin Historisk Arbog*, January 2012, 154.
2 Flender, *Rescue in Denmark*, 118.
3 Flender, *Rescue in Denmark*, 118.
4 Flender, *Rescue in Denmark*, 122.
5 Kaznelson, "Northern Light in White Coats," 154.
6 Kaznelson, "Northern Light in White Coats," 156.
7 Kaznelson, "Northern Light in White Coats," 157.
8 Kaznelson, "Northern Light in White Coats," 158.
9 Goldberger, *Rescue of the Danish Jews*, 162.
10 Goldberger, *Rescue of the Danish Jews*, 166–69.

CHAPTER 17

1 Veisz, *Henny and Her Boat*, 29–31.
2 Pundik, *In Denmark It Could Not Happen*, 109–12.
3 Veisz, *Henny and Her Boat*, 31.

4 Veisz, *Henny and Her Boat*, 43–48. Details of the boat, the crew, and the voyages of the *Gerda III* all come from Howard Veisz and his very fine and thoroughly researched *Henny and Her Boat*.
5 Lidegaard, *Countrymen*, 331.
6 Veisz, *Henny and Her Boat*, 55–56. This is disputed by Lidegaard in *Countrymen*.
7 Veisz, *Henny and Her Boat*, 54.

CHAPTER 18
1 Rhodes, *Making of the Atomic Bomb*, 484–85.
2 Rhodes, *Making of the Atomic Bomb*, 484–85.

CHAPTER 19
1 Sofie Lene Bak, *Nothing to Speak Of*, trans. Virginia Raynolds Laursen (Copenhagen: The Danish Jewish Museum, 2011), 74.
2 Bak, *Nothing to Speak Of*, 76.
3 Flender, *Rescue in Denmark*, 154.
4 Flender, *Rescue in Denmark*, 155.
5 Lidegaard, *Countrymen*, 192.
6 Pundik, *In Denmark It Could Not Happen*, 65.
7 Pundik, *In Denmark It Could Not Happen*, 66–67.
8 Bertelsen, *Oktober 43*, 104.
9 Bertelsen, *Oktober 43*, 108.
10 Bertelsen, *Oktober 43*, 109.
11 Lidegaard, *Countrymen*, 289.
12 Veisz, *Henny and Her Boat*, 31–36.
13 Veisz, *Henny and Her Boat*, 49.
14 Veisz, *Henny and Her Boat*, 50.

CHAPTER 20
1 Bak, *Nothing to Speak Of*, 109.
2 Emmy Werner, *A Conspiracy of Decency* (Boulder, CO: Westview Press, 2002), 90.
3 Goldberger, *Rescue of the Danish Jews*, 94.
4 Pundik, *In Denmark It Could Not Happen*, 96–98.
5 Bak, *Nothing to Speak Of*, 110–11.
6 Bak, *Nothing to Speak Of*, 111.
7 Werner, *Conspiracy of Decency*, 92.
8 Goldberger, *Rescue of the Danish Jews*, 124.
9 Goldberger, *Rescue of the Danish Jews*, 130–31. Sam Besekow's account.
10 Bak, *Nothing to Speak Of*, 113.

CHAPTER 21
1 Bak, *Nothing to Speak Of*, 86.
2 Bak, *Nothing to Speak Of*, 88.
3 Werner, *Conspiracy of Decency*, 104.
4 Werner, *Conspiracy of Decency*, 105.
5 Werner, *Conspiracy of Decency*, 106.
6 Werner, *Conspiracy of Decency*, 107.
7 Werner, *Conspiracy of Decency*, 106–7.
8 Bak, *Nothing to Speak Of*, 95.

9 Yahil, *Rescue of Danish Jewry*, 161.
10 Bak, *Nothing to Speak Of*, 95–96.
11 Werner, *Conspiracy of Decency*, 108.
12 Werner, *Conspiracy of Decency*, 111.
13 Bak, *Nothing to Speak Of*, 97.
14 Yahil, *Rescue of Danish Jewry*, 311–12.

CHAPTER 22

1 Kieler, *Resistance Fighter*, 73.
2 Kieler, *Resistance Fighter*, 125–26.
3 Kieler, *Resistance Fighter*, 154.
4 Thomas, *Giant-Killers*, 198.
5 Biography of Bent Faurschou Hviid, Nationalmuseet Frihedsmuseet Modstands-database (resistance database), https://modstand.natmus.dk.
6 "Henny Sinding," United States Holocaust Memorial Museum, Oral History Collections, filmed interview.
7 Veisz, *Henny and Her Boat*, 63.
8 Kieler, *Resistance Fighter*, 125.

CHAPTER 23

1 Kieler, *Resistance Fighter*, 128.
2 Kieler, *Resistance Fighter*, 131.
3 Kieler, *Resistance Fighter*, 134–42.

CHAPTER 24

1 Kieler, *Resistance Fighter*, 143–45; Thomas, *Giant-Killers*, 201–4.

CHAPTER 25

1 Kieler, *Resistance Fighter*, 131. See footnote regarding this meeting years later.

CHAPTER 26

1 Thomas, *Giant-Killers*, 204.
2 Veisz, *Henny and Her Boat*, 67-68; Kieler, *Resistance Fighter*, 147.
3 Kieler, *Resistance Fighter*, 150.

CHAPTER 27

1 Kieler, *Resistance Fighter*, 153.
2 Kieler, *Resistance Fighter*, 155. Kieler quotes Mix from a report he wrote after the action.
3 Kieler, *Resistance Fighter*, 158.
4 Kieler, *Resistance Fighter*, 158.
5 Veisz, *Henny and Her Boat*, 73.
6 Kieler, *Resistance Fighter*, 163.
7 Kieler, *Resistance Fighter*, 166.

CHAPTER 28

1 Veisz, *Henny and Her Boat*, 83–84.
2 Veisz, *Henny and Her Boat*, 84.
3 Freedom Council pamphlet, "Are You a Nazi?", December 1943, from History of Denmark on lex.dk, https://danmarkshistorien.lex.dk.

4 Soren Tange Rasmussen, "Peter Group: German Terror in Denmark 1944–45," from History of Denmark on lex.dk
5 Ibid.
6 Anna Bech Lund and Elena Nielsen, "Hvidstengruppen 1943–1944," from History of Denmark on lex.dk.
7 Ibid.

CHAPTER 29

1 Kieler, *Resistance Fighter*, 167–69.
2 Kieler, *Resistance Fighter*, 172.
3 Kieler, *Resistance Fighter*, 185.
4 Kieler, *Resistance Fighter*, 194.
5 Veisz, *Henny and Her Boat*, 77.
6 Veisz, *Henny and Her Boat*, 78–79.
7 Kieler, *Resistance Fighter*, 199.
8 Veisz, *Henny and Her Boat*, 80.

CHAPTER 30

1 Bak, *Nothing to Speak Of*, 122.
2 Bak, *Nothing to Speak Of*, 126.
3 Bak, *Nothing to Speak Of*, 46.
4 Bak, *Nothing to Speak Of*, 49.
5 Goldberger, *Rescue of the Danish Jews*, 135.
6 Werner, *Conspiracy of Decency*, 96.
7 Werner, *Conspiracy of Decency*, 95.
8 Yahil, *Rescue of Danish Jewry*, 346.
9 Yahil, *Rescue of Danish Jewry*, 358.
10 Yahil, *Rescue of Danish Jewry*, 361.
11 Yahil, *Rescue of Danish Jewry*, 362.
12 Yahil, *Rescue of Danish Jewry*, 362.

CHAPTER 31

1 Werner, *Conspiracy of Decency*, 127.
2 Werner, *Conspiracy of Decency*, 130.
3 Petrow, *Bitter Years*, 251.

CHAPTER 32

1 Kieler, *Resistance Fighter*, 208.
2 Kieler, *Resistance Fighter*, 218–19.
3 Kieler, *Resistance Fighter*, 224.
4 Kieler, *Resistance Fighter*, 226.
5 Kieler, *Resistance Fighter*, 231.
6 Kieler, *Resistance Fighter*, 234.

CHAPTER 33

1 Kieler, *Resistance Fighter*, 240.
2 Kieler, *Resistance Fighter*, 242.

CHAPTER 34

1 Kieler, *Resistance Fighter*, 243.

CHAPTER 35

1 Werner, *Conspiracy of Decency*, 133.
2 Petrow, *Bitter Years*, 289.

CHAPTER 37

1 Petrow, *Bitter Years*, 290.
2 Petrow, *Bitter Years*, 293.

CHAPTER 38

1 Kieler, *Resistance Fighter*, 254.
2 Kieler, *Resistance Fighter*, 256.
3 Kieler, *Resistance Fighter*, 256.
4 Kieler, *Resistance Fighter*, 259.
5 Kieler, *Resistance Fighter*, 266.
6 Kieler, *Resistance Fighter*, 267.
7 Kieler, *Resistance Fighter*, 271.
8 Kieler, *Resistance Fighter*, 279.
9 Kieler, *Resistance Fighter*, 283.
10 Kieler, *Resistance Fighter*, 284.
11 Kieler, *Resistance Fighter*, 286.
12 Kieler, *Resistance Fighter*, 291.
13 Kieler, *Resistance Fighter*, 291.

CHAPTER 39

1 Veisz, *Henny and Her Boat*, 87–88.
2 Jorgen Kieler, *Hvorfor Gjorde I Det?*, vol. 1 (Copenhagen: Gyldendal), 145–46.

CHAPTER 40

1 Petrow, *Bitter Years*, 315–16.
2 Petrow, *Bitter Years*, 318.
3 Petrow, *Bitter Years*, 318.

CHAPTER 41

1 Klaus Velschow, "The Bombing of the Shellhus," *Dansk Militærhistorie*, milhist.dk/the-bombing-of-the-shellhus.

CHAPTER 42

1 Petrow, *Bitter Years*, 320–21.
2 Petrow, *Bitter Years*, 322.
3 Petrow, *Bitter Years*, 322.
4 Petrow, *Bitter Years*, 323.

CHAPTER 43

1 Kieler, *Resistance Fighter*, 302.
2 Kieler, *Resistance Fighter*, 308.
3 Kieler, *Resistance Fighter*, 308–9.

CHAPTER 44

1 Yahil, *Rescue of Danish Jewry*, 316.
2 Yahil, *Rescue of Danish Jewry*, 316.
3 Yahil, *Rescue of Danish Jewry*, 317.
4 Yahil, *Rescue of Danish Jewry*, 317.
5 Flender, *Rescue in Denmark*, 252.
6 Pundik, *In Denmark It Could Not Happen*, 166–67.